COLES NOTES TOTAL STUDY EDITION

King Lear

COLES NOTES TOTAL STUDY EDITION

King Lear

Complete Text + Commentary + Glossary

John Wiley & Sons Canada, Ltd.

Coles Notes Total Study Edition King Lear

Published by:

John Wiley & Sons Canada, Ltd.

6045 Freemont Blvd.

Mississauga, Ontario

L5R 4J3

Copyright © 2012 John Wiley & Sons Canada, Ltd.

ISBN: 978-1-118-48673-3

Printed in the United States of America

1 2 3 4 5 DP 16 15 14 13 12

WILEY

COLES NOTES TOTAL STUDY EDITION

King Lear

TABLE OF CONTENTS

Introduction: King Lear **1**

Introduction to William Shakespeare......................... 1

Introduction to Early Modern England..................... 7

Introduction to King Lear................................ 17

Character Map 23

Act I	Scene 1	*King Lear's palace* 27
	Scene 2	*The Earl of Gloucester's castle* 40
	Scene 3	*The Duke of Albany's palace*................ 48
	Scene 4	*A hall in the same* 50
	Scene 5	*A court before the same*.................. 64
Act II	Scene 1	*A court in the castle of the Earl of Gloucester*...................... 71
	Scene 2	*Before Gloucester's castle*................. 77
	Scene 3	*A wood* 85
	Scene 4	*Before Gloucester's castle. Kent in the stocks* ... 87
Act III	Scene 1	*A heath*............................. 103
	Scene 2	*Another part of the heath* 106
	Scene 3	*A room in Gloucester's castle*............. 110
	Scene 4	*The heath, before a hovel* 112
	Scene 5	*A room in Gloucester's castle* 120
	Scene 6	*A farmhouse adjoining the castle* 122
	Scene 7	*A room in Gloucester's castle* 127

Act IV   **Scene 1**   *A heath* *137*

            Scene 2   *Before the Duke of Albany's palace* *142*

            Scene 3   *The French camp near Dover* *147*

            Scene 4   *The same* *150*

            Scene 5   *Gloucester's castle* *152*

            Scene 6   *The country near Dover* *155*

            Scene 7   *The French camp* *168*

Act V   **Scene 1**   *The British camp near Dover* *177*

            Scene 2   *A field between the two camps* *182*

            Scene 3   *The British camp* *184*

Review **201**

Resource Centre **210**

Reading Group Discussion Guide **214**

KING LEAR

INTRODUCTION TO WILLIAM SHAKESPEARE

William Shakespeare, or the "Bard" as people fondly call him, permeates almost all aspects of our society. He can be found in our classrooms, on our televisions, in our theatres, and in our cinemas. Speaking to us through his plays, Shakespeare comments on his life and culture, as well as our own. Actors still regularly perform his plays on the modern stage and screen. The 1990s, for example, saw the release of cinematic versions of *Romeo and Juliet, Hamlet, Othello, A Midsummer Night's Dream,* and many more of his works.

In addition to the popularity of Shakespeare's plays as he wrote them, other writers have modernized his works to attract new audiences. For example, *West Side Story* places *Romeo and Juliet* in New York City, and *A Thousand Acres* sets *King Lear* in Iowa corn country. Beyond adaptations and productions, his life and works have captured our cultural imagination. The twentieth century witnessed the production of a play and film about two minor characters from Shakespeare's *Hamlet* in *Rosencrantz and Guildenstern are Dead* and a fictional movie about Shakespeare's early life and poetic inspiration in *Shakespeare in Love.*

Despite his monumental presence in our culture, Shakespeare remains enigmatic. He does not tell us which plays he wrote alone, on which plays he collaborated with other playwrights, or which versions of his plays we should read and perform. Furthermore, with only a handful of documents available about his life, he does not tell us much about Shakespeare the person, forcing critics and scholars to look to historical references to uncover the true-life great dramatist.

Anti-Stratfordians—modern scholars who question the authorship of Shakespeare's plays—have used this lack of information to argue that William Shakespeare either never existed or, if he did exist, did not write any of the plays we attribute to him. They believe that another historical figure, such as Francis Bacon or Queen Elizabeth I, used the name as a cover. Whether or not a man named William Shakespeare ever actually existed is ultimately secondary to the recognition that the group of plays bound together by that name does exist and continues to educate, enlighten, and entertain us.

An engraved portrait of Shakespeare by an unknown artist, ca. 1607.
Culver Pictures, Inc./SuperStock

Family life

Though scholars are unsure of the exact date of Shakespeare's birth, records indicate that his parents—Mary and John Shakespeare—baptized him on April 26, 1564, in the small provincial town of Stratford-upon-Avon—so named because it sat on the banks of the Avon river. Because common practice was to baptize infants a few days after they were born, scholars generally recognize April 23, 1564 as Shakespeare's birthday. Coincidentally, April 23 is the day of St. George, the patron saint of England, as well as the day upon which Shakespeare would die 52 years later. William was the third of Mary and John's eight children and the first of four sons. The house in which scholars believe Shakespeare to have been born stands on Henley Street and, despite many modifications over the years, you can still visit it today.

Shakespeare's father

Prior to William Shakespeare's birth, John Shakespeare lived in Snitterfield, where he married Mary Arden, the daughter of his landlord. After moving to Stratford in 1552, he worked as a glover, a money-lender, and a dealer in agricultural products such as wool and grain. He also pursued public office and achieved a variety of posts including bailiff, Stratford's highest elected position—equivalent to a small town's mayor. At the height of his career, sometime near 1576, he petitioned the Herald's Office for a coat of arms and thus the right to be a gentleman. But the rise from the middle class to the gentry did not come right away, and the costly petition expired without being granted.

About this time, John Shakespeare mysteriously fell into financial difficulty. He became involved in serious litigation, was assessed heavy fines, and even lost his seat on the town council. Some scholars suggest that this decline could have resulted from religious discrimination. The Shakespeare family may have supported Catholicism, the practice of which was illegal in England. However, other scholars point out that not all religious dissenters (both Catholics and radical Puritans) lost their posts due to their religion. Whatever the cause of his decline, John did regain some prosperity toward the end of his life. In 1596, the Herald's Office granted the Shakespeare family a coat of arms at the petition of William, by then a successful playwright in London. And John, prior to his death in 1601, regained his seat on Stratford's town council.

Childhood and education

Our understanding of William Shakespeare's childhood in Stratford is primarily speculative because children do not often appear in the legal records from which many scholars attempt to reconstruct Shakespeare's life. Based on his father's local prominence, scholars speculate that Shakespeare most likely attended King's New School, a school that usually employed Oxford graduates and was generally well-respected. Shakespeare would have started *petty school*—the rough equivalent to modern preschool—at the age of 4 or 5. He would have learned to read on a *hornbook*, which was a sheet of parchment or paper on which the alphabet and the Lord's Prayer were written. This sheet was framed in wood and covered with a transparent piece of horn for durability. After two years in petty school, he would have transferred to grammar school, where his school day probably lasted from 6 or 7 o'clock in the morning (depending on the time of year) until 5 o'clock in the evening, with only a handful of holidays.

While in grammar school, Shakespeare would primarily have studied Latin, reciting and reading the works of classical Roman authors such as Plautus, Ovid, Seneca, and Horace. Traces of these authors' works can be seen in his dramatic texts. Toward his last years in grammar school, Shakespeare probably acquired some basic skills in Greek as well. Thus the remark made by Ben Jonson, Shakespeare's well-educated friend and contemporary playwright,

Shakespeare's birthplace in Stratford-upon-Avon.
SuperStock

that Shakespeare knew "small Latin and less Greek" is accurate. Jonson is not saying that when Shakespeare left grammar school he was only semiliterate; he merely indicates that Shakespeare did not attend University, where he would have gained more Latin and Greek instruction.

Wife and children

When Shakespeare became an adult, the historical records documenting his existence began to increase. In November 1582, at the age of 18, he married 26-year-old Anne Hathaway from the nearby village of Shottery. The disparity in their ages, coupled with the fact that they baptized their first daughter, Susanna, only six months later in May 1583, has caused a great deal of modern speculation about the nature of their relationship. However, sixteenth-century conceptions of marriage differed slightly from our modern notions. Though all marriages needed to be performed before a member of the clergy, many of Shakespeare's contemporaries believed that a couple could establish a relationship through a premarital contract by exchanging vows in front of witnesses. This contract removed the social stigma of pregnancy before marriage. (Shakespeare's plays contain instances of marriage prompted by pregnancy, and *Measure for Measure* includes this kind of premarital contract.) Two years later, in February

1585, Shakespeare baptized his twins Hamnet and Judith. Hamnet would die at the age of 11 when Shakespeare was primarily living away from his family in London.

For seven years after the twins' baptism, the records remain silent on Shakespeare. At some point, he travelled to London and became involved with the theatre, but he could have been anywhere between 21 and 28 years old when he did. Though some have suggested that he may have served as an assistant to a schoolmaster at a provincial school, it seems likely that he went to London to become an actor, gradually becoming a playwright and gaining attention.

The plays: On stage and in print

The next mention of Shakespeare comes in 1592 by a university wit named Robert Greene, when Shakespeare apparently was already a rising actor and playwright for the London stage. Greene, no longer a successful playwright, tried to warn other university wits about Shakespeare. He wrote:

> *For there is an upstart crow, beautified with our feathers, that with his "Tiger's heart wrapped in a player's hide" supposes he is as well able to bombast out a blank verse as the best of you, and, being an absolute Johannes Factotum, is in his own conceit the only Shake-scene in a country.*

This statement comes at a point in time when men without a university education, like Shakespeare, were starting to compete as dramatists with the university wits. As many critics have pointed out, Greene's statement recalls a line from *3 Henry VI*, which reads, "O tiger's heart wrapped in a woman's hide!" (I.4.137). Greene's remark does not indicate that Shakespeare was generally disliked. On the contrary, another university wit, Thomas Nashe, wrote of the great theatrical success of *Henry VI*, and Henry

Chettle, Greene's publisher, later printed a flattering apology to Shakespeare. What Greene's statement does show us is that Shakespeare's reputation for poetry had reached enough prominence to provoke the envy of a failing competitor.

In the following year, 1593, the government closed London's theatres due to an outbreak of the bubonic plague. Publication history suggests that during this closure, Shakespeare may have written his two narrative poems, *Venus and Adonis,* published in 1593, and *The Rape of Lucrece,*

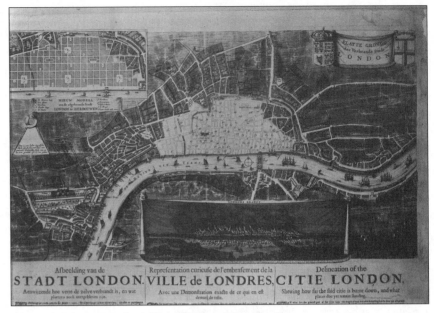

A ground plan of London after the fire of 1666, drawn by Marcus Willemsz Doornik.
Guildhall Library, London/AKG, Berlin/SuperStock

published in 1594. These are the only two works that Shakespeare seems to have helped into print; each carries a dedication by Shakespeare to Henry Wriothesley, Earl of Southampton.

Stage success

When the theatres reopened in 1594, Shakespeare joined the Lord Chamberlain's Men, an acting company. Though uncertain about the history of his early dramatic works, scholars believe that by this point he had written *The Two Gentlemen of Verona, The Taming of the Shrew,* the *Henry VI* trilogy, and *Titus Andronicus.* During his early years in the theatre, he primarily wrote history plays, with his romantic comedies emerging in the 1590s. Even at this early stage in his career, Shakespeare was a success. In 1597, he was able to purchase New Place, one of the two largest houses in Stratford, and secure a coat of arms for his family.

In 1597, the lease expired on the Lord Chamberlain's playhouse, called The Theatre. Because the owner of The Theatre refused to renew the lease, the acting company was forced to perform at various playhouses until the 1599 opening of the now famous Globe theatre, which was literally built with lumber from The Theatre. (The Globe, later destroyed by fire, has recently been reconstructed in London and can be visited today.)

Recent scholars suggest that Shakespeare's great tragedy *Julius Caesar* may have been the first of Shakespeare's plays performed in the original playhouse. When this open-air theatre on the Thames River opened, financial papers list Shakespeare's name as one of the principal investors. Already an actor and a playwright, Shakespeare was now becoming a "Company Man." This new status allowed him to share in the profits of the theatre rather than merely getting paid for his plays, some of which publishers were beginning to release in quarto format.

Publications

A *quarto* was a small, inexpensive book typically used for leisure books such as plays; the term itself indicates that the printer folded the paper four times. The modern day equivalent of a quarto would be a paperback. In contrast, the first collected works of Shakespeare were in folio format, which means that the printer folded each sheet only once. Scholars call the collected edition of Shakespeare's works the *First Folio*. A folio was a larger and more prestigious book than a quarto, and printers generally reserved the format for works such as the Bible.

No evidence exists that Shakespeare participated in the publication of any of his plays. Members of Shakespeare's acting company printed the First Folio seven years after Shakespeare's death. Generally, playwrights wrote their works to be performed on stage, and publishing them was a novel innovation at the time. Shakespeare probably would not have thought of them as books in the way we do. In fact, as a principal investor in the acting company (which purchased the play as well as the exclusive right to perform it), he may not have even thought of them as his own. He would probably have thought of his plays as belonging to the company.

For this reason, scholars have generally characterized most quartos printed before the First Folio as "bad" by arguing that printers pirated the plays and published them illegally. How would a printer have received a pirated copy of a play? The theories range from someone stealing a copy to an actor (or actors) selling the play by relating it from memory to a printer. Many times, major differences exist between a quarto version of the play and a folio version, causing uncertainty about which is Shakespeare's true creation. *Hamlet,* for example, is almost twice as long in the Folio as in quarto versions. Recently, scholars have come to realize the value of the different versions. The *Norton Shakespeare,* for example, includes all three versions of *King Lear*—the Quarto, the Folio, and the *conflated* version (the combination of the Quarto and Folio).

Prolific productions

The first decade of the 1600s witnessed the publication of additional quartos as well as the production of most of Shakespeare's great tragedies, with *Julius Caesar* appearing in 1599 and *Hamlet* in 1600–1601. After the death of Queen Elizabeth in 1603, the Lord Chamberlain's Men became the King's Men under James I, Elizabeth's successor. Around the time of this transition in the English monarchy, the famous tragedy *Othello* (1603–1604) was most likely written and performed, followed closely by *King Lear* (1605–1606), *Antony and Cleopatra* (1606), and *Macbeth* (1606) in the next two years.

Shakespeare's name also appears as a major investor in the 1609 acquisition of an indoor theatre known as the Blackfriars. This last period of Shakespeare's career, which includes plays that considered the acting conditions both at the Blackfriars and the open-air Globe theatre, consists primarily of romances or tragicomedies such as *The Winter's Tale* and *The Tempest*. On June 29, 1613, during a performance of *All is True*, or *Henry VIII*, the thatching on top of the Globe caught fire and the playhouse burned to the ground. After this incident, the King's Men moved solely into the indoor Blackfriars theatre.

Final days

During the last years of his career, Shakespeare collaborated on a couple of plays with contemporary dramatist John Fletcher, even possibly coming out of retirement—which scholars believe began sometime in 1613—to work on *The Two Noble Kinsmen* (1613–1614). Three years later, Shakespeare died on April 23, 1616. Though the exact cause of death remains unknown, a vicar from Stratford in the mid-seventeenth-century wrote in his diary that Shakespeare, perhaps celebrating the marriage of his daughter, Judith, contracted a fever during a night of revelry with fellow literary figures Ben Jonson and Michael Drayton. Regardless, Shakespeare may have felt his death was imminent in March of that year because he altered his will. Interestingly, his will mentions no book or theatrical manuscripts, perhaps indicating the lack of value that he put on printed versions of his dramatic works and their status as company property.

Seven years after Shakespeare's death, John Heminge and Henry Condell, fellow members of the King's Men, published his collected works. In their preface, they claim that they are publishing the true versions of Shakespeare's plays partially as a response to the previous quarto printings of 18 of his plays, most of these with multiple printings. This Folio contains 36 plays to which scholars generally add *Pericles* and *The Two Noble Kinsmen*. This volume of Shakespeare's plays began the process of constructing Shakespeare not only as England's national poet but also as a monumental figure whose plays would continue to captivate imaginations at the end of the millenium with no signs of stopping. Ben Jonson's prophetic line about Shakespeare in the First Folio— "He was not of an age, but for all time!"—certainly holds true.

Chronology of Shakespeare's plays

1590–1591	*The Two Gentlemen of Verona*
	The Taming of the Shrew
1591	*2 Henry VI*
	3 Henry VI
1592	*1 Henry VI*
	Titus Andronicus
1592–1593	*Richard III*
	Venus and Adonis
1593–1594	*The Rape of Lucrece*
1594	*The Comedy of Errors*
1594–1595	*Love's Labour's Lost*
1595	*Richard II*
	Romeo and Juliet
	A Midsummer Night's Dream
1595–1596	*Love's Labour's Won*
	(This manuscript was lost.)
1596	*King John*

1596–1597	*The Merchant of Venice*
	1 Henry IV
1597–1598	*The Merry Wives of Windsor*
	2 Henry IV
1598	*Much Ado About Nothing*
1598–1599	*Henry V*
1599	*Julius Caesar*
1599–1600	*As You Like It*
1600–1601	*Hamlet*
1601	*Twelfth Night, or What You Will*
1602	*Troilus and Cressida*
1593–1603	*Sonnets*
1603	*Measure for Measure*
1603–1604	*A Lover's Complaint*
	Othello
1604–1605	*All's Well That Ends Well*
1605	*Timon of Athens*
1605–1606	*King Lear*
1606	*Macbeth*
	Antony and Cleopatra
1607	*Pericles*
1608	*Coriolanus*
1609	*The Winter's Tale*
1610	*Cymbeline*
1611	*The Tempest*
1612–1613	*Cardenio* (with John Fletcher; this manuscript was lost.)
1613	*All is True (Henry VIII)*
1613–1614	*The Two Noble Kinsmen* (with John Fletcher)

This chronology is derived from Stanley Wells and Gary Taylor's *William Shakespeare: A Textual Companion*, which is listed in the "Works consulted" section on the next page.

A note on Shakespeare's language

Readers encountering Shakespeare for the first time usually find Early Modern English difficult to understand. Yet rather than serving as a barrier to Shakespeare, the richness of this language should form part of our appreciation of the Bard.

One of the first things readers usually notice about the language is the use of pronouns. Like the King James Version of the Bible, Shakespeare's pronouns are slightly different from our own and can cause confusion. Words like "thou" (you), "thee" and "ye" (objective cases of you), and "thy" and "thine" (your/yours) appear throughout Shakespeare's plays. You may need a little time to get used to these changes. You can find the definitions for other words that commonly cause confusion in the glossary column on the right side of each page in this edition.

Iambic pentameter

Though Shakespeare sometimes wrote in prose, he wrote most of his plays in poetry, specifically blank verse. Blank verse consists of lines in unrhymed *iambic pentameter. Iambic* refers to the stress patterns of the line. An *iamb* is an element of sound that consists of two beats—the first unstressed (da) and the second stressed (DA). A good example of an iambic line is Hamlet's famous line "To be or not to be," in which you do not stress "to," "or," and "to," but you do stress "be," "not," and "be." *Pentameter* refers to the *meter* or number of stressed syllables in a line. *Penta*-meter has five stressed syllables. Thus, Juliet's line "But soft, what light through yonder window breaks?" (II.2.2) is a good example of an iambic pentameter line.

Wordplay

Shakespeare's language is also verbally rich because he, along with many dramatists of his period, had a fondness for wordplay. This wordplay often takes the forms of double meanings, called *puns,* where a word can mean more than one thing in a given context. Shakespeare often employs these puns as a way of illustrating the distance between what is on the surface—*apparent* meanings—and what meanings lie underneath. Though recognizing these puns may be difficult at first, the glosses in the right-hand column point many of them out to you.

If you are encountering Shakespeare's plays for the first time, the following reading tips may help ease you into the text. Shakespeare's lines were meant to be spoken; therefore, reading them aloud or speaking them should help with comprehension. Also, though most of the lines are poetic, do not forget to read complete sentences—move from period to period as well as from line to line. Although Shakespeare's language can be difficult at first, the rewards of immersing yourself in the richness and fluidity of the lines are immeasurable.

Works consulted

For more information on Shakespeare's life and works, see the following:

Bevington, David, ed. *The Complete Works of Shakespeare.* New York: Longman, 1997.

Evans, G. Blakemore, ed. *The Riverside Shakespeare.* Boston: Houghton Mifflin Co., 1997.

Greenblatt, Stephen, ed. *The Norton Shakespeare.* New York: W.W. Norton and Co., 1997.

Kastan, David Scott, ed. *A Companion to Shakespeare.* Oxford: Blackwell, 1999.

McDonald, Russ. *The Bedford Companion to Shakespeare: An Introduction with Documents.* Boston: Bedford-St. Martin's Press, 1996.

Wells, Stanley and Gary Taylor. *William Shakespeare: A Textual Companion.* New York: W.W. Norton and Co., 1997.

INTRODUCTION TO EARLY MODERN ENGLAND

William Shakespeare (1564–1616) lived during a period in England's history that people have generally referred to as the English Renaissance. The term *renaissance,* meaning rebirth, was applied to this period of English history as a way of celebrating what was perceived as the rapid development of art, literature, science, and politics: in many ways, the rebirth of classical Rome.

Recently, scholars have challenged the name "English Renaissance" on two grounds. First, some scholars argue that the term should not be used because women did not share in the advancements of English culture during this time period; their legal status was still below that of men. Second, other scholars have challenged the basic notion that this period saw a sudden explosion of culture. A rebirth of civilization suggests that the previous period of time was not civilized. This second group of scholars sees a much more gradual transition between the Middle Ages and Shakespeare's time.

Some people use the terms *Elizabethan* and *Jacobean* when referring to periods of the sixteenth and seventeenth centuries. These terms correspond to the reigns of Elizabeth I (1558–1603) and James I (1603–1625). The problem with these terms is that they do not cover large spans of time; for example, Shakespeare's life and career span both monarchies.

Scholars are now beginning to replace Renaissance with the term Early Modern when referring to this time period, but people still use both terms interchangeably. The term *Early Modern* recognizes that this period established many of the foundations of our modern culture. Though critics still disagree about the exact dates of the period, in general, the dates range from 1450 to 1750. Thus, Shakespeare's life clearly falls within the Early Modern period.

Shakespeare's plays live on in our culture, but we must remember that Shakespeare's culture differed greatly from our own. Though his understanding of human nature and relationships seems to apply to our modern lives, we must try to understand the world he lived in so we can better understand his plays. This introduction helps you do just that. It examines the intellectual, religious, political, and social contexts of Shakespeare's work before turning to the importance of the theatre and the printing press.

Intellectual context

In general, people in Early Modern England looked at the universe, the human body, and science very differently from the way we do. But while we do not share their same beliefs, we must not *think* of people during Shakespeare's time as lacking in intelligence or education. Discoveries made during the Early Modern period concerning the universe and the human body provide the basis of modern science.

Cosmology

One subject we view very differently than Early Modern thinkers is *cosmology*. Shakespeare's contemporaries believed in the astronomy of Ptolemy, an intellectual from Alexandria in the second century A.D. Ptolemy thought that the earth stood at the centre of the universe, surrounded by nine concentric rings. The celestial bodies circled the earth in the following order: the moon, Mercury, Venus, the sun, Mars, Jupiter, Saturn, and the stars. The entire system was controlled by the *primum mobile*, or Prime Mover, which initiated and maintained the movement of the celestial bodies. No one had yet discovered the last three planets in our solar system, Uranus, Neptune, and Pluto.

In 1543, Nicolaus Copernicus published his theory of a sun-based solar system, in which the sun stood at the centre and the planets revolved around it. Though this theory appeared prior to Shakespeare's birth, people didn't really start to change their minds until 1610, when Galileo used his telescope to confirm Copernicus's theory. David Bevington asserts in the general introduction to his edition of Shakespeare's works that during most of Shakespeare's writing career, the cosmology of the universe was in question, and this sense of uncertainty influences some of his plays.

Universal hierarchy

Closely related to Ptolemy's hierarchical view of the universe is a hierarchical conception of the earth (sometimes referred to as the Chain of Being). During the Early Modern period, many people believed that all of creation was organized hierarchically. God existed at the top, followed by the angels, men, women, animals, plants, and rocks. (Because all women were thought to exist below all men on the chain, we can easily imagine the confusion that Elizabeth I caused when she became queen of England. She was literally "out of order," an expression that still exists in our society.) Though the concept of this hierarchy is a useful one when beginning to study Shakespeare, keep in mind that distinctions in this hierarchical view were not always clear and that we should not reduce all Early Modern thinking to a simple chain.

Elements and humours

The belief in a hierarchical scheme of existence created a comforting sense of order and balance that carried over into science as well. Shakespeare's contemporaries generally accepted that four different elements composed everything in the universe: earth, air, water, and fire. People associated these four elements with four qualities of being. These qualities—hot, cold, moist, and dry—appeared in different combinations in the elements. For example, air was hot and moist; water was cold and moist; earth was cold and dry; and fire was hot and dry.

In addition, people believed that the human body contained all four elements in the form of *humours*—blood, phlegm, yellow bile, and black bile—each of which corresponded to an element. Blood corresponded to air (hot and moist), phlegm to water (cold and moist), yellow bile to fire (hot and dry), and black bile to earth (cold and dry). When someone was sick, physicians generally believed that the patient's humours were not in the proper balance. For example, if someone were diagnosed with an abundance of blood, the physician would bleed the patient (using leeches or cutting the skin) in order to restore the balance.

Shakespeare's contemporaries also believed that the humours determined personality and temperament. If a person's dominant humour was blood, he was considered light-hearted. If dominated by yellow bile (or choler), that person was irritable. The dominance of phlegm led a person to be dull and kind. And if black bile prevailed, he was melancholy or sad. Thus, people of Early Modern England often used the humours to explain behaviour and emotional outbursts. Throughout Shakespeare's plays, he uses the concept of the humours to define and explain various characters.

In *King Lear,* the title character has a highly irritable personality and can therefore be considered as having a choleric temperament. Goneril, the king's oldest daughter, speaks in Act I, Scene 1, Line 299 about Lear's "infirm and choleric years." Throughout the play, King Lear displays an explosive and extroverted personality.

Religious context

Shakespeare lived in an England full of religious uncertainty and dispute. From the Protestant Reformation to the translation of the Bible into English, the Early Modern era is punctuated with events that have greatly influenced modern religious beliefs.

The Reformation

Until the Protestant Reformation, the only Christian church was the Catholic, or "universal," church. Beginning in Europe in the early sixteenth century, religious thinkers such as Martin Luther and John Calvin, who claimed that the Roman Catholic Church had become corrupt and was no longer following the word of God, began what has become known as the Protestant Reformation. The Protestants ("protestors") believed in salvation by faith rather than works. They also believed in the primacy of the Bible and advocated giving all people access to reading the Bible.

Many English people initially resisted Protestant ideas. However, the Reformation in England began in 1527 during the reign of Henry VIII, prior to Shakespeare's birth. In that year, Henry VIII decided to divorce his wife, Catherine of Aragon, for her failure to produce a male heir. (Only one of their children, Mary, survived past infancy.) Rome denied Henry's petitions for a divorce, forcing him to divorce Catherine without the Church's approval, which he did in 1533.

A portrait of King Henry VIII, artist unknown, ca. 1542.
National Portrait Gallery, London/SuperStock

The Act of Supremacy

The following year, the Pope excommunicated Henry VIII while Parliament confirmed his divorce and the legitimacy of his new marriage through the *Act of Succession*. Later in 1534, Parliament passed the *Act of Supremacy*, naming Henry the "Supreme Head of the Church in England." Henry persecuted both radical Protestant reformers and Catholics who remained loyal to Rome.

Henry VIII's death in 1547 brought Edward VI, his 10-year-old son by Jane Seymour (the king's third wife), to the throne. This succession gave Protestant reformers the chance to solidify their break with the Catholic Church. During Edward's reign, Archbishop Thomas Cranmer established the foundation for the Anglican Church through his 42 articles of religion. He also wrote the first *Book of Common Prayer*, adopted in 1549, which was the official text for worship services in England.

Bloody Mary

Catholics continued to be persecuted until 1553, when the sickly Edward VI died and was succeeded by Mary, his half-sister and the Catholic daughter of Catherine of Aragon. The reign of Mary witnessed the reversal of religion in England through the restoration of Catholic authority and obedience to Rome. Protestants were executed in large numbers, which earned the monarch the nickname *Bloody Mary*. Many Protestants fled to mainland Europe to escape persecution.

Elizabeth, the daughter of Henry VIII and Anne Boleyn, outwardly complied with the mandated Catholicism during her half-sister Mary's reign, but she restored Protestantism when she took the throne in 1558 after Mary's death. Thus, in the space of single decade, England's throne passed from Protestant to Catholic to Protestant, with each change carrying serious and deadly consequences.

Though Elizabeth reigned in relative peace from 1558 to her death in 1603, religion was still a serious concern for her subjects. During Shakespeare's life, a great deal of religious dissent existed in England. Many Catholics, who remained loyal to Rome and their church, were persecuted for their beliefs. At the other end of the spectrum, the Puritans were persecuted for their belief that the Reformation was not complete. (The English pejoratively applied the term *Puritan* to religious groups that wanted to continue purifying the English church by such measures as removing the *episcopacy,* or the structure of bishops.)

The Great Bible

One thing agreed upon by both the Anglicans and Puritans was the importance of a Bible written in English. Translated by William Tyndale in 1525, the first authorized Bible in English, published in 1539, was known as the Great Bible. This Bible was later revised during Elizabeth's reign into what was known as the Bishop's Bible. As Stephen Greenblatt points out in his introduction to the *Norton Shakespeare,* Shakespeare would probably have been familiar with both the Bishop's Bible, heard aloud in Mass, and the Geneva Bible, which was written by English exiles in Geneva. The last authorized Bible produced during Shakespeare's lifetime came within the last decade of his life when James I's commissioned edition, known as the King James Bible, appeared in 1611.

Political context

Politics and religion were closely related in Shakespeare's England. Both of the monarchs under whom Shakespeare lived had to deal with religious and political dissenters.

Elizabeth I

Despite being a Protestant, Elizabeth I tried to take a middle road on the religious question. She allowed Catholics to practice their religion in private as long as they outwardly appeared Anglican and remained loyal to the throne.

Elizabeth's monarchy was one of absolute supremacy. Believing in the divine right of kings, she styled herself as being appointed by God to rule England. To oppose the Queen's will was the equivalent of opposing God's will. Known as *passive obedience,*

this doctrine did not allow any opposition even to a tyrannical monarch because God had appointed the king or queen for reasons unknown to His subjects on earth. However, as Bevington notes, Elizabeth's power was not as absolute as her rhetoric suggested. Parliament, already well-established in England, reserved some power, such as the authority to levy taxes, for itself.

Elizabeth I lived in a society that restricted women from possessing any political or personal autonomy and power. As queen, Elizabeth violated and called into question many of the prejudices and practices against women. In a way, her society forced her to "overcome" her sex in order to rule effectively. However, her position did nothing to increase the status of women in England.

A portrait of Elizabeth I by George Gower, ca. 1588. National Portrait Gallery, London/SuperStock

One of the rhetorical strategies that Elizabeth adopted in order to rule effectively was to separate her position as monarch of England from her natural body—to separate her *body politic* from her *body natural*. In addition, throughout her reign, Elizabeth brilliantly negotiated between domestic and foreign factions—some of whom were anxious about a female monarch and wanted her to marry—appeasing both sides without ever committing to one.

She remained unmarried throughout her 45-year reign, partially by styling herself as the Virgin Queen whose purity represented England herself. Her refusal to marry and her habit of hinting and promising marriage with suitors both foreign and domestic helped Elizabeth maintain internal and external peace. Not marrying allowed her to retain her independence, but it left the succession of the English throne in question. In 1603, on her deathbed, she named James VI, King of Scotland and son of her cousin Mary, as her successor.

James I

When he assumed the English crown, James VI of Scotland became James I of England. (Some historians refer to him as James VI and I.) Like Elizabeth, James was a strong believer in the divine right of kings and their absolute authority.

Upon his arrival in London to claim the English throne, James made his plans to unite Scotland and England clear. However, a long-standing history of enmity existed between the two countries. Partially as a result of this history and the influx of Scottish courtiers into English society, anti-Scottish prejudice abounded in England. When James asked Parliament for the title of "King of Great Britain," he was denied.

As scholars such as Bevington have pointed out, James was less successful than Elizabeth in negotiating between the different religious and political factions in England. Although he was a Protestant, he began to have problems with the Puritan sect of the House of Commons, which ultimately led to a rift between the court (which also started to have Catholic sympathies) and the Parliament. This rift between the monarchy and Parliament eventually escalated into the civil war that would erupt during the reign of James's son, Charles I.

In spite of its difficulties with Parliament, James's court was a site of wealth, luxury, and extravagance. James I commissioned elaborate feasts, masques, and pageants, and in doing so he more than doubled the royal debt. Stephen Greenblatt suggests that Shakespeare's *The Tempest* may reflect this extravagance through Prospero's magnificent banquet and accompanying masque. Reigning from 1603 to 1625, James I remained the King of England throughout the last years of Shakespeare's life.

Social context

Shakespeare's England divided itself roughly into two social classes: the aristocrats (or nobility) and everyone else. The primary distinctions between these two classes were ancestry, wealth, and power. Simply put, the aristocrats were the only ones who possessed all three.

Aristocrats were born with their wealth, but the growth of trade and the development of skilled professions began to provide wealth for those not born with it. Although the notion of a middle class did not begin to develop until after Shakespeare's death, the possibility of some social mobility did exist in Early Modern England. Shakespeare himself used the wealth gained from the theatre to move into the lower ranks of the aristocracy by securing a coat of arms for his family.

Shakespeare was not unique in this movement, but not all people received the opportunity to increase their social status. Members of the aristocracy feared this social movement and, as a result, promoted harsh laws of apprenticeship and fashion, restricting certain styles of dress and material. These laws dictated that only the aristocracy could wear certain articles of clothing, colours, and materials. Though enforcement was a difficult task, the Early Modern aristocracy considered dressing above one's station a moral and ethical violation.

The status of women

The legal status of women did not allow them much public or private autonomy. English society functioned on a system of patriarchy and hierarchy (see "Universal Hierarchy" earlier in this introduction), which means that men controlled society beginning with the individual family. In fact, the family metaphorically corresponded to the state. For example, the husband was the king of his family. His authority to control his family was absolute and based on divine right, similar to that of the country's king. People also saw the family itself differently than today, considering apprentices and servants part of the whole family.

The practice of *primogeniture*—a system of inheritance that passed all of a family's wealth through the first male child—accompanied this system of patriarchy. Thus, women did not generally inherit their family's wealth and titles. In the absence of a male heir, some women, such as Queen Elizabeth, did. But after women married, they lost almost all of their already limited legal rights, such as the right to inherit, to own property, and to sign contracts. In all likelihood, Elizabeth I would have lost much of her power and authority had she married.

Furthermore, women did not generally receive an education and could not enter certain professions, including acting. Society relegated women to the domestic sphere of the home.

The role of women in *King Lear* is an unusual one, because in this play the three female characters possess extraordinary power. The king's two oldest daughters—Goneril and Regan—are married women. Yet they are also regents, and their actions are commanding. They are anything but subservient

Elizabethan wives. In the play's first scene, you will see how the youngest daughter Cordelia defies tradition to hold to her personal beliefs.

Daily life

Daily life in Early Modern England began before sunup—exactly how early depended on one's station in life. A servant's responsibilities usually included preparing the house for the day. Families usually possessed limited living space. Even among wealthy families, multiple family members tended to share a small number of rooms, suggesting that privacy may not have been important or practical.

Working through the morning, Elizabethans usually had lunch about noon. This midday meal was the primary meal of the day, much like dinner is for modern families. The workday usually ended around sundown or 5 p.m., depending on the season. Before an early bedtime, Elizabethans usually ate a light repast and then settled in for a couple of hours of reading (if the family members were literate and could bear the high cost of books) or socializing.

Mortality rates

Mortality rates in Early Modern England were high compared to our standards, especially among infants. Infection and disease ran rampant because physicians did not realize the need for antiseptics and sterile equipment. As a result, communicable diseases often spread very rapidly in cities, particularly London.

In addition, the bubonic plague frequently ravaged England, with two major outbreaks—from 1592–1594 and in 1603—occurring during Shakespeare's lifetime. People did not understand the plague and generally perceived it as God's punishment. (We now know that the plague was spread by fleas and could not be spread directly from human to human.) Without a cure or an understanding of what transmitted the disease, physicians could do nothing to stop the thousands of deaths that resulted from each outbreak. These outbreaks had a direct effect on Shakespeare's career, because the government often closed the theatres in an effort to impede the spread of the disease.

London life

In the sixteenth century, London, though small compared to modern cities, was the largest city of Europe, with a population of about 200,000 inhabitants in the city and surrounding suburbs. London was a crowded city without a sewer system, which facilitated epidemics such as the plague. In addition, crime rates were high in the city due to inefficient law enforcement and the lack of street lighting.

Despite these drawbacks, London was the cultural, political, and social heart of England. As the home of the monarchy and most of England's trade, London was a bustling metropolis. Not surprisingly, a young Shakespeare moved to London to begin his professional career.

The theatre

Most theatres were not actually located within the city of London. Rather, theatre owners built them on the South bank of the Thames River (in Southwark) across from the city in order to avoid the strict regulations that applied within the city's walls. These restrictions stemmed from a mistrust of public performances as locations of plague and riotous behavior. Furthermore, because theatre performances took place during the day, they took labourers away from their jobs. Opposition to the theatres also came from Puritans, who believed that they fostered immorality. Therefore, theatres moved out of the city, to areas near other sites of restricted activities, such as dog fighting, bear- and bull-baiting, and prostitution.

Despite the move, the theatre was not free from censorship or regulation. In fact, a branch of the government known as the Office of the Revels attempted to ensure that plays did not present politically or socially sensitive material. Prior to each

The recently reconstructed Globe theatre.
Chris Parker/PAL

performance, the Master of the Revels would read a complete text of each play, cutting out offending sections or, in some cases, not approving the play for public performance.

Performance spaces

Theatres in Early Modern England were quite different from our modern facilities. They were usually open-air, relying heavily on natural light and good weather. The rectangular stage extended out into an area that people called the *pit*—a circular, uncovered area about 21 metres in diameter. Audience members had two choices when purchasing admission to a theatre. Admission to the pit, where the lower classes (or *groundlings*) stood for the performances, was the cheaper option. People of wealth could purchase a seat in one of the three covered tiers of seats that ringed the pit. At full capacity, a public theatre in Early Modern England could hold between 2,000 and 3,000 people.

The stage, which projected into the pit and was raised about 1.5 metres above it, had a covered portion called the *heavens*. The heavens enclosed theatrical equipment for lowering and raising actors to and from the stage. A trapdoor in the middle of the stage provided theatrical graves for characters such as Ophelia in *Hamlet* and also allowed ghosts, such as Banquo in *Macbeth,* to rise from the earth. A wall separated the back of the stage from the actors' dressing room, known as the *tiring house*. At each end of the wall stood a door for major entrances and exits. Above the wall and doors stood a gallery directly above the stage, reserved for the wealthiest spectators. Actors occasionally used this area when a performance called for a difference in height—for example, to represent Juliet's balcony or the walls of a besieged city. A good example of this type of theatre was the original Globe theatre in London in which Shakespeare's company, the Lord Chamberlain's Men (later the King's Men), staged its plays. However, indoor theatres, such as the Blackfriars, differed slightly because the pit was filled with chairs that faced a rectangular stage. Because only the wealthy could afford the cost of admission, the public generally considered these theatres private.

As you read the play, you will discover that staging *King Lear* in an Early Modern theatre must have been a challenge even for its author. Keen imagination was a must, because in this drama the stage has to represent a royal court, an earl's castle, a storm-ridden heath, a courtyard, a hut, a farmhouse, French and British military encampments, and the cliffs of Dover!

Actors and staging

Performances in Shakespeare's England do not appear to have employed scenery. However, theatre companies developed their costumes with great care and expense. In fact, a playing company's costumes were its most valuable items. These extravagant costumes were the object of much controversy because some aristocrats feared that the actors could use them to disguise their social status on the streets of London.

Costumes also disguised a player's gender. All actors on the stage during Shakespeare's lifetime were men. Young boys whose voices had not reached maturity played female parts. This practice no doubt influenced Shakespeare's and his contemporary playwrights' thematic explorations of cross-dressing.

Though historians have managed to reconstruct the appearance of the Early Modern theatre, such as the recent construction of the Globe in London, much of the information regarding how plays were performed during this era has been lost. Scholars of Early Modern theatre have turned to the scant external and internal stage directions in manuscripts in an effort to find these answers. While a hindrance for modern critics and scholars, the lack of detail about Early Modern performances has allowed modern directors and actors a great deal of flexibility and room to be creative.

Certain performance challenges specific to *King Lear* are mentioned in the commentaries accompanying the play. In Shakespeare's time, the players needed to demonstrate amazing flexibility to tell this

Shakespeare in Love *shows how the interior of the Globe would have appeared.*
Everett Collection

story. The young boys playing the female roles had not only to be convincing as women but believable as women assuming other roles within the play. Another interesting aspect of this play's production is the range of costuming: everything from the royal robes of the king to the mud and blanket of Tom o' Bedlam.

The printing press

If not for the printing press, many Early Modern plays may not have survived until today. In Shakespeare's time, printers produced all books by *sheet*—a single large piece of paper that the printer would fold in order to produce the desired book size. For example, a folio required folding the sheet once, a quarto four times, an octavo eight, and so on. Sheets would be printed one side at a time; thus, printers had to simultaneously print multiple nonconsecutive pages.

In order to estimate what section of the text would be on each page, the printer would *cast off* copy. After the printer made these estimates, *compositors* would set the type upside down, letter by letter. This process of setting type produced textual errors, some of which a proofreader would catch. When a proofreader found an error, the compositors would fix the piece or pieces of type. Printers called corrections made after printing began *stop-press* corrections because they literally had to stop the press to fix the error. Because of the high cost of paper, printers would still sell the sheets printed before they made the correction.

Printers placed frames of text in the bed of the printing press and used them to imprint the paper. They then folded and grouped the sheets of paper into gatherings, after which the pages were ready for sale. The buyer had the option of getting the new play bound.

The printing process was crucial to the preservation of Shakespeare's works, but the printing of drama in Early Modern England was not a standardized practice. Many of the first editions of Shakespeare's plays appear in quarto format and, until recently, scholars regarded them as "corrupt." In fact, scholars still debate how close a relationship exists between what appeared on the stage in the sixteenth and seventeenth centuries and what appears on the printed page. The inconsistent and scant appearance of stage directions, for example, makes it difficult to determine how close this relationship was.

We know that the practice of the theatre allowed the alteration of plays by a variety of hands other than the author's, further complicating any efforts to extract what a playwright wrote and what was changed by either the players, the printers, or the government censors. Theatre was a collaborative environment. Rather than lament our inability to determine authorship and what exactly Shakespeare wrote, we should work to understand this collaborative nature and learn from it.

In the "Introduction to *King Lear*" that follows, you will find a discussion of the textual history of this drama. *Lear* presents us with a perfect example of the differences between foul papers and other editions. *King Lear* exists in two different forms, and among some dozen quarto editions of the play, discrepancies and alterations are found in each.

Shakespeare wrote his plays for the stage, and the existing published texts reflect the collaborative nature of the theater as well as the unavoidable changes made during the printing process. A play's first written version would have been the author's *foul papers,* which invariably consisted of blotted lines and revised text. From there, a scribe would recopy the play and produce a *fair copy*. The theatre manager would then copy out and annotate this copy into a playbook (what people today call a *promptbook*).

At this point, scrolls of individual parts were copied out for actors to memorize. (Due to the high cost of paper, theatre companies could not afford to provide their actors with a complete copy of the play.) The government required the company to send the playbook to the Master of the Revels, the government official who would make any necessary changes or mark any passages considered unacceptable for performance.

Printers could have used any one of these copies to print a play. We cannot determine whether a printer used the author's version, the modified theatrical version, the censored version, or a combination when printing a given play. Refer to the "Publications" section of the "Introduction to William Shakespeare" for further discussion of the impact printing practices have on our understanding of Shakespeare's works.

Works cited

For more information regarding Early Modern England, consult the following works:

Bevington, David. "General Introduction." *The Complete Works of William Shakespeare*. Updated Fourth edition. New York: Longman, 1997.

Greenblatt, Stephen. "Shakespeare's World." *Norton Shakespeare*. New York: W.W. Norton and Co., 1997.

Kastan, David Scott, ed. *A Companion to Shakespeare*. Oxford: Blackwell, 1999.

McDonald, Russ. *The Bedford Companion to Shakespeare: An Introduction with Documents*. Boston: Bedford-St. Martin's Press, 1996.

INTRODUCTION TO *KING LEAR*

The Tragedy of King Lear is arguably Shakespeare's greatest tragedy, if not indeed his greatest play. Respected Shakespeare critic Jan Kott argues that Shakespeare's *King Lear* is a giant among masterpieces of art. Kott writes, "Modern criticism compares *King Lear* to Bach's *Mass in B Minor*, to Beethoven's Fifth and Ninth Symphonies, to Wagner's *Parsifal*, to Michelangelo's *Last Judgment*, to Dante's *Purgatory* and *Inferno*." However, *King Lear* is not the most popular play of Shakespeare's repertoire, because it presents production challenges both in terms of staging and for the actor who takes on the part of Lear. In spite of these performance difficulties, *Lear* is an immensely moving play.

As the "Introduction to Early Modern England" explains, the era during which Shakespeare lived and wrote was a period of great change. England sent her ships on voyages of discovery and exploration, which brought new images and ideas to English thinkers and artisans. The Spanish Armada suffered defeat at English hands, and religious reformation was reflected up and down the social scale. A new type of nobility graced the royal court; a certain new wealth and status grew among English citizens. Perhaps most significantly, Early Modern thinkers began to promote the importance of the individual; previous generations had been convinced by the teachings of the church that humanity was the lowest form of life. Shakespeare's *Lear* emerged from this exciting period.

A study in evil

Shakespeare wrote *Lear* at a time when he was also creating some of his best comedies and some of his greatest tragedies. Critic Ernest Dowden writes that from the years 1601 to 1608, "It seems Shakespeare needed to sound the depths of the human heart, to inquire into the darkest and saddest parts of human life, to study the great mystery of evil." This evil becomes the stuff of tragedy in *King Lear*—tragedy that is traditional in the respect that human action often brings about catastrophe coupled with the death of persons in high places.

Of all the Shakespearean tragedies, Dowden sees *Lear* as "the one in which the passions assume the largest proportion, act upon the widest theatre, and

Nigel Hawthorne plays Lear in a Barbican production in October 1999.
Henrietta Butler/PAL.

attain their absolute extremes." As we watch the development of Lear throughout the drama, we observe tremendous outbursts of passion as the very depths of the king's emotions are plumbed and his entire outlook on life undergoes drastic changes. Perhaps more than any other tragedy, *King Lear* reveals the agony of a tortured mind.

Lear's debut

Scholars have a difficult time determining when Shakespeare wrote many of his plays, but evidence surrounding the *King Lear* text provides clues about when the play was written. On November 26, 1607, John Busby and Nathaniel Butter made the follow-

ing entry in the Stationer's Register (a public record that documented performances and publications): "A booke called Master William Shakespeare his historye of King Lear, as yt was played before the King's maiestie at Whitehall vppon Sainct Stephens night [December 26] at Christmas Last, by his maiesties servantes playinge vsually at the Globe on the Banksyde." This entry indicates that King James and his court most likely watched a performance of *King Lear* during the Christmas season of 1606. (The Stationer's Register also contains an entry dated May 13, 1606, that indicates an imitation of *Lear* by the dramatist Sharplan called *The Fleer; Lear,* then, may be dated even earlier than May 1606.)

Historical records of eclipses also give us a hint as to *Lear's* date of creation. Notable eclipses were visible in England on September 27 and October 2, 1605; in *Lear,* the character Gloucester refers to "these late eclipses of the sun and moon." During Shakespeare's time, people believed that eclipses were serious, significant events. Shakespeare surely drew on contemporary events and superstitions in composing his play texts.

Sources for the story

Modern audiences tend to value originality highly when judging the worth of artistic works. When Shakespeare wrote *King Lear,* however, originality was not nearly so important. Early Modern artists often based their works on well-known legends and current events, and Shakespeare was no exception. For example, in *Lear,* Shakespeare uses well-known names of Roman and Anglo-Saxon origin to christen his characters. *Gloucester* is a Roman name, and *Edgar, Kent,* and *Edmund* all share Anglo-Saxon roots. (Shakespeare had a brother named Edmund, an actor who died in 1607.) Shakespeare also did not create the idea of the "love test," which King Lear uses in Act I, Scene 1 to decide which of his daughters loves him the most. The "love test" has roots in many cultures.

Many scholars believe that Shakespeare's primary source for *Lear* is a tale published in 1587 in the second edition of Raphael Holinshed's *The First Volume of the Chronicles of England, Scotland, and Ireland.* The story centres around a British king named Leir who ruled during the time of Joash of Judah. The king subjects his daughters—Gonorilla, Regan, and Cordeilla—to a test of affections. Displeased with Cordeilla's response, Leir denies her an inheritance. He marries off the two older sisters: Gonorilla to the Duke of Cornwall and Regan to the Duke of Albania. (An additional source for this story of Lear and his daughters appears in the *Historia Regnum Brittanaiae* by the Welsh priest Geoffrey of Monmouth, circa 1135.)

Shakespeare pulled from other sources to create the subplot about Gloucester and his sons. Those sources include two poems that were written during Shakespeare's lifetime: *Arcadia* by Sir Philip Sidney and *The Faerie Queene* by Edmund Spenser. Shakespeare even used a religious pamphlet (called a tract) written in 1603 as a source for the names of the demons that the character Edgar claims are plaguing him in Act III, Scene 4.

Despite having an abundance of sources, however, certain aspects of *King Lear* remain original with Shakespeare. None of the sources presents the king as a madman, and the character of loyal Kent does not appear anywhere else. The horrific storm and the characters of the Fool and Oswald are also pure Shakespeare. And the ending of the play—one of the more heartrending in drama—owes nothing to Shakespeare's sources, either.

Audience recognition

Because parts of the Lear story were already familiar to his audience, Shakespeare enjoyed the advantage of not having to provide elaborate *exposition,* or set-up information, for his play. The title itself, *The Tragedy of King Lear,* somewhat prepares an audience

for the drama. Shakespeare also relies on his audiences' acceptance of certain concepts, including the idea that a king's successes or failures are reflected in the kingdom over which he rules. As the "Introduction to Early Modern England" explains, Shakespeare's contemporaries believed that kings were divinely chosen to rule. Lear's action in the first scene of dividing his kingdom and giving up his rule would have instantly sounded warning bells for Early Modern audiences.

Interestingly, a lawsuit in England in 1603 may have also prepared Shakespeare's audiences for the story of *Lear.* Stephen Greenblatt writes that in 1603, "[t]he two elder daughters of a doddering gentleman named Sir Brian Annesley attempted to get their father legally certified as insane, thereby enabling themselves to take over his estate, while his youngest daughter vehemently protested on her father's behalf. The youngest daughter's name happened to be Cordell, a name uncannily close to that of Lear's youngest daughter, Cordelia, who tries to save her father from the malevolent designs of her older sisters."

Critical response

But even though early audiences for this play may have recognized much of its subject matter as familiar, not everyone gave the play a glowing review. In fact, in 1681, a man named Nahum Tate actually rewrote the play's ending because he found Shakespeare's version too tragic. The effects of that change were far-reaching; for more than 150 years, Tate's revision was played before audiences. Fortunately, the original ending has been restored.

Clockwise from top left: Cordelia, Lear, the Fool, and Gloucester as portrayed in the 1984 film starring Laurence Olivier. Everett Collection

presents a terrific challenge for an actor; Lear is sometimes overpowering and difficult, sometimes weak and desperate.

Quarto versus Folio text

Another favourite subject for critics of *King Lear* has to do with the issue of the "master text." *King Lear* was first published in a quarto edition in 1608. This quarto, called Q1, is also known as the *Pied Bull* quarto. Scholars generally agree that this version of *Lear* was printed from Shakespeare's own copy of the play (his *foul papers*) and contains many spelling and punctuation errors. In 1619, three years after Shakespeare's death, another quarto edition was printed (Q2). This second quarto contains far fewer errors but does not seem to be based upon the same papers as Q1. In 1623, the First Folio, or collected edition,

Production challenges

Even with the return of Shakespeare's version of *Lear,* critical response to the play is often mixed. *Lear* is difficult to stage. For example, if the sights and sounds of the storm are produced realistically, Lear's voice gets lost. Other production challenges include deciding upon a setting, presenting the battle between Edgar and Edmund in Act V, and enacting the blinding of Gloucester. The character of Lear also

of Shakespeare's plays was printed. The Folio (F) text contains correct spellings but also contains stage directions absent in the Q1 text. In the Folio version, for the first time, the play is divided into scenes and acts. The Folio divisions of acts and scenes were modified in 1709, when Nicholas Rowe worked on the text and created a version of the play that is the most familiar to modern audiences.

The Quarto and Folio versions differ significantly. To begin with, the Quarto text calls the play a history, while the Folio indicates that it is a tragedy. Q1 contains 283 lines not found in the Folio, and the Folio contains some 100 lines not found in Q1. Certain changes in wording—or even the omission of an entire scene—create different views of the action in the play. So which version is the correct one? Which one reflects Shakespeare's final version? Some scholars feel that the Folio version contains Shakespeare's own revisions. Other scholars and editors choose to mix the two texts (as is done in this study edition), producing what is termed a *conflated* text that arguably includes the best of all versions.

Plot and subplot

Critic Edwin Muir, in *The Politics of King Lear,* tells us that "of the great tragedies *King Lear* is the only one in which two ideas of society are directly confronted and the old generation and the new generation are set face to face, each assured of its own right to power." Two sets of characters, each representing two generations, are introduced in the first scene. The play opens as the Earl of Gloucester and the Earl of Kent discuss both Lear's plan to divide his kingdom and also the bastardy of Gloucester's son Edmund. From the start, Gloucester and his sons will create a subplot that mirrors the action of the main plot between Lear and his three daughters. A conflict between generations is evident from the start.

The main plot involves Lear, who divides his kingdom between his elder daughters Regan and Goneril while angrily disinheriting his youngest daughter Cordelia. His decision quickly proves unreasonable, and the consequences are tragic. We meet good characters in the play, such as the loyal Earl of Kent, and evil characters, such as Regan, Goneril, and Edmund. The clash of good and evil culminates in one of the most distressing final scenes of any play.

Lear carries the body of Cordelia in a 1997 Old Vic production. Billie Rafaeli/PAL

At first introduction, Lear is a regal monarch—"every inch a king." As the play progresses, Lear deteriorates into madness. The tragedy that engulfs the king swallows nearly all those near him as well, both friend and foe, which accounts for part of the enormity of the drama. The outcome of these complicated events has been called, ironically, both pessimistic and hopeful.

Themes

The *King Lear* reader can discover a wealth of meaning within this drama by looking for several key concepts and themes. The conflict between good and evil is primary among these concepts. Jan Kott writes that "of the twelve major characters, half are just and good, the other half, unjust and bad. It is a division as consistent and abstract as in a morality play." Just as a morality play deals in absolutes and in religious issues of good and evil, so does *King Lear* deal with biblical analogies and allusion.

Power

Also important is the notion of power—who has it, how one obtains it, how one defines it, and how it plays into *King Lear*. With this look at power should also come an investigation of issues such as age and gender. We can consider, for example, the treatment of the elderly by their offspring. And we can think about the power and placement of women in Shakespeare's time as compared with the position of women in society and the home today.

Nature

Nature, in varying forms, is another concept prevalent in *Lear*. Lear's view of nature is one that holds certain values, such as respect for one's parents and loyalty to one's king, to be important regardless of circumstance. Edmund, however, sees nature as a repository of sensuality and self-advancement. To Edmund, as well as to several other characters in the play, the natural impulse of humanity is to better oneself at the expense of others.

In highlighting this lower sense of nature, Shakespeare makes frequent use of animal imagery, often attributing various animal behaviours to the characters. We also find numerous references to the gods and to astronomical events. The contrast of these images—those of the beast world and those of the heavens—add interest to the play, further the development of the characters' personalities, and help to define two distinct worlds between which humans generally live out their lives.

Doubling

Doubling (to create either oppositions or parallels) adds tremendously to the *King Lear* experience. At various times, fools are contrasted with wise men, reason is set opposite to nature, the upper class is set apart from the beggar, and the family is paralleled by society. False service, as in the case of Oswald, is contrasted with true service, represented by Kent. The selfish and false love of Regan and Goneril is a foil for the honest devotion of Cordelia.

The Machiavel

The play also addresses the meaning of truly knowing oneself and humanity's real relationship—if any—to the divine. Additionally, a key image in *King Lear* is that of the "Machiavel"—the self-serving villain. *The Prince*, written by Niccolo Machiavelli, contains a philosophy that tended to preoccupy Shakespeare and his contemporaries. Machiavelli wrote that in order to become a ruler and maintain that position, a person should use every means at his or her disposal to gain control. Murder of the family of a deposed ruler was but one of the ways Machiavelli suggested that a new ruler ensure that his authority was not questioned or overthrown. Edmund, the illegitimate son of Gloucester, is often described in Machiavellian terms, and his methods and actions are as deliberate and self-serving as any described in *The Prince*.

Finally, the reader of *King Lear* can benefit from spending time with the play. An "easy" drama often requires at least a second reading, and *Lear* is admittedly difficult, not only in theme but in language as well. Although some readers may complain that *Lear* would be more easily understood if written in contemporary terms, Shakespeare's poetic language allows for vivid imagery and metaphor. With careful attention to context, you may find that what initially appear to be hurdles in *King Lear* can be overcome and even enjoyed.

CHARACTERS IN THE PLAY

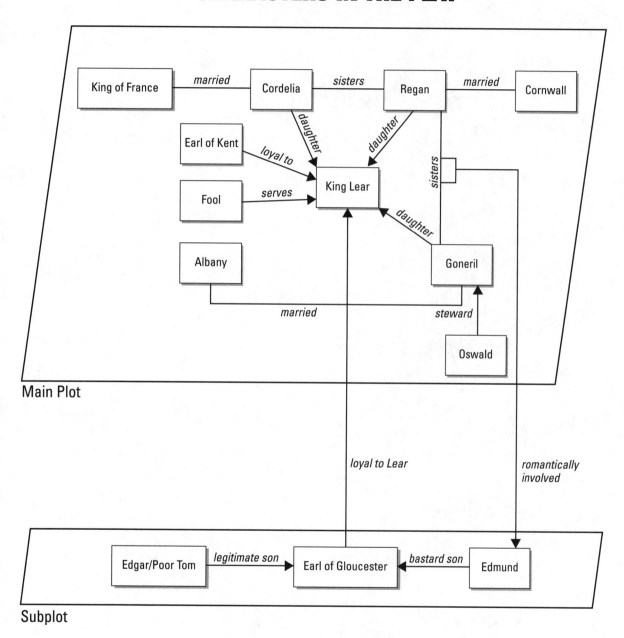

Main Plot

Subplot

COLES NOTES TOTAL STUDY EDITION

KING LEAR
ACT I

Scene 1 27

Scene 2 40

Scene 3 48

Scene 4 50

Scene 5 64

Cordelia *It is no vicious blot, murder, or foulness,*
No unchaste action or dishonoured step,
That hath deprived me of your grace and favour;
But even for want of that for which I am richer—
A still-soliciting eye, and such a tongue
That I am glad I have not, though not to have it
Hath lost me in your liking.

Act I, Scene 1

This scene introduces most of the major characters. We find that King Lear divides his kingdom between his older daughters Goneril and Regan, disinherits his youngest daughter Cordelia, and banishes the loyal Earl of Kent. By the end of the scene we get a glimpse of the conspiratorial natures of Goneril and Regan.

ACT I, SCENE 1
King Lear's palace.

[Enter KENT, GLOUCESTER, and EDMUND]

Kent I thought the King had more affected the
Duke of Albany than Cornwall.

Gloucester It did always seem so to us; but now,
in the division of the kingdom, it appears not which
of the dukes he values most, for equalities are so   5
weighed that curiosity in neither can make choice of
either's moiety.

Kent Is not this your son, my lord?

Gloucester His breeding, sir, hath been at my
charge. I have so often blushed to acknowledge him   10
that now I am brazed to't.

Kent I cannot conceive you.

Gloucester Sir, this young fellow's mother could;
whereupon she grew round-wombed, and had indeed,
sir, a son for her cradle ere she had a husband for   15
her bed. Do you smell a fault?

Kent I cannot wish the fault undone, the issue of
it being so proper.

Gloucester But I have a son, Sir, by order of law,
some year elder than this who yet is no dearer in my   20
account: though this knave came something saucily
to the world before he was sent for, yet was his
mother fair, there was good sport at his making, and
the whoreson must be acknowledged. Do you know
this noble gentleman, Edmund?   25

Edmund No, my lord.

Gloucester My Lord of Kent. Remember him
hereafter as my honourable friend.

NOTES

1.   *more affected:* had more affection for.

2.   *Albany:* northern Britain.

5–7.   *equalities...moiety:* Their shares are so equal that even a close examination cannot decide which share is to be preferred.

9.   *breeding:* rearing.

10.   *charge:* expense.

11.   *brazed:* become brazen.

12.   *conceive:* understand.

17.   *issue:* result; child.

18.   *proper:* handsome.

19.   *by...law:* legitimate.

Edmund My services to your lordship.

Kent I must love you, and sue to know you better.   30

Edmund Sir, I shall study deserving.

Gloucester He hath been out nine years, and away
he shall again. *[Sound a sennet]*
The King is coming.

*[Enter one bearing a coronet, then KING LEAR, then the
DUKES OF CORNWALL and ALBANY, next GONERIL,
REGAN, CORDELIA, and Attendants.]*

Lear Attend the lords of France and Burgundy,   35
Gloucester.

Gloucester I shall, my lord. *[Exit with EDMUND]*

Lear Meantime we shall express our darker purpose.
Give me the map there. Know that we have divided
In three our kingdom; and 'tis our fast intent
To shake all cares and business from our age,   40
Conferring them on younger strengths while we
Unburdened crawl toward death. Our son of Cornwall,
And you our no less loving son of Albany,
We have this hour a constant will to publish
Our daughter's several dowers, that future strife   45
May be prevented now. The princes, France and
Burgundy,
Great rivals in our youngest daughter's love,
Long in our court have made their amorous sojourn,
And here are to be answered. Tell me, my daughters
(Since now we will divest us both of rule,   50
Interest of territory, cares of state),
Which of you shall we say doth love us most,
That we our largest bounty may extend
Where nature doth with merit challenge. Goneril,
Our eldest-born, speak first.   55

Goneril Sir, I love you more than word can wield
the matter;
Dearer than eyesight, space, and liberty;
Beyond what can be valued, rich or rare;
No less than life, with grace, health, beauty, honour;
As much as child e'er loved, or father found;   60

31. *I...deserving:* I shall do my best to deserve your favour.

s.d. *sennet:* trumpet call used to announce a procession.

s.d. *coronet:* small crown worn by those of lesser rank than king.

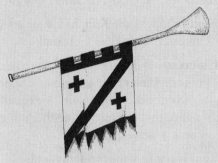

A sennet announces the king's arrival.

37. *darker:* more secret.

44. *constant will:* firm intention.

45. *several:* separate.

51. *Interest:* possession.

54. *Where...challenge:* where affection has an equal claim on my generosity.

A love that makes breath poor, and speech unable.
Beyond all manner of so much I love you.

Cordelia *[Aside]* What shall Cordelia speak?
    Love, and be silent.

Lear Of all these bounds, even from this line to this,
With shadowy forests and with champains riched,   65
With plenteous rivers and wide-skirted meads,
We make thee lady. To thine and Albany's issues
Be this perpetual.—What says our second daughter,
Our dearest Regan, wife of Cornwall?

Regan I am made of that self mettle as my sister,   70
And prize me at her worth. In my true heart
I find she names my very deed of love;
Only she comes too short, that I profess
Myself an enemy to all other joys
Which the most precious square of sense possesses,   75
And find I am alone felicitate
In your dear Highness' love.

Cordelia *[Aside]*   Then poor Cordelia;
And yet not so, since I am sure my love's
More ponderous than my tongue.

Lear To thee and thine hereditary ever   80
Remain this ample third of our fair kingdom,
No less in space, validity, and pleasure
Than that conferred on Goneril.—Now, our joy,
Although our last and least; to whose young love
The vines of France and milk of Burgundy   85
Strive to be interest; what can you say to draw
A third more opulent than your sisters? Speak.

Cordelia Nothing, my lord.

Lear Nothing?

Cordelia Nothing.   90

Lear Nothing will come of nothing. Speak again.

Cordelia Unhappy that I am, I cannot heave
My heart into my mouth. I love your Majesty
According to my bond, no more nor less.

Lear How, how, Cordelia? Mend your speech a little,   95
Lest you may mar your fortunes.

---

61.   *breath:* the power to speak.

62.   *Beyond...much:* beyond all these things.

65.   *champains riched:* rich in fertile fields.

66.   *wide-skirted meads:* extensive pasture lands.

67.   *issues:* children.

70.   *self mettle:* same material.

75.   *most precious square:* measurement (carpenter's rule).

      most precious...possesses: feeling in the highest degree possible.

76.   *felicitate:* made happy.

78–79.   *love's...tongue:* love is heavier than my words.

82.   *validity:* value.

85.   *milk:* pasture lands.

86.   *be interest:* establish a claim.

      draw: acquire.

Cordelia   Good my lord,
You have begot me, bred me, loved me. I
Return those duties back as are right fit,
Obey you, love you, and most honour you.
Why have my sisters husbands if they say   100
They love you all? Haply, when I shall wed,
That lord whose hand must take my plight shall carry
Half my love with him, half my care and duty.
Sure I shall never marry like my sisters,
To love my father all.   105

Lear But goes thy heart with this?

Cordelia   Ay, my good lord.

Lear So young, and so untender?

Cordelia So young, my lord, and true.

Lear Let it be so, thy truth then be thy dower!
For, by the sacred radiance of the sun,   110
The mysteries of Hecate and the night,
By all the operation of the orbs
From whom we do exist and cease to be,
Here I disclaim all my paternal care,
Propinquity and property of blood,   115
And as a stranger to my heart and me
Hold thee from this for ever. The barbarous Scythian,
Or he that makes his generation messes
To gorge his appetite, shall to my bosom
Be as well neighboured, pitied, and relieved,   120
As thou my sometime daughter.

Kent   Good my liege—

Lear Peace, Kent!
Come not between the dragon and his wrath.
I loved her most, and thought to set my rest
On her kind nursery.—Hence and avoid my sight!—   125
So be my grave my peace as here I give
Her father's heart from her! Call France. Who stirs!
Call Burgundy. Cornwall and Albany,

---

101.   *Haply:* it may happen.

102.   *plight:* promise made at betrothal.

111.   *Hecate:* goddess of the moon and of witchcraft.

112.   *orbs:* stars.

114.   *disclaim:* renounce.

115.   *Propinquity:* relationship.

            property: identity.

117.   *Scythian:* person of South Russia; worst kind of savage.

118–119.   *Or...appetite:* or he that feeds gluttonously upon his own children.

120.   *relieved:* helped in distress.

123.   *dragon:* The Dragon of Britain was Lear's heraldic device.

124.   *set my rest:* to risk all; also means to find rest or live with.

125.   *nursery:* care.

            avoid: depart from.

With my two daughters' dowers digest the third;
Let pride, which she calls plainness, marry her.   130
I do invest you jointly with my power,
Preeminence, and all the large effects
That troop with majesty. Ourself, by monthly course,
With reservation of an hundred knights,
By you to be sustained, shall our abode   135
Make with you by due turn. Only we shall retain
The name, and all th' addition to a king. The sway,
Revenue, execution of the rest,
Belov'd sons, be yours; which to confirm,
This coronet part between you.

Kent   Royal Lear,   140
Whom I have ever honoured as my king,
Loved as my father, as my master followed,
As my great patron thought on in my prayers—

Lear The bow is bent and drawn; make from the
     shaft.

Kent Let it fall rather, though the fork invade   145
    The region of my heart. Be Kent unmannerly
    When Lear is mad. What wouldst thou do, old man?
    Think'st thou that duty shall have dread to speak
    When power to flattery bows? To plainness
      honour's bound
    When majesty falls to folly. Reserve thy state,   150
    And in thy best consideration check
    This hideous rashness. Answer my life my judgment
    Thy youngest daughter does not love thee least,
    Nor are those empty-hearted whose low sounds
    Reverb no hollowness.

Lear   Kent, on thy life, no more!   155

Kent My life I never held but as a pawn
    To wage against thine enemies; ne'er fear to lose it,
    Thy safety being motive.

Lear   Out of my sight!

Kent See better, Lear, and let me still remain
    The true blank of thine eye.   160

Lear Now by Apollo—

---

132.   *Preeminence:* authority.

132–133. *large...majesty:* outward show of power that goes with rule.

133.   *Ourself:* form of the royal we.

       course: turn.

137.   *addition:* title of honour.

145.   *fork:* point of a forked arrow.

147.   *old man:* as spoken Kent to Lear, insulting to a still ruling king.

148–150. *Think'st...folly:* An honourable man is not afraid to speak dutifully when a king acts in error.

160.   *blank:* aim; the centre of the target.

Kent   Now by Apollo, King,
Thou swear'st thy gods in vain.

Lear   O vassal! Miscreant!
[Grasping his sword]

Albany, Cornwall Dear Sir, forbear!

Kent Kill thy physician, and thy fee bestow
Upon the foul disease. Revoke thy gift,   165
Or, whilst I can vent clamour from my throat,
I'll tell thee thou dost evil.

Lear   Hear me, recreant,
On thine allegiance, hear me!
That thou hast sought to make us break our vows,
Which we durst never yet, and with strained pride   170
To come betwixt our sentence and our power,
Which nor our nature nor our place can bear,
Our potency made good, take thy reward.
Five days we do allot thee for provision
To shield thee from disasters of the world,   175
And on the sixth to turn thy hated back
Upon our kingdom. If, on the tenth day following,
Thy banished trunk be found in our dominions,
The moment is thy death. Away. By Jupiter,
This shall not be revoked.   180

Kent Fare thee well, King. Sith thus thou wilt appear,
Freedom lives hence, and banishment is here.
[To Cordelia] The gods to their dear shelter take
      thee, maid,
That justly think'st and hast most rightly said.
[To Regan and Goneril] And your large speeches may
      your deeds approve,   185
That good effects may spring from words of love.
Thus Kent, O princes, bids you all adieu;
He'll shape his old course in a country new. *[Exit]*

*[Flourish. Enter GLOUCESTER, with FRANCE and
      BURGUNDY; Attendants]*

Gloucester Here's France and Burgundy, my noble lord.

---

162.   *Miscreant:* misbeliever (not an unbeliever, which has a religious connotation).

165.   *vent clamour:* utter a cry.

167.   *recreant:* traitor.

168.   *On thine allegiance:* solemn command; disobedience is treason.

170.   *strained:* excessive.

173.   *Our...good:* My power is now being asserted.

174.   *Five...provision:* The Quarto version of the text allows Kent only four days to gather supplies.

178.   *trunk:* body.

181.   *Sith:* since.

184.   *large:* fine-sounding.

s.d.   *Flourish:* trumpet fanfare.

Lear My Lord of Burgundy,   190
We first address toward you, who wish this king
Hath rivalled for our daughter. What in the least
Will you require in present dower with her,
Or cease your quest of love?

Burgundy   Most royal Majesty,
crave no more than hath your Highness offered,   195
Nor will you tender less.

Lear   Right noble Burgundy,
When she was dear to us, we did hold her so;
But now her price is fallen. Sir, there she stands.
If aught within that little seeming substance,
Or all of it, with our displeasure pieced   200
And nothing more, may fitly like your Grace,
She's there, and she is yours.

Burgundy   I know no answer.

Lear Will you, with those infirmities she owes,
Unfriended, new adopted to our hate,
Dow'red with our curse, and strangered with our oath, 205
Take her, or leave her?

Burgundy   Pardon me, royal sir.
Election makes not up on such conditions.

Lear Then leave her, sir, for by the pow'r that made me
I tell you all her wealth. *[to France]* For you, great King,
I would not from your love make such a stray   210
To match you where I hate; therefore beseech you
T' avert your liking a more worthier way
Than on a wretch whom nature is ashamed
Almost t' acknowledge hers.

France   This is most strange,
That she whom even but now was your best object,   215
The argument of your praise, balm of your age,
The best, the dearest, should in this trice of time
Commit a thing so monstrous to dismantle
So many folds of favour. Sure her offence

---

193. *require:* request.

    present: immediate.

196. *tender:* offer.

197. *dear:* beloved and valuable.

199. *little...substance:* creature that seems so small; part of Lear's anger here is that so small a body seems to hold so proud a heart.

200. *pieced:* added to it.

201. *fitly like:* suitably please.

203. *owes:* possesses.

205. *strangered...oath:* made a stranger to me by my oath.

207. *Election...conditions:* One doesn't choose one's wife on such conditions.

216. *argument:* topic or subject.

218. *dismantle:* to take off (as a robe or other garment).

Must be of such unnatural degree   220
That monsters it, or your fore-vouched affection
Fall'n into taint; which to believe of her
Must be a faith that reason without miracle
Should never plant in me.

Cordelia   I yet beseech your Majesty,
If for I want that glib and oily art   225
To speak and purpose not since what I well intend
I'll do't before I speak, that you make known
It is no vicious blot, murder, or foulness,
No unchaste action or dishonoured step,
That hath deprived me of your grace and favour;   230
But even for want of that for which I am richer—
A still-soliciting eye, and such a tongue
That I am glad I have not, though not to have it
Hath lost me in your liking.

Lear   Better thou
Hadst not been born than not t' have pleased me
    better.   235

France It is but this? A tardiness in nature
Which often leaves the history unspoke.
That it intends to do. My lord of Burgundy,
What say you to the lady? Love's not love
When it is mingled with regards that stands   240
Aloof from th' entire point. Will you have her?
She is herself a dowry.

Burgundy   Royal King,
Give but that portion which yourself proposed,
And here I take Cordelia by the hand,
Duchess of Burgundy.   245

Lear Nothing. I have sworn. I am firm.

Burgundy I am sorry then you have so lost a father
That you must lose a husband.

Cordelia   Peace be with Burgundy.
Since that respects of fortune are his love,
I shall not be his wife.   250

---

221. *monsters it:* makes it a monster.

or: before.

222. *Fall'n into taint:* become bad (as in spoiled or rotten).

222–224. *which...me:* so contrary to reason that only a miracle could make me believe it.

225. *for I want:* because I lack.

226. *and purpose not:* and not mean it.

232. *still-soliciting:* always begging favours.

234. *lost me in:* deprived me of.

236. *tardiness in nature:* slowness of habitual character.

240–241. *When...point:* when love is mixed with other motives (such as the amount of dowry) that have nothing to do with love itself.

France Fairest Cordelia, that art most rich being poor,
   Most choice forsaken, and most loved despised,
   Thee and thy virtues here I seize upon.
   Be it lawful I take up what's cast away.
   Gods, gods! 'Tis strange that from their cold'st neglect   255
   My love should kindle to inflamed respect.
   Thy dow'rless daughter, King, thrown to my chance,
   Is queen of us, of ours, and our fair France.
   Not all the dukes of wat'rish Burgundy
   Can buy this unprized precious maid of me.   260
   Bid them farewell, Cordelia, though unkind.
   Thou losest here, a better where to find.

Lear Thou hast her, France; let her be thine, for we
   Have no such daughter, nor shall ever see
   That face of hers again. Therefore be gone   265
   Without our grace, our love, our benison.
   Come, noble Burgundy.

*[Flourish. Exeunt LEAR, BURGUNDY, CORNWALL,
ALBANY, GLOUCESTER and Attendants]*

France Bid farewell to your sisters.

Cordelia The jewels of our father, with washed eyes
   Cordelia leaves you. I know you what you are;   270
   And, like a sister, am most loath to call
   Your faults as they are named. Love well our father.
   To your professed bosoms I commit him;
   But yet, alas, stood I within his grace,
   I would prefer him to a better place.   275
   So farewell to you both.

Regan Prescribe not us our duty.

Goneril   Let your study
   Be to content your lord, who hath received you
   At fortune's alms. You have obedience scanted,
   And well are worth the want that you have wanted.   280

Cordelia Time shall unfold what plighted cunning hides,
   Who covers faults, at last with shame derides.
   Well may you prosper.

---

256.   *inflamed respect:* warmer affection.

259.   *wat'rish:* double meaning: feeble and with many rivers.

266.   *benison:* blessing.

269.   *The jewels...father:* creatures my father values so highly.

       washed: weeping but also clear-sighted.

279.   *scanted:* neglected.

280.   *And...wanted:* and well deserve the same lack of love you have shown.

281.   *plighted:* pleated or folded; also plaited, as in women's hair braids.

France   Come, my fair Cordelia.

[Exit FRANCE and CORDELIA]

Goneril Sister, it is not little I have to say of what
most nearly appertains to us both. I think our father   285
will hence to-night.

Regan That's most certain, and with you; next
month with us.

Goneril You see how full of changes his age is. The
observation we have made of it hath not been little. He   290
always loved our sister most, and with what poor
judgment he hath now cast her off appears too grossly.

Regan 'Tis the infirmity of his age; yet he hath
ever but slenderly known himself.

Goneril The best and soundest of his time hath been   295
but rash; then must we look from his age to receive
not alone the imperfections of long-ingraffed condition,
but therewithal the unruly waywardness that infirm
and choleric years bring with them.

Regan Such unconstant starts are we like to have   300
from him as this of Kent's banishment.

Goneril There is further compliment of leave-taking
between France and him. Pray you let us hit
together; if our father carry authority with such
disposition as he bears, this last surrender of his will   305
but offend us.

Regan We shall further think of it.

Goneril We must do something, and i' th' heat.

[Exeunt]

284–308. *Sister...heat:* The abrupt change from rhyme to prose marks a change from the emotion of previous segments to the frankness of the sisters.

297. *long-ingraffed:* long-standing.

300. *unconstant starts:* sudden outbursts.

302. *compliment:* formality; possibly spoken with sarcasm given the anger between the two kings.

303–304. *hit together:* agree or work together.

305. *disposition:* frame of mind.

306. *offend:* injure.

308. *i' th' heat:* while the iron is hot; while the topic is raised; while the getting is good.

COMMENTARY

In *King Lear*, Shakespeare names for us 21 characters, along with an assortment of officers, knights, messengers, and so on. In this first scene, you meet 11 of these characters in Shakespeare's setup, or *exposition*, of the play. The introductions include all but one member of the two primary families of the drama: the royal family of King Lear and the family of the Earl of Gloucester.

The first players to enter the stage are the Earl of Kent, the Earl of Gloucester, and Edmund, Gloucester's son. At first, the two earls discuss King Lear's proposal to divide his kingdom between Lear's sons-in-law, the Dukes of Cornwall and Albany. The Dukes are married to Lear's elder daughters Regan and Goneril, respectively.

Edmund's illegitimacy

The talk between the earls turns quickly from matters of state to matters of family as Gloucester introduces Edmund to Kent. Gloucester makes plain the fact that Edmund is illegitimate; he displays no outward regret at having a son out of wedlock. In a sense, Gloucester ridicules Edmund by making light of his son's illegitimacy, especially given that Gloucester has a legitimate son as well. Edmund's facial expressions, which prove that he is both embarrassed and angry, give us our first hint that Edmund bears ill will toward his father.

The arrival of Lear and his entourage is signalled by a trumpet flourish (a pronounced entrance both appreciated and expected by Shakespeare's Early Modern audiences). When Lear appears, accompanied by his married daughters Goneril and Regan, their husbands the Dukes of Albany and Cornwall, and his youngest daughter Cordelia, the language of the play shifts. While Kent and Gloucester converse in prose, the type of language used by regular citizens, Lear and his daughters speak in somewhat formal, courtly language.

The love test

The change from prose to iambic pentameter verse takes place as Lear forces his daughters into a "love test." During this kind of test, the head of a family—usually a monarch or nobleman—issues a challenge to his children. His offspring must respond by trying to outdo each another in praising their father. The love test challenge

was a standard of court life—one of the expected charades. The children's responses were also supposed to be standard. (No one expected anything less than glowing praise, and if we were to grade Goneril and Regan on their performances in this scene, we would assuredly assign them an "A.")

Lear's reasons for dividing his kingdom among his three daughters may initially seem wise to modern readers. He says, "Know that we have divided / In three our kingdom . . . that future strife / May be prevented now" (38–46). But to an Early

Lear divides his land and weakens the power of the crown in this opening scene.

Modern audience, a king's division of his kingdom and relinquishing of rule could only spell disaster. The idea of kingship—and fatherhood, for that matter—was linked to the divine in Elizabethan thought. Lear's announcement disrupts the accepted hierarchical order in Lear's kingdom and family. (See the "Introduction to Early Modern England" for further discussion of the belief in a hierarchy of creation.)

Though he renounces the responsibilities of rule, Lear apparently plans to retain the respect due to a king and the other perks of his position. Rather than simply dividing his kingdom and making a graceful exit, Lear uses his royal power and authority not only to test the love of his daughters but also to divide his kingdom based upon the results of that test. Because Goneril and Regan offer such fabulous descriptions of their undying love for Lear, the king metes out generous portions of his kingdom to these two daughters, both of whom claim that their foremost goal in life is to continue in the love of their father, a man they love more than they do their husbands!

"Nothing"

Faced with the task of professing her love for her father, Cordelia proves unable to utter the expected speeches of praise that Goneril and Regan have so expertly pronounced. When Lear asks what Cordelia can say to persuade him to give her a bigger share of his kingdom than he will give the other two sisters,

Cordelia says a single word—"Nothing" (90). Lear's pride—both as king and as father—is injured to the extent that he disinherits Cordelia. Kent berates the king for making such a foolish decision, but Lear refuses to listen to his loyal advisor and goes so far as to banish Kent from the kingdom.

Cordelia's response is a powerful one in several respects. The word "Nothing" is strong enough to send her father into a rage. But the response is also powerful in contrast to the flowery words spoken by Regan and Goneril, who claim that their love for their father surpasses all. Cordelia says "Nothing" because the love and respect she holds for her father are founded upon her "bond" to him. Hers is a more profound and honest sentiment than the words spoken by Goneril and Regan.

The word "Nothing" also has Christian overtones in the context of the play. Though the action of *King Lear* is set before the time of Christ, Shakespeare's audiences would have understood the Christian allusions. In Christian theology, no amount of prayer or flattery can save the soul of humanity; only the unselfish and steady love of the Creator and His Son can accomplish that salvation. Cordelia, by refusing to offer hollow praise to her father, stands precisely in the position of humanity, which has nothing to offer the deity but the duty required by the Christian bond. Lear reacts not with the unconditional love of a Christian lord toward his subject but rather with spite and sullen pride.

Disinheriting Cordelia

Lear strips Cordelia of her dowry and then offers her in marriage to the Duke of Burgundy. Many scholars debate why Lear offers Cordelia first to the duke instead of to the King of France. In earlier historical periods, Burgundy was more than simply one part of France. The Dukes of Burgundy were nearly as powerful as the French kings, and the dukes were traditionally allied with Britain. Lear may consider the security of the kingdom when offering Cordelia to Burgundy. Lear also may want to keep Cordelia closer to home by wedding her to the duke. However, Lear's action may be purely spiteful; perhaps he is unwilling to see Cordelia elevated to the rank of queen, a title Regan and Goneril can never hold.

Laurence Olivier stars as Lear in the 1984 film version directed by Michael Elliott. Everett Collection

In any case, the duke refuses to marry Cordelia because her dowry is gone. The duke proves that he cares more about the money than about Cordelia. Almost by default, the King of France wins Cordelia as his wife; this king does not concern himself with material goods, and he claims that his affection for Cordelia has grown as he has observed both her honour and the actions of her father.

The opening scene establishes a parallel between Kent and Cordelia. Lear has overlooked the true love that Cordelia offers him in favour of the formalistic love speeches that Goneril and Regan recite. Likewise, Lear does not appreciate the true and loyal service of Kent. Both Kent and Cordelia are thrust from Lear's kingdom and supposedly from Lear's heart as well, primarily because neither offender chooses to speak the false truth of the court, proclaiming instead the plain truth that Lear refuses to believe.

Regan and Goneril's anger

This scene also begins to examine the relationship between Lear and his elder daughters. Goneril and Regan are both married women, regents in the kingdom and in their own homes as wives of dukes. For these women to be put to the "test"—to be asked publicly to bow and scrape before their father and loudly magnify his virtues and their love for him—is probably an insult. Lear himself was outraged when Kent berated his judgment in a public setting. Goneril and Regan very probably feel anger at being forced to publicly profess their love for their father.

The elder sisters' anger toward their father has other sources as well. They know that Cordelia is Lear's "joy"; Lear offers to give her the largest portion of the kingdom if she will only speak the right words. Cordelia has clearly been Lear's favorite; "I loved her most," he says, "and thought to set my rest / On her kind nursery" (124–125). The elder sisters can see this preference plainly; Goneril reminds Regan that Lear "always loved our sister most" (291). The elder sisters' anger at this favoritism is hardly surprising. To fuel their frustration even more, at the scene's end, they are forced into being caretakers and hosts for their father because Cordelia has been renounced.

But while Goneril and Regan's anger with their father may seem somewhat justified, their actions throughout the play indicate that they are corrupt, unloving daughters. Critic William Hazlitt sees Goneril and Regan as "thoroughly hateful"; he does not "even like to repeat their names." When Cordelia refers to her sisters as the "jewels of our father," her words are bitterly ironic (269). Cordelia knows that her father's care and well-being should be left "to a better place" than the households of the elder sisters (275).

The daughters' duty

Regan's response to Cordelia's admonition that the sisters take good care of Lear is chilling: "Prescribe not us our duty" (277). Goneril, however, is quick to turn the tables. Goneril reminds Cordelia that her duty is to satisfy her soon-to-be husband, the King of France. She also declares that Cordelia herself has fallen short of duty to Lear—she has "scanted" obedience in her refusal to shower her father with lavish praise (279).

Having bid their sister a cold farewell, the hypocritical elder sisters conference immediately. Their discussion is openly disrespectful to their father, contrasting sharply with their public declarations of love and pointing out further how unfair the judgment against Cordelia has been. Lear's age and changeable nature disturb Goneril and Regan; they feel that Lear's mental state, which supposedly has never been good, is fast approaching a crisis. Lear's mental crisis would likely have a negative effect upon his daughters and their households.

Goneril and Regan seem stunned by Lear's foolish actions in this scene. The sisters are concerned that their father may, at some point, do the same thing to them that he has so rashly done to Cordelia. Consequently, Goneril and Regan must remain alert and prepare in advance for that possibility. Note that Goneril is the instigator here. She urges the conference about Lear with Regan, and she finds Regan's agreement to "further think of it" insufficient (307). For Goneril the answer to their fears is immediate action, not just brainstorming: "We must do something, and i' th' heat" (308).

Poor judgment

A parallel between Lear and Gloucester becomes apparent in the plans that Regan and Goneril make to take advantage of their father's poor judgment. (Note that poor judgment is itself a concept to observe throughout the play.) Gloucester has exercised poor judgment in speaking of Edmund's bastardy in the presence of Edmund and Kent. Lear has exercised poor judgment in banishing Kent and in disinheriting Cordelia. Interestingly, this pattern of ill-advised thought and actions, so obvious in the parents, is continued in some of the children. In the second scene of the play, Edmund will take blatant advantage of Gloucester's gullibility, and later in the drama Edgar will do the same, for different and much more noble purposes.

Act I, Scene 2

The bastard Edmund, son of the Earl of Gloucester, maligns his brother Edgar to Gloucester. Edmund's evil nature becomes apparent as he also manages to dupe Edgar into believing that he is concerned for his safety in light of Gloucester's anger.

ACT I, SCENE 2
The Earl of Gloucester's castle.

[Enter EDMUND, alone, with a letter]

Edmund Thou, Nature art my goddess; to thy law
My services are bound. Wherefore should I
Stand in the plague of custom, and permit
The curiosity of nations to deprive me,
For that I am some twelve or fourteen moonshines   5
Lag of a brother? Why bastard? Wherefore base,
When my dimensions are as well compact,
My mind as generous, and my shape as true,
As honest madam's issue? Why brand they us
With base? With baseness? Bastardy base? Base?   10
Who, in the lusty stealth of nature, take
More composition and fierce quality
Than doth, within a dull, stale tired bed,
Go to th' creating a whole tribe of fops
Got 'tween asleep and wake? Well then,   15
Legitimate Edgar, I must have your land.
Our father's love is to the bastard Edmund
As to th' legitimate. Fine word, 'legitimate.'
Well, my legitimate, if this letter speed,
And my invention thrive, Edmund the base   20
Shall top th' legitimate. I grow, I prosper.
Now, gods, stand up for bastards.

[Enter GLOUCESTER]

Gloucester Kent banished thus? And France
     in choler parted?
And the King gone to-night? prescribed his pow'r?
Confined to exhibition? All this done   25
Upon the gad? Edmund, how now? What news?

Edmund So please your lordship, none.

Gloucester Why so earnestly seek you to put up
     that letter?

NOTES

2-6. *Wherefore...brother?:* Why should I let myself be plagued by custom and nice distinctions that deprive me of my natural rights just because I am a year younger than my legitimate brother?

4. *curiosity of nations:* picky distinctions made by society.

7. *compact:* put together.

8. *generous:* noble.

12. *More composition...quality:* more fibre and ferocity.

14. *fops:* fools or dandies.

15. *Got:* conceived.

19. *speed:* prosper or accomplish its purpose.

24. *prescribed:* signed away.

25. *Confined to exhibition:* reduced to a mere pension.

26. *gad:* spur of the moment.

Edmund I know no news, my lord.

Gloucester What paper were you reading?   30

Edmund Nothing, my lord.

Gloucester No? What needed then that terrible
dispatch of it into your pocket? The quality of nothing
hath not such need to hide itself. Let's see.
Come, if it be nothing, I shall not need spectacles.   35

Edmund I beseech you, sir, pardon me. It is a letter
from my brother that I have not all o'er-read;
and for so much as I have perused, I find it not fit
for your o'erlooking.

Gloucester Give me the letter, sir.   40

Edmund I shall offend, either to detain or give it. The
contents, as in part I understand them, are to
blame.

Gloucester Let's see, let's see.

Edmund I hope, for my brother's justification, he   45
wrote this but as an essay or taste of my virtue.

Gloucester *[reads]* "This policy and reverence of
age makes the world bitter to the best of our times;
keeps our fortunes from us till our oldness cannot
relish them. I begin to find an idle and fond bond-   50
age in the oppression of aged tyranny, who sways,
not as it hath power, but as it is suffered. Come
to me, that of this I may speak more. If our father
would sleep till I wake him, you should enjoy half
his revenue for ever, and live the beloved of your   55
brother, Edgar."
Hum! Conspiracy? "Sleep till I wake him, you
should enjoy half his revenue." My son Edgar! Had
he a hand to write this? A heart and brain to breed
it in? When came you to this? Who brought it?   60

Edmund It was not brought me, my lord; there's
the cunning of it. I found it thrown in at the casement
of my closet.

Gloucester You know the character to be your
brother's?   65

---

31.   *Nothing, my lord:* Note how the Gloucester story begins with nothing.

32–33.   *What…pocket?:* Why did you put it in your pocket so quickly?

39.   *o'erlooking:* reading.

46.   *essay:* trial or test.

47–48.   *policy…age:* custom of respecting old men.

48.   *best…times:* when we are still young.

50.   *idle and fond:* useless and foolish.

52.   *suffered:* allowed; tolerated.

62.   *casement:* window.

63.   *closet:* room.

64.   *character:* handwriting.

Edmund If the matter were good, my lord, I durst
swear it were his; but in respect of that, I would
fain think it were not.

Gloucester It is his.

Edmund It is his hand, my lord; but I hope his   70
heart is not in the contents.

Gloucester Has he never before sounded you in this
business?

Edmund Never, my lord. But I have heard him oft
maintain it to be fit that, sons at perfect age, and   75
fathers declined, the father should be as ward to the
son, and the son manage his revenue.

Gloucester O villain, villain! His very opinion in the
letter. Abhorred villain, unnatural, detested, brutish
villain; worse than brutish! Go, sirrah, seek him.   80
I'll apprehend him. Abominable villain! Where
is he?

Edmund I do not well know, my lord. If it shall
please you to suspend your indignation against my
brother till you can derive from him better testimony   85
of his intent, you should run a certain course;
where, if you violently proceed against him, mistaking
his purpose, it would make a great gap in your
own honour and shake in pieces the heart of his
obedience. I dare pawn down my life for him that   90
he hath writ this to feel my affection to your honour,
and to no other pretence of danger.

Gloucester Think you so?

Edmund If your honour judge it meet, I will place
you where you shall hear us confer of this and by an   95
auricular assurance have your satisfaction, and that
without any further delay than this very evening.

Gloucester He cannot be such a monster.

Edmund Nor is not, sure.

Gloucester To his father, that so tenderly and   100
entirely loves him. Heaven and earth! Edmund, seek
him out; wind me into him, I pray you; frame the

68. *fain:* gladly.

75. *at perfect age:* at full maturity.

80. *sirrah:* familiar form of address of parents to children or master to servant.

86. *run a certain course:* know what you are doing and not be surprised.

91. *feel:* test.

102. *wind...him:* worm your way into his confidence for me.

business after your own wisdom. I would unstate
myself to be in a due resolution.

Edmund I will seek him, sir, presently; convey the
business as I shall find means, and acquaint you withal.

Gloucester These late eclipses in the sun and moon
portend no good to us. Though the wisdom of nature
can reason it thus and thus, yet nature finds itself
scourged by the sequent effects. Love cools, friendship
falls off, brothers divide. In cities, mutinies; in
countries, discord; in palaces, treason; and the bond
cracked 'twixt son and father. This villain of mine
comes under the prediction, there's son against
father; the King falls from bias of nature, there's
father against child. We have seen the best of our
time. Machinations, hollowness, treachery, and all
ruinous disorders follow us disquietly to our graves.
Find out this villain, Edmund, it shall lose thee nothing;
do it carefully. And the noble and true-hearted
Kent banished; his offence, honesty. 'Tis strange.

[Exit]

Edmund This is the excellent foppery of the world, that
when we are sick in fortune, often the surfeits of
our own behaviour, we make guilty of our disasters
the sun, the moon, and stars; as if we were villains
on necessity; fools by heavenly compulsion; knaves,
thieves, and treachers by spherical predominance;
drunkards, liars, and adulterers by an enforced
obedience of planetary influence; and all that we are
evil in, by a divine thrusting on. An admirable evasion
of whoremaster man, to lay his goatish disposition
on the charge of a star. My father compounded
with my mother under the Dragon's Tail, and my
nativity was under Ursa Major, so that it follows I am
rough and lecherous. Fut! I should have been that
I am, had the maidenliest star in the firmament
twinkled on my bastardizing. Edgar—
[Enter EDGAR]
and pat he comes, like the catastrophe of the old

105

110

115

120

125

130

135

103–104. *I...resolution:* I would lose my earldom to learn the truth (prophetic).

105. *presently:* immediately.

convey: manage or complete.

107. *late:* recent.

109. *reason:* explain.

110. *sequent:* subsequent or resultant.

115. *bias of nature:* natural inclination.

Edmund chides men who blame their "goatish disposition[s]" on the stars.

122. *foppery:* folly.

123. *surfeits:* eating to excess.

126–127. *knaves...predominance:* criminal because the planets or stars fated us that way when we were born.

128–129. *drunkards...influence:* We are this way due to the influence of the stars.

131–132. *to...star:* to say some star caused him to have the morals of a goat or lecher.

134. *Ursa Major:* Great Bear constellation.

135. *Fut!:* exclamation of contempt.

138. *catastrophe:* final episode.

comedy. My cue is villainous melancholy, with a sigh
like Tom o' Bedlam.—O, these eclipses do portend   140
these divisions. Fa, sol, la, mi.

Edgar How now, brother Edmund; what serious
contemplation are you in?

Edmund I am thinking, brother, of a prediction I
read this other day, what should follow these   145
eclipses.

Edgar Do you busy yourself with that?

Edmund I promise you, the effects he writes of
succeed unhappily; as of unnaturalness between the
child and the parent; death, dearth, dissolutions of   150
ancient amities; divisions in state, menaces and
maledictions against king and nobles; needless
diffidences, banishment of friends, dissipation of
cohorts, nuptial breaches, and I know not what.

Edgar How long have you been a sectary astro-   155
nomical?

Edmund Come, come, when saw you my father
last?

Edgar The night gone by.

Edmund Spake you with him?   160

Edgar Ay, two hours together.

Edmund Parted you in good terms? Found you no
displeasure in him by word nor countenance?

Edgar None at all.

Edmund Bethink yourself wherein you may have   165
offended him; and at my entreaty forbear his
presence until some little time hath qualified the
heat of his displeasure, which at this instant so
rageth in him that with the mischief of your person
it would scarcely allay.   170

Edgar Some villain hath done me wrong.

Edmund That's my fear. I pray you have a continent forbearance till the speed of his rage goes
slower; and, as I say, retire with me to my lodging,

139–140. *My...Bedlam:* I will pretend to be melancholy and sigh like a lunatic discharged from Bethlehem hospital.

141. The Folio version of the text adds a stage direction here: *He reads a book.*

149. *succeed:* follow.

150. *dearth:* famine.

151. *amities:* friendships.

151–152. *menaces and maledictions:* threats and curses.

153. *diffidences:* mistrusts.

153–154. *dissipation of cohorts:* breaking up of established friendships.

155–156. *sectary astronomical:* follower of a group of astrologers.

167. *qualified:* lessened.

169–170. *with...allay:* It would scarcely be lessened even if he did you bodily injury.

172–173. *continent forbearance:* mature self-control.

from whence I will fitly bring you to hear my   175
lord speak. Pray ye, go; there's my key. If you do
stir abroad, go armed.

Edgar Armed, brother?

Edmund Brother, I advise you to the best. Go
armed. I am no honest man if there be any good   180
meaning toward you. I have told you what I have
seen and heard; but faintly, nothing like the image
and horror of it. Pray you, away.

Edgar Shall I hear from you anon?

Edmund I do serve you in this business.   185
[Exit EDGAR]
A credulous father, and a brother noble,
Whose nature is so far from doing harms
That he suspects none; on whose foolish honesty
My practices ride easy. I see the business.
Let me, if not by birth, have lands by wit;   190
All with me's meet that I can fashion fit. *[Exit]*

191.   *meet:* suitable.

fashion fit: make fit my purposes.

COMMENTARY

Entering alone as Scene 2 opens, Edmund presents us with a *soliloquy*. A conventional part of Shakespearean dramas, the soliloquy serves several purposes, including the elaboration and development of an individual character. Alone on stage, the player has the opportunity to reveal many things not brought out in dialogue. The character's beliefs and plans come alive during a soliloquy, and the audience glimpses how good—or in Edmund's case, how evil—a character truly can be.

As well as developing character, the soliloquy also serves to further the plot by passing along information impossible to portray reasonably on stage. For example, when Edmund speaks to the goddess Nature in lines 1 and 2, he issues a formal pledge that explains much of the plot that will follow. Edmund has two goals: to discredit Edgar in the eyes of Gloucester and to make himself into a man of means by acquiring an inheritance of his own. By turning Gloucester against Edgar, Edmund hopes to achieve both of these goals. If Edmund's pledge had been a silent one, we wouldn't know the reasons for Edmund's later actions.

Nature

The concept of Nature is important in this play, and we should note that more than one type of Nature is represented in this drama. The Nature in which Edmund operates is animalistic; the common acts of decency and morality that we expect from human beings are not present in him. Later in the play, we shall see that Lear operates and believes in a different level of Nature—a higher plateau in which morality and decency are the expected norms.

Edmund's illegitimacy explains his pledge to the animalistic world of Nature. The law of the society that Edmund lives in stands to rob him of everything he desires in life: respect, position, and wealth. That's because society's laws reward the legitimate and punish the illegitimate. To Edmund, therefore, the rule of "survival of the fittest" reigns supreme; the law of Nature affords him a chance to succeed. Edmund questions the accepted order; indeed, he pledges to overthrow that order in favour of the individual's right to success.

Deceiving Gloucester

Because the soliloquy has revealed Edmund's true intentions, we realize that he must play-act in front of Gloucester and Edgar in order to convince them to distrust each other. Pretending to be reluctant, Edmund tells Gloucester that the letter he holds looks like it was written by Edgar. Feigning anguish, Edmund looks on as Gloucester reads the treacherous remarks that Edgar has supposedly written. Believing that Edgar is ridiculing him, Gloucester learns that his legitimate son is anxious to spend his inheritance.

Gloucester is already upset; he finds the recent banishments and unpleasantness at court difficult to comprehend and quite against his sensual nature that loves pleasure, not strife. With ease, Edmund convinces his father that Edgar has been disloyal. Gloucester's emotional reaction is all too predictable; he refers to his legitimate son as an "Abhorred villain, unnatural, detested, brutish/villain" (79–80).

Edmund is well aware of his father's tendency to place importance upon the portents of the sky. Here, his timing is perfect, because Gloucester blames "[t]hese late eclipses in the sun and moon" for Edgar's treachery and the recent upheavals at court as well (107).

Gloucester's selective blindness

Gloucester's willingness to see Edgar as a traitor cannot be blamed entirely on Edmund. As seen in Gloucester's brazen discussion with Kent about Edmund's parentage in Scene 1, Gloucester often decides what is right and what is wrong based not on moral absolutes but rather on what benefits him personally. His judgment is questionable. Gloucester is quick to believe Edmund's case with only the flimsiest of circumstantial evidence. When Gloucester cannot identify Edgar's handwriting with certainty, he defers to Edmund for identification—even though Edmund has been away for nine years. This selective blindness is characteristic of Gloucester and will have horrific consequences later in the drama.

While taking advantage of Gloucester's gullibility, Edmund also demonstrates his belief that his father's superstitions are ridiculous. He may be criticizing the beliefs of the Elizabethan people in general. Critic Northrop Frye writes that "in Shakespeare's day astrology was taken seriously because of the assumption God had made the world primarily for the benefit of man. . . . Stars aren't just there; they've been put there for a purpose and that's why the configurations of stars can spell out the destinies of men and women."

Edmund simply doesn't believe that the stars have influence over the lives of humans. With sarcasm, Edmund says, "My father compounded with / my mother under the Dragon's Tail, and my / nativity was under Ursa Major, so that it follows I am / rough and lecherous" (132–135). In saying this, he defies the notion that the alignment of the stars when he was conceived has somehow created his unsavoury personality. But Edmund plays the role of a believer, even when explaining Gloucester's anger to Edgar. He tells his brother that the recent eclipses "do portend / these divisions" (140–141).

Brother's keeper

Having successfully deceived Gloucester, Edmund now turns his attention to Edgar. Pretending to have studied the signs in the heavens, Edmund predicts that divisions are coming. He claims to foresee friendships crumble, marriages dissolve, parents distrust their children, and nations struggle both internally and with foreign enemies.

Ironically, we shall see later in the drama that all of Edmund's predictions come true. At this point, however, his words seem somewhat silly to Edgar, who is astonished that his brother busies himself with such astronomical playthings. What does seem noteworthy to Edgar, however, is the fact that Edmund is so willing to come to his aid. Edmund's role-playing is so astute that Edgar believes he is trustworthy in the role of brother's keeper.

Sure of his brother's honesty, Edgar easily falls in line with each step of Edmund's plan, earning Edmund's scorn as he does. Edmund says with disgust that he has "[a] credulous father, and a brother noble, / Whose nature is so far from doing harms / That he suspects none" (186–188). The scene closes as Edmund gloats over the ease with which his machinations are proceeding.

Edmund's final remark in this scene, "All with me's meet that I can fashion fit" expresses the modern concept, "Let the end justify the means" (191). This single-mindedness of purpose describes the evil developing in the character of Edmund.

Throughout this scene, parallels in the overall story continue to take shape. Edmund takes advantage of poor judgment, a recurring theme, by recognizing that neither his father nor his brother exhibit any suspicion about what Edmund has told them. Certain characters begin to hint of "doubles" in the play. As discussed in the commentary for Act I, Scene 1, Lear's double is Gloucester. In this scene, we start to notice that the roles of Goneril and Regan are mirrored in Edmund. Finally, Cordelia can be paired with Edgar; both are children whose "price has fallen" because their fathers are foolish men deceived by their other offspring.

Act I, Scene 3

Goneril instructs her steward Oswald to be negligent in serving her father, King Lear. Presumably, Goneril hopes to cajole her father into meekness by causing his needs and desires to go unmet. We find Oswald to be extremely willing to serve his lady and the lady very familiar with her servant.

ACT I, SCENE 3
The Duke of Albany's palace.

[Enter GONERIL and OSWALD, her Steward]

Goneril Did my father strike my gentleman for
    chiding of his fool?

Oswald Ay, madam.

Goneril By day and night, he wrongs me! Every hour
  He flashes into one gross crime or other
  That sets us all at odds. I'll not endure it.   5
  His knights grow riotous, and himself upbraids us
  On every trifle. When he returns from hunting,
  I will not speak with him. Say I am sick.
  If you come slack of former services,
  You shall do well; the fault of it I'll answer.   10

[Horns within]

Oswald He's coming, madam; I hear him.

Goneril Put on what weary negligence you please,
  You and your fellows. I'd have it come to question.
  If he distaste it, let him to my sister,
  Whose mind and mine I know in that are one,   15
  Not to be overruled. Idle old man,
  That still would manage those authorities
  That he hath given away. Now, by my life,
  Old fools are babes again, and must be used
  With checks as flatteries, when they are seen abused.   20
  Remember what I have said.

Oswald   Well, madam.

NOTES

13. *come to question:* come to a showdown.

16. *Idle:* foolish.

19–20. *Old...abused:* Old men are like babies: scold, not flatter, when they are naughty.

Goneril And let his knights have colder looks
    among you.
What grows of it, no matter; advise your fellows so.
I would breed from hence occasions, and I shall,
That I may speak. I'll write straight to my sister   25
To hold my course. Prepare for dinner. *[Exeunt]*

24.   *breed...occasions:* find excuses for taking action.

COMMENTARY

In this brief scene, we meet Goneril's steward, Oswald, for the first time. Some sense of wrongdoing is apparent between the two, although the play offers no direct indication of any improper relationship. Goneril discusses with Oswald her frustration with having a house full of her father's attendants. She speaks much more openly with him than you might expect a mistress to speak to her servant. With Oswald, Shakespeare creates another parallel; his loyalty to Goneril will prove to be strong and remind us of Kent's loyalty to Lear.

The dialogue here also elaborates Goneril's role as instigator. Although Regan rarely seems to have inspirations of her own, Goneril is quite creative when making plans to strip Lear of any remaining power. In this scene, she urges Oswald to let Lear's needs and desires go unmet and unsatisfied. With such neglect, Goneril hopes not only to reduce the threat Lear and his knights present to an ordered household but also to establish a modicum of control over her father. Echoing the exchange between Edmund and Gloucester in the previous scene, here again a child preys upon the weaknesses of an aging parent in order to gain power and advantage.

Act I, Scene 4

The disguised but loyal Kent requests and receives employment as one of Lear's band of knights and servants. Also in this scene we meet the Fool, a fascinating character who serves the king as a court jester. The conflict between Goneril and Lear becomes obvious.

ACT I, SCENE 4
A hall in the same.

[Enter KENT, disguised]

Kent If but as well I other accents borrow
That can my speech defuse, my good intent
May carry through itself to that full issue
For which I razed my likeness. Now, banished Kent,
If thou canst serve where thou dost stand condemned,   5
So may it come, thy master whom thou lov'st
Shall find thee full of labours.

[Horns within. Enter LEAR, Knight, and Attendants]

Lear Let me not stay a jot for dinner; go get it ready.
[Exit an Attendant] How now, what art
thou?   10

Kent A man, sir.

Lear What dost thou profess? What wouldst thou
with us?

Kent I do profess to be no less than I seem, to
serve him truly that will put me in trust, to love him   15
that is honest, to converse with him that is wise and
says little, to fear judgment, to fight when I cannot
choose, and to eat no fish.

Lear What art thou?

Kent A very honest-hearted fellow, and as poor as   20
the King.

Lear If thou be'st as poor for a subject as he's for
a king, thou art poor enough. What wouldst thou?

Kent Service.

Lear Who wouldst thou serve?   25

NOTES

2. *defuse:* disguise.

4. *razed:* shaved; changed.

7. *full of labours:* excellent in service.

s.d. *within:* offstage.

18. *to eat no fish:* not a Catholic; not observing fast days.

Kent You.

Lear Dost thou know me, fellow?

Kent No, sir, but you have that in your countenance
which I would fain call master.

Lear What's that?   30

Kent Authority.

Lear What services canst thou do?

Kent I can keep honest counsel, ride, run, mar a
curious tale in telling it and deliver a plain message
bluntly. That which ordinary men are fit for I am   35
qualified in, and the best of me is diligence.

Lear How old art thou?

Kent Not so young, sir, to love a woman for singing,
nor so old to dote on her for anything. I have
years on my back forty-eight.   40

Lear Follow me; thou shalt serve me. If I like
thee no worse after dinner, I will not part from thee
yet. Dinner, ho, dinner! Where's my knave? my
fool? Go you and call my fool hither.
[Exit an Attendant. Enter OSWALD]
You, you, sirrah, where's my daughter?   45

Oswald So please you—*[Exit]*

Lear What says the fellow there? Call the clotpoll
back. *[Exit Knight]* Where's my fool? Ho, I think
the world's asleep.
[Enter Knight]
How now? Where's that mongrel?   50

Knight He says, my lord, your daughter is not
well.

Lear Why came not the slave back to me when I
called him?

Knight Sir, he answered me in the roundest man-   55
ner, he would not.

Lear He would not?

---

28.   *countenance:* bearing; face; demeanor.

33.   *keep honest counsel:* keep secret things.

33–34.   *mar...it:* He is not a typical courtier; he is not given
to elaborate storytelling.

46.   *So please you:* Sorry, I am busy.

47.   *clotpoll:* blockhead.

55.   *roundest:* plainest; rudest; most insolent.

Knight My lord, I know not what the matter is;
but to my judgment your Highness is not entertained
with that ceremonious affection as you were wont.   60
There's a great abatement of kindness appears as
well in the general dependants as in the Duke
himself also and your daughter.

Lear Ha? Say'st thou so?

Knight I beeseech you pardon me, my lord, if I be   65
mistaken; for my duty cannot be silent when I think
your Highness wronged.

Lear Thou but rememb'rest me of mine own
conception. I have perceived a most faint neglect of late,
which I have rather blamed as mine own jealous   70
curiosity than as a very pretense and purpose of
unkindness. I will look further into't. But where's my
fool? I have not seen him this two days.

Knight Since my young lady's going into France,
sir, the fool hath much pined away.   75

Lear No more of that; I have noted it well. Go
you and tell my daughter I would speak with her.
[Exit Knight]
Go you, call hither my Fool. *[Exit an Attendant]*
[Enter OSWALD]
O, you, sir, you! Come you hither, sir. Who am I,
sir?   80

Oswald My lady's father.

Lear 'My lady's father'? My lord's knave, you
whoreson dog, you slave, you cur!

Oswald I am none of these, my lord; I beseech
your pardon.   85

Lear Do you bandy looks with me, you rascal?

[Strikes him]

Oswald I'll not be strucken, my lord.

Kent Nor tripped neither, you base football player.

[Trips up his heels]

---

59.   *entertained:* treated or served.

60.   *ceremonious affection:* formal manners.

68.   *rememb'rest:* remind.

70–71.   *jealous curiosity:* excessive suspicion.

71.   *pretense:* deliberate intention.

86.   *bandy:* to exchange; to fight by means of staring.

88.   *football:* a lower-class street game in Elizabethan times.

Lear I thank thee, fellow. Thou serv'st me, and
I'll love thee.   90

Kent Come, sir, arise, away. I'll teach you differences. Away, away. If you will measure your
lubber's length again, tarry; but away. Go to! Have
you wisdom? So. *[Pushes him out]*

Lear Now, my friendly knave, I thank thee. There's   95
earnest of thy service. *[Gives money]*
[Enter Fool]

Fool Let me hire him too. Here's my coxcomb.
[Offers Kent his cap]

Lear How now, my pretty knave? How dost thou?

Fool Sirrah, you were best take my coxcomb.

Kent Why, fool?   100

Fool Why? For taking one's part that's out of favour. Nay, an thou canst not smile as the wind sits,
thou'lt catch cold shortly. There, take my coxcomb.
Why, this fellow has banished two on's daughters, and did
the third a blessing against his will. If thou   105
follow him, thou must needs wear my coxcomb—
How, now, nuncle? Would I had two coxcombs and
two daughters.

Lear Why, my boy?

Fool If I gave them all my living, I'd keep my   110
coxcombs myself. There's mine; beg another of thy
daughters.

Lear Take heed, sirrah—the whip.

Fool Truth's a dog must to kennel; he must be
whipped out, when the Lady Brach may stand by th'   115
fire and stink.

Lear A pestilent gall to me.

Fool Sirrah, I'll teach thee a speech.

Lear Do.

91–92   *differences:* how to tell high class from low class.

92-93.   *If you. . . again:* if you want to be tripped again.

96.   *earnest:* money given in advance upon promise of service or purchase.

97.   *coxcomb:* professional fool's headgear shaped like rooster comb or head tuft.

The Fool offers Kent his coxcomb.

102.   *an...sits:* if you cannot get on the good side of those in power.

110.   *living:* property.

113.   *the whip:* Refers to the precariousness of the Fool's position. In March of 1605, Stone, a professional fool, was whipped for commentary on a diplomatic mission about to set sail for Spain.

115.   *Lady Brach:* the pet bitch.

117.   *A pestilent gall to me:* This fool rubs me on a sore spot.

Fool Mark it, nuncle.   120
  Have more than thou showest,
  Speak less than thou knowest,
  Lend less than thou owest,
  Ride more than thou goest,
  Learn more than thou trowest,   125
  Set less than thou throwest;
  Leave thy drink and thy whore,
  And keep in-a-door,
  And thou shalt have more
  Than two tens to a score.   130

Kent This is nothing, Fool.

Fool Then 'tis like the breath of an unfee'd lawyer—
  you gave me nothing for't. Can you make no
  use of nothing, nuncle?

Lear Why, no, boy. Nothing can be made out of   135
  nothing.

Fool *[to Kent]* Prithee tell him, so much the rent of his
  land comes to; he will not believe a fool.

Lear A bitter fool.

Fool Dost thou know the difference, my boy, between   140
  a bitter fool and a sweet one?

Lear No, lad; teach me.

Fool That lord that counselled thee
  To give away thy land,
  Come place him here by me—   145
  Do thou for him stand.
  The sweet and bitter fool
  Will presently appear;
  The one in motley here,
  The other found out there.   150

Lear Dost thou call me fool, boy?

Fool All thy other titles thou hast given away; that
  thou wast born with.

Kent This is not altogether fool, my lord.

Fool No, faith; lords and great men will not let   155
  me. If I had a monopoly out, they would have part

125. *trowest:* know or believe.

126. *Set...throwest:* Don't bet more than you can afford to lose.

129–130. *And thou...score:* and then your money will increase.

149. *motley:* multicoloured fabric worn by a fool.

on't. And ladies too, they will not let me have all the
fool to myself; they'll be snatching. Nuncle, give
me an egg, and I'll give thee two crowns.

Lear What two crowns shall they be?   160

Fool Why, after I have cut the egg i' th' middle and
eat up the meat, the two crowns of the egg. When thou
clovest thy crown i' th' middle and gav'st away both
parts, thou bor'st thine ass on thy back o'er the dirt.
Thou hadst little wit in thy bald crown when thou   165
gav'st thy golden one away. If I speak like myself
in this, let him be whipped that first finds it so.
[Sings] Fools had ne'er less grace in a year,
For wise men are grown foppish,
And know not how their wits to wear,   170
Their manners are so apish,

Lear When were you wont to be so full of songs,
sirrah?

Fool I have used it, nuncle, e'er since thou mad'st
thy daughters thy mothers; for when thou gav'st   175
them the rod, and put'st down thine own breeches,
[Sings] Then they for sudden joy did weep,
And I for sorrow sung,
That such a king should play bo-peep
And go the fools among.   180
Prithee, nuncle, keep a schoolmaster that can teach thy
fool to lie. I would fain learn to lie.

Lear An you lie, sirrah, we'll have you whipped.

Fool I marvel what kin thou and thy daughters are.
They'll have me whipped for speaking true; thou'lt   185
have me whipped for lying; and sometimes I am
whipped for holding my peace. I had rather be any
kind o' thing than a fool, and yet I would not be thee,
nuncle: thou hast pared thy wit o' both sides and
left nothing i' th' middle. Here comes one o' the   190
parings.

[Enter GONERIL]

Lear How now, daughter? What makes that frontlet on? You are too much of late i' th' frown.

157–158. *ladies...snatching:* probably refers to traditionally phallic-shaped ornament worn by fools.

168–171. *Fools...apish:* There is no job left for fools these days because wise men are so much like fools.

177–180. *Then...among:* The original music for this song probably came from a 1609 copy of *Pammelia, Musick's Miscellanie.* The Fool's words here are adapted from a song about a Protestant martyr, "The Ballad of John Careless."

183. *An:* if.

192–193. *frontlet:* frown on forehead.

Fool Thou wast a pretty fellow when thou hadst
no need to care for her frowning. Now thou art an O   195
without a figure. I am better than thou are now: I
am a fool, thou art nothing. [To *Goneril*] Yes, for-
sooth, I will hold my tongue. So your face bids me,
though you say nothing. Mum, mum.
He that keeps nor crust nor crumb,   200
Weary of all, shall want some.—
[Points at Lear] That's a shealed peascod.

Goneril Not only, sir, this your all-licensed fool,
But other of your insolent retinue
Do hourly carp and quarrel, breaking forth   205
In rank and not-to-be-endured riots. Sir,
I had thought by making this well known unto you
To have found a safe redress, but now grow fearful,
By what yourself too late have spoke and done,
That you protect this course, and put it on   210
By your allowance; which if you should, the fault
Would not 'scape censure, nor the redresses sleep,
Which, in the tender of a wholesome weal,
Might in their working do you that offence,
Which else were shame, that then necessity   215
Will call discreet proceeding.

Fool For you know, nuncle,
The hedge-sparrow fed the cuckoo so long
That it's had it head bit off by it young.
So out went the candle, and we were left darkling.   220

Lear Are you our daughter?

Goneril I would you would make use of your good
wisdom.
(Whereof I know you are fraught) and put away
These dispositions which of late transport you   225
From what you rightly are.

Fool May not an ass know when the cart draws the horse?
Whoop, Jug, I love thee!

Lear Does any here know me? This is not Lear.
Does Lear walk thus? speak thus? Where are his eyes?

195–196. *O without a figure:* a valueless zero with no other digit in front of it.

202. *shealed peascod:* shelled peapod.

203. *all-licensed:* allowed to take all liberties.

210. *put it on:* encourage it.

211. *allowance:* approval.

213–216. *Which...proceeding:* If you continue to be a nuisance, I will be forced to keep the peace through measures that will annoy you. Although shameful to a father, my actions in this instance would be justified.

218. *cuckoo:* The word puns on horns and cuckolds in Elizabethan plays. (A cuckold is a husband deceived by an unfaithful wife.) The cuckoo bird has unusual and disorderly habits, including its practice of laying its eggs in the nest of some smaller bird who then hatches and feeds the foster bird after the young cuckoo has pushed the legitimate offspring out of the nest.

219. *it:* its.

Either his notion weakens, his discernings   230
Are lethargied—Ha! Waking? 'Tis not so.
Who is it that can tell me who I am?

Fool Lear's shadow.

Lear I would learn that; for, by the marks of sovereignty,
Knowledge, and reason, I should be false persuaded   235
I had daughters.

Fool Which they will make an obedient father.

Lear Your name, fair gentlewoman?

Goneril This admiration, sir, is much o' th' savour
Of other your new pranks. I do beseech you   240
To understand my purposes aright.
As you are old and reverend, should be wise.
Here do you keep a hundred knights and squires,
Men so disordered, so deboshed, and bold
That this our court, infected with their manners,   245
Shows like a riotous inn. Epicurism and lust
Makes it more like a tavern or a brothel
Than a graced palace. The shame itself doth speak
For instant remedy. Be then desired
By her that else will take the thing she begs   250
A little to disquantity your train,
And the remainders that shall still depend
To be such men as may besort your age,
Which know themselves, and you.

Lear   Darkness and devils!
Saddle my horses; call my train together.   255
Degenerate bastard, I'll not trouble thee:
Yet have I left a daughter.

Goneril You strike my people, and your disordered rabble
Make servants of their betters.

[*Enter ALBANY*]

Lear Woe that too late repents.—O, sir, are you come?   260
Is it your will? Speak, sir.—Prepare my horses.

---

230.   *notion:* understanding.

233.   *Lear's shadow:* In the Quarto version, this is spoken by Lear and followed by a question mark.

239.   *admiration:* pretended astonishment.

244.   *deboshed:* debauched.

246.   *Epicurism:* self-indulgent, riotous living.

Ingratitude! thou marble-hearted fiend,
More hideous when thou show'st thee in a child
Than the sea-monster.

Albany   Pray, sir, be patient.

Lear Detested kite, thou liest.   265
My train are men of choice and rarest parts,
That all particulars of duty know
And in the most exact regard support
The worships of their name. O most small fault,
How ugly didst thou in Cordelia show!   270
Which, like an engine, wrenched my frame of nature
From the fixed place; drew from my heart all love
And added to the gall. O Lear, Lear, Lear!
Beat at this gate that let thy folly in
[Strikes his head]
And thy dear judgment out. Go, go, my people.   275

Albany My lord, I am guiltless, as I am ignorant
Of what hath moved you.

Lear   It may be so, my lord.
Hear, Nature, hear; dear goddess, hear:
Suspend thy purpose if thou didst intend
To make this creature fruitful.   280
Into her womb convey sterility,
Dry up in her the organs of increase,
And from her derogate body never spring
A babe to honour her. If she must teem,
Create her child of spleen, that it may live   285
And be a thwart disnatured torment to her.
Let it stamp wrinkles in her brow of youth,
With cadent tears fret channels in her cheeks,
Turn all her mother's pains and benefits
To laughter and contempt, that she may feel   290
How sharper than a serpent's tooth it is
To have a thankless child. Away, away! *[Exit]*

Albany Now, gods that we adore, wherof comes this?

Goneril Never afflict yourself to know more of it,
But let his disposition have that scope   295
As dotage gives it.

265.   *kite:* the lowest birds of prey; eaters of feces.

266.   *parts:* accomplishments.

268–269.   *in...name:* are worthy of their honorable titles.

273.   *gall:* bitterness.

Lear calls Goneril a *"[d]etested kite."*

282.   *increase:* childbearing.

283.   *derogate:* unworthy; debased.

284.   *teem:* conceive.

285.   *spleen:* malice.

286.   *thwart disnatured:* perverse and unnatural.

288.   *cadent:* falling; *cadence:* measured.

[Enter LEAR]

Lear What, fifty of my followers at a clap?
  Within a fortnight?

Albany   What's the matter, sir?

Lear I'll tell thee. *[To Goneril]* Life and death, I
        am ashamed
  That thou hast power to shake my manhood thus!   300
  That these hot tears, which break from me perforce,
  Should make thee worth them. Blasts and fogs upon thee!
  Th' untented woundings of a father's curse
  Pierce every sense about thee! Old fond eyes,
  Beweep this cause again I'll pluck ye out   305
  And cast you, with the waters that you loose,
  To temper clay. Yea, is it come to this?
  Ha! Let it be so. Yet have I left a daughter,
  Who I am sure is kind and comfortable.
  When she shall hear this of thee, with her nails   310
  She'll flay thy wolfish visage. Thou shalt find
  That I'll resume the shape which thou dost think
  I have cast off for ever.

[Exit LEAR with KENT and Attendants]

Goneril   Do you mark that?

Albany I cannot be so partial, Goneril,
  To the great love I bear you—   315

Goneril Pray you, content.—What, Oswald, ho!
  [To Fool] You, sir, more knave than fool, after your
        master!

Fool Nuncle Lear, nuncle Lear, tarry. Take the fool
  with thee.
  A fox, when one has caught her,   320
  And such a daughter,
  Should sure to the slaughter,
  If my cap would buy a halter.
  So the fool follows after.

[Exit]

---

300.   *shake my manhood:* make me cry.

303–304. *untented woundings . . . about thee!:* There will be
no lifting of Lear's curse; a tent is a small roll of cloth
used to clean out a wound.

314.   *partial:* biased

Goneril This man hath had good counsel—a hundred   325
      knights!
   'Tis politic and safe to let him keep
   At point a hundred knights—yes, that on every dream,
   Each buzz, each fancy, each complaint, dislike,
   He may enguard his dotage with their pow'rs
   And hold our lives in mercy.—Oswald, I say!   330

Albany Well, you may fear too far.

Goneril   Safer than trust too far.
   Let me still take away the harms I fear,
   Not fear still to be taken. I know his heart.
   What he hath uttered I have writ my sister.
   If she sustain him and his hundred knights,   335
   When I have showed th' unfitness—
   [Enter OSWALD]
                                 How now, Oswald?
   What, have you writ that letter to my sister?

Oswald Ay, madam.

Goneril Take you some company, and away to horse.
   Inform her full of my particular fear,   340
   And thereto add such reasons of your own
   As may compact it more. Get you gone,
   And hasten your return. *[Exit Oswald]* No, no, my lord,
   This milky gentleness and course of yours,
   Though I condemn not, yet under pardon,   345
   You are much more ataskèd for want of wisdom
   Than praised for harmful mildness.

Albany How far your eyes may pierce I cannot tell;
   Striving to better, oft we mar what's well.

Goneril Nay then—   350

Albany Well, well; th' event.

[Exeunt]

---

326.   *politic:* wise or good policy.

327.   *At point:* fully armed.

328.   *buzz:* rumour.

332–333.   *Let...taken:* May I always dispose of what I fear rather than live in fear always.

342.   *compact it more:* make my argument more convincing.

344.   *milky...course:* weak behaviour.

346.   *ataskèd:* taken to task.

351.   *th' event:* We will see what happens.

COMMENTARY

In Scene 4, Kent appears in disguise, playing the role of a man in search of a master. At court in Act I, Scene 1, Kent promised to "shape his old course in a country new." Although Kent has not changed his geographical country, he has changed his personal landscape by assuming a different identity. His course, or service, however, remains the same as before; he petitions to be taken into Lear's service.

Kent's heroism

Interestingly, in a play named for a king, Kent seems to be quite the hero. Classical heroes are dedicated to a cause, display unfailing loyalty, function well in disguise, and seek higher morals and values. With every right and reason to remain angry with Lear and to leave the king to his own devices, Kent instead rises above the average. He assumes the disguise and characteristics of a mere indentured ruffian for the purpose of continuing to protect his beloved king.

Note that when Lear asks Kent, "[W]hat art thou?," Kent replies, "A man, sir" (9–11). At first offering no name, status, or qualifications, Kent presents himself as symbolically unadorned: simply a human being. Kent is divested of position, name, and title. He stands before his old master as nothing more than stark humanity, and as the play progresses, we shall see this vision of stark humanity emerge in almost every character. Yet in the act of continuing to serve his king, Kent is more humane in his humanity than are many of the other characters encountered thus far.

In his loyalty, Kent is quick-tempered and aggressive—traits that will get him into trouble in the future. When Oswald slights Lear and one of Lear's knights reports that the king is not being served well, Kent's temper is roused. After Lear strikes Oswald for his insolence, Kent trips the steward and promises to teach him "differences" (91). Kent's action pleases Lear, who gives Kent money and calls him a "friendly knave" (95). In this scene, Kent and Oswald are like two boisterous boys playing a game of dare. But later, we will see just how deadly such a game can become when Kent again lets his temper and zeal get the better of him.

The Fool's role

Another character introduced in this scene is Lear's Fool. Shakespeare's fools and clowns are the subjects of much discussion because they play such important and dynamic roles in his plays. Placed in positions where they can watch the goings-on at court, fools tend to serve as foils and sounding boards for their masters. The Fool in *King Lear* is no exception. Privy to the innermost feelings of his king, the Fool also observes the outcomes of Lear's rash judgments and will comment upon those judgments throughout the drama.

In this scene, the Fool provides commentary on two mistakes that Lear has made. First, in lines 168–171, the Fool sings about masters usurping the roles of professional fools. The Fool castigates Lear for giving away his kingly authority, suggesting that because Lear no longer has the authority of a crown, then perhaps Lear should don the coxcomb, or fool's cap. In a second snippet of song in lines 177–180, the Fool makes plain his discontent over the parcelling out of the kingdom. While the Fool admits that Regan and Goneril have benefited immensely, he also recognizes Lear's almost infantile behavior when making such divisions.

Second, the Fool hints at his disagreement with Lear's disowning of Cordelia. "Why, this fellow has banished two on's daughters," says the Fool, "and did the third a blessing against his will" (104–105). The Fool's remarks here are sarcastic; the Fool does not believe at all that Lear has done right by his youngest child. In some respects the Fool, according to the limitations of his profession, serves as the "true blank" of Lear's eye that Kent wished to be in Scene 1.

Notice that Lear cannot help but be reminded of Cordelia through this scene. Having listened to the Fool's rhymed proverbs in lines 121–130, Kent remarks, "This is nothing, Fool" (131). The word "nothing" appears twice more in the Fool's next lines, and Lear himself comments that "nothing can be made out of / nothing" (135–136). Though Lear's comment about a "bitter fool" is ostensibly directed at the Fool, Lear may also be starting to see himself as something of a fool who grows decidedly bitter (139).

Lear's neglect

As Lear confronts Goneril about her servants' neglect, he begins to discover how his authority is being usurped. Having given up the responsibilities of rule, Lear feels that it is now time to enjoy an unencumbered rest—a time to play and bask in the care of his children. Instead, Lear finds that in giving up his responsibility, he has also lost all respect due him as a king.

Amazed that he is not being taken seriously, Lear remarks: "Does any here know me? This is not Lear" (228). At this particular juncture the king begins to question his own identity; indeed, Lear voices the question, "Who is it that can tell me who I am?" (232). The Fool's response—"Lear's shadow"—answers Lear's question ambiguously, with two meanings possible (233). The Fool may mean that Lear is now but a shadow of his former self, or he may mean that only the shadow of the old Lear can explain to Lear his current status. In either case, some clues now surface about how much of Lear's sense of self has been wrapped up in his power and authority as king and father. To be effectively stripped of both of these titles renders Lear susceptible and weak.

Lear versus Goneril

As a sense of his ineffectuality dawns, Lear attempts in two ways to reestablish some superiority. His first strategy is to position himself above his daughter Goneril in the hierarchy of creation—the "Great Chain of Being." Lear compares ingratitude in a child to ingratitude in a sea monster; he finds the sea monster more appealing. Lear also calls Goneril a "[d]etested kite" and a "creature" (265, 280). This attempt to elevate himself

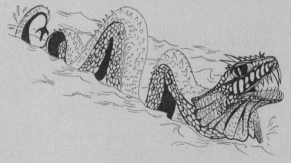

Lear finds a sea monster more appealing than his daughter Goneril.

by degrading Goneril to the rank of a beast represents just one example of the animal imagery with which Shakespeare fills this play. A great deal of scholarship focuses on this imagery, and within the play certain persons are compared, either explicitly or through the use of simile, to a lengthy list of creatures: lions, sheep, horses, dogs, cows, hogs, wolves, polecats, monkeys, foxes, bears, civet cats, wrens, flies, pelicans, butterflies, owls, rats, crows, mice, choughs, water newts, tadpoles, worms, frogs, kites, serpents, dragons, and spotted toads.

Lear's second strategy is to effect the stance of titan—or at least prophet—as he demands a curse upon Goneril, revealing that he views Nature differently than Edmund does. Lear's Nature is one that applauds human morality, respect, and dignity—not one that wallows in the more animalistic sensuality and raging desire. Just as Lear tries to affirm his humanity by relegating Goneril to the status of a beast, so does Lear further that affirmation by engaging in an activity that is uniquely human: invoking the divine.

Near the end of this scene, as Lear rails at his daughter, Goneril's husband Albany seems to be completely ineffectual in mediating this father-daughter quarrel. Albany's comments here are sparse; in the Quarto text his remarks are even more spare as his request to Lear— "Pray, sir, be patient"—is absent (264). (For a discussion of the differences between the Quarto and Folio versions of this play, see the "Introduction to *King Lear*.")

Lear says that having a "thankless child" is "sharper than a serpent's tooth."

Albany's weakness

Despite Goneril's powerful personality, Albany is not free of responsibility concerning his wife's actions. Regent or no, Goneril is still the wife of this Duke, and her actions reflect upon her husband. Earlier in the scene, the knight describes the atmosphere in Goneril's household to Lear this way: "There's a great abatement of kindness appears as / well in the general dependants as in the Duke / himself also and your daughter" (61–63).

Given the mastery that Albany allows Goneril over the household and the fact that he shrinks from her to avoid confrontation, Albany does not seem like the type of person to purposely neglect or affront Lear. Rather, Albany more likely has simply ignored or been blind to what goes on in his own household. Goneril, her plans, and her little kingdom all form a situation that Albany appears to have taken "too little care of"—another example of poor judgment. And just as the audience recognizes the folly of both Lear and Gloucester in previous scenes, so the audience sees in this scene that Albany has abdicated rule in his own home. None of these three characters can foresee the impact his mistakes in judgment will have.

As the scene draws to a close, a basis develops for several conflicts that arise in later scenes. First, Lear makes comparisons between Goneril and Regan. Angered and insulted by Goneril, Lear remarks, "Yet have I left a daughter, / Who I am sure is kind and comfortable" (308–309). This daughter, Regan, is Lear's hope for the salvation of his honour. Lear is certain that Regan will "flay" Goneril's "wolfish visage" in retaliation for the manner in which Lear has been treated in the house of Goneril (311). Soon, however, Regan proves to be equally as unloving and unkind as her sister.

Second, Goneril commissions Oswald to deliver a letter to Regan. Note again the ease with which this mistress and steward conspire together. Goneril instructs Oswald to "inform her [Regan] full of my particular fear, / And thereto add such reasons of your own / As may compact it more" (340–342). Goneril wants to inform her sister not only of what has occurred in Goneril's home but also how to react when Lear appears at Regan's door and asks to be welcomed and served. As later revealed, Oswald finds his postal mission to be something more than the simple delivery of Goneril's message. In finding Regan, Oswald will also find Kent.

Note also how Goneril and Regan—mainly through the direction of the former—are allies at this point in the play. The control of their father, especially with an eye toward reducing his entourage of 100 knights, is their common goal, and to this end they indeed initially "hit together." Soon, however, both women become aware of Edmund, and with this awareness will come a parting of the ways. The common goal the sisters now share will acquire a new face and a new direction—one that elevates personal desire above the common good.

Act I, Scene 5

Lear sends Kent with letters to Gloucester and Regan. The Fool comments upon Lear's errors in judgment. Lear leaves the home of Goneril.

ACT I, SCENE 5
A court before the same.

[Enter LEAR, KENT, and FOOL]

Lear Go you before to Gloucester with these letters. Acquaint my daughter no further with anything
you know than comes from her demand out of the letter. If your diligence be not speedy, I shall be there
afore you.   5

Kent I will not sleep, my lord, till I have delivered your
letter. *[Exit]*

Fool If a man's brains were in's heels, were't not
in danger of kibes?

Lear Ay, boy.   10

Fool Then I prithee be merry. Thy wits shall not
go slipshod.

Lear Ha, ha, ha.

Fool Shalt see thy other daughter will use thee
kindly; for though she's as like this as a crab's like   15
an apple, yet I can tell what I can tell.

Lear What canst tell, boy?

Fool She will taste as like this as a crab does to a crab.
Thou canst tell why one's nose stands i' th' middle
on's face?   20

Lear No.

Fool Why, to keep one's eyes of either side 's nose,
that what a man cannot smell out he may spy into.

Lear I did her wrong.

NOTES

1.   *Gloucester:* the locale, not the man.

9.   *kibes:* chapped heels.

11-12.   *Thy...slipshod:* You need no slippers because you
have no brains in your feet to cause chapped
heels.

24.   *her:* Lear is thinking of Cordelia.

Fool Canst tell how an oyster makes his shell? 25

Lear No.

Fool Nor I neither; but I can tell why a snail has a house.

Lear Why?

Fool Why, to put 's head in; not to give it away to 30 his daughters, and leave his horns without a case.

Lear I will forget my nature. So kind a father!— Be my horses ready?

Fool Thy asses are gone about 'em. The reason why the seven stars are no moe than seven is a pretty 35 reason.

Lear Because they are not eight.

Fool Yes indeed. Thou wouldst make a good fool.

Lear To take 't again perforce—Monster ingratitude!

Fool If thou wert my fool, nuncle, I'll have thee 40 beaten for being old before thy time.

Lear How's that?

Fool Thou shouldst not have been old till thou hadst been wise.

Lear O, let me not be mad, not mad, sweet heaven! 45 Keep me in temper; I would not be mad! *[Enter a Gentleman]* How now, are the horses ready?

Gentleman Ready, my lord.

Lear Come, boy.

Fool She that's a maid now, and laughs at my departure, 50 Shall not be a maid long, unless things be cut shorter.

[Exeunt]

---

31.   *case:* shelter.

38.   *To take. . . perforce:* Lear is considering retaking his position by force.

46.   *in temper:* sane.

50-51.   *She that's. . . shorter:* The maid who laughs when I leave will not be a maid long; she is a fool and will lose her virginity unless men are castrated.

COMMENTARY

Lear prepares to leave Goneril's home, and he sends Kent ahead with letters to pave the way with what Lear assumes will be a receptive Regan. Kent leaves, and Lear and the Fool are left in dialogue. Traditionally, fools tend to point out their masters' errors in these dialogues, leading the conversation in such a way that the master seems almost as much a fool as is the professional clown.

The Fool lives up to the traditional expectation in this scene, for the Fool is quite critical of Lear's confidence in Regan. "Shalt see thy other daughter will use thee / kindly; for though she's as like this as a crab's like / an apple, yet I can tell what I can tell," quips the Fool sarcastically (14–16). Not for a minute does the Fool believe Lear will be better treated by Regan than by Goneril, and it becomes apparent that Lear, despite his bravado, may harbor such doubts as well.

A hint of madness

Some of Lear's "unconstant starts," which Regan complained of in Scene 1, become evident in this scene.

Over and over again Lear catches himself in slips of speech, inattention, or wandering thoughts. His remark in line 24—"I did her wrong"—undoubtedly refers to Cordelia. In lines 269–270 of Scene 4, Lear looked back to the reason he disinherited his youngest daughter: "O most small fault, / How ugly didst thou in Cordelia show!" In line 32 of this scene, Lear fears he will "forget [his] nature" and then abruptly asks about the readiness of his horses. Lear even briefly voices the possibility of reassuming his kingly rule—"To take 't again perforce"—as he considers the "Monster ingratitude" of Goneril (38–39).

The beginning of Lear's journey into madness can be seen here. Earlier, in Scene 4, Lear struck his head, punishing the "gate that let thy folly in." Now Lear no longer speaks in metaphor. The distraught king cries, "O, let me not be mad, not mad, sweet heaven! / Keep me in temper; I would not be mad!" (45–46). This titan who demanded love as a commodity in Scene 1 is now realizing the effects of designating love, loyalty, and affection as items that can be bartered.

Notes

Notes

COLES NOTES TOTAL STUDY EDITION

KING LEAR
ACT II

Scene 1 71

Scene 2 77

Scene 3 85

Scene 4 87

Lear *You see me here, you gods, a poor old man,*
As full of grief as age, wretched in both.
If it be you that stirs these daughters' hearts
Against their father, fool me not so much
To bear it tamely; touch me with noble anger,
And let not women's weapons, water drops,
Stain my man's cheeks.

Act II, Scene 1

Rumors circulate about a conflict between Albany and Cornwall. Edmund spreads more false tales about Edgar and wins the support of Cornwall.

ACT II, SCENE 1
A court in the castle of the Earl of Gloucester.

[Enter EDMUND and CURAN severally]

Edmund Save thee, Curan.

Curan And you, sir. I have been with your father, and given him notice that the Duke of Cornwall and Regan his Duchess will be here with him this night.

Edmund How comes that?   5

Curan Nay, I know not. You have heard of the news abroad—I mean the whispered ones, for they are yet but ear-kissing arguments?

Edmund Not I. Pray you, what are they?

Curan Have you heard of no likely wars toward, 'twixt   10
the Dukes of Cornwall and Albany?

Edmund Not a word.

Curan You may do, then, in time. Fare you well, sir.

[Exit]

Edmund The Duke be here to-night? The better best!
This weaves itself perforce into my business.   15
My father hath set guard to take my brother,
And I have one thing of a queasy question
Which I must act. Briefness and fortune, work!
Brother, a word: descend. Brother, I say!
[Enter EDGAR]
My father watches. O sir, fly this place.   20
Intelligence is given where you are hid.
You have now the good advantage of the night.
Have you not spoken 'gainst the Duke of Cornwall?
He's coming hither; now i' th' night, i' th' haste,

NOTES

s.d.   *severally:* separately and from different directions.

8.   *ear-kissing:* whispered.

17.   *queasy question:* needs delicate handling.

19.   *descend:* from chamber where he had been hiding.

And Regan with him. Have you nothing said   25
Upon his party 'gainst the Duke of Albany?
Advise yourself.

Edgar   I am sure on't, not a word.

Edmund I hear my father coming. Pardon me:
In cunning I must draw my sword upon you.
Draw, seem to defend yourself; now quit you well.—   30   **30.**   *quit you well:* defend yourself well.
Yield! Come before my father! Light ho, here!—
Fly, brother.—Torches, torches!—So farewell.
[Exit EDGAR]
Some blood drawn on me would beget opinion   **33.**   *beget opinion:* give the impression.
Of my more fierce endeavour. *[Wounds his arm]*
     I have seen drunkards
Do more than this in sport.—Father, father!   35
Stop, stop! No help?

[Enter GLOUCESTER and Servants with torches]

Gloucester Now, Edmund, where's the villain?

Edmund Here stood he in the dark, his sharp sword out,
Mumbling of wicked charms, conjuring the moon   **38–39.**   *Mumbling...mistress:* This is the type of story
To stand auspicious mistress.   Gloucester is sure to like.

Gloucester   But where is he?   40

Edmund Look, sir, I bleed.

Gloucester   Where is the villain, Edmund?

Edmund Fled this way, sir, when by no means he could—

Gloucester Pursue him, ho! Go after. *[Exit some
     Servants]* By no means what?

Edmund Persuade me to the murder of your lordship;
But that I told him the revenging gods   45
'Gainst parricides did all their thunders bend;
Spoke with how manifold and strong a bond
The child was bound to th' father—sir, in fine,   **48.**   *in fine:* in short.
Seeing how loathly opposite I stood
To his unnatural purpose, in fell motion   50   **50.**   *fell:* fearful.
With his prepared sword he charges home
My unprovided body, latched mine arm;   **52.**   *unprovided:* unguarded.
                                                                          latched: stabbed.
And when he saw my best alarumed spirits
Bold in the quarrel's right, roused to th' encounter,   **53.**   *alarumed spirits:* stoutest spirits called out by the
                                                                          alarm.

Or whether gasted by the noise I made,   55
Full suddenly he fled.

Gloucester   Let him fly far.
Not in this land shall he remain uncaught;
And found—dispatch. The noble Duke my master,
My worthy arch and patron, comes to-night:
By his authority I will proclaim it   60
That he which finds him shall deserve our thanks,
Bringing the murderous coward to the stake;
He that conceals him, death.

Edmund When I dissuaded him from his intent
And found him pight to do it, with curst speech   65
I threatened to discover him. He replied,
"Thou unpossessing bastard; dost thou think,
If I would stand against thee, would the reposal
Of any trust, virtue, or worth in thee
Make thy words faithed? No. What I should deny   70
(As this I would, ay, though thou didst produce
My very character) I'll turn it all
To thy suggestion, plot, and damned practice;
And thou must make a dullard of the world,
If they not thought the profits of my death   75
Were very pregnant and potential spirits
To make thee seek it."

Gloucester   O strange and fast'ned villain!
Would he deny his letter, said he? [I never got him.]
[Tucket within]
Hark, the Duke's trumpets. I know not why he comes.
All ports I'll bar; the villain shall not 'scape;   80
The Duke must grant me that. Besides, his picture
I will send far and near, that all the kingdom
May have due note of him; and of my land,
Loyal and natural boy, I'll work the means
To make thee capable.   85

[Enter CORNWALL, REGAN, and Attendants]

Cornwall How now, my noble friend? Since I came hither
(Which I can call but now) I have heard strange news.

Regan If it be true, all vengeance comes too short
Which can pursue th' offender. How dost, my lord?

55.	*gasted:* terrified.
58.	*dispatch:* kill him.
59.	*arch:* support.
65.	*pight:* determined.
	curst: angry.
70.	*faithed:* believed.
73.	*suggestion:* idea.
	practice: habit.
74–77.	*And thou...it:* People would be stupid indeed to believe your motive wasn't to profit by my death.
76.	*pregnant...spirits:* obvious and powerful arguments.
77.	*fast'ned:* confirmed.
s.d.	*tucket:* a type of trumpet call.
84.	*natural boy:* one who behaves properly as son toward father.
85.	*capable:* able to inherit lawfully.

Gloucester O madam, my old heart is cracked, is cracked. 90

Regan What, did my father's godson seek your life?
He whom my father named, your Edgar?

Gloucester O lady, lady, shame would have it hid.

Regan Was he not companion with the riotous knights
That tended upon my father? 95

Gloucester I know not, madam. 'Tis too bad, too bad.

Edmund Yes, madam, he was of that consort.

Regan No marvel then though he were ill affected.
'Tis they have put him on the old man's death,
To have th' expense and waste of his revenues. 100
I have this present evening from my sister
Been well informed of them, and with such cautions
That, if they come to sojourn at my house,
I'll not be there.

Cornwall   Nor I, assure thee, Regan.
Edmund, I hear that you have shown your father 105
A childlike office.

Edmund   It was my duty, sir.

Gloucester He did bewray his practice, and received
This hurt you see, striving to apprehend him.

Cornwall Is he pursued?

Gloucester   Ay, my good lord.

Cornwall If he be taken, he shall never more 110
Be feared of doing harm. Make your own purpose,
How in my strength you please. For you, Edmund,
Whose virtue and obedience doth this instant
So much commend itself, you shall be ours.
Natures of such deep trust we shall much need; 115
You we first seize on.

Edmund   I shall serve you, sir,
Truly, however else.

Gloucester   For him I thank your Grace.

Cornwall You know not why we came to visit you?

Regan Thus out of season, threading dark-eyed night.
Occasions, noble Gloucester, of some prize, 120

---

97. *consort:* group.

98. *though he were ill affected:* having thoughts of treason.

106. *childlike office:* an appropriate duty from son to father.

107. *bewray:* reveal.

111–112. *Make...please:* Use my authority for any action you care to take.

119. *threading...night:* making our way through the darkness.

Wherein we must have use of your advice.
Our father he hath writ, so hath our sister,
Of differences, which I best thought it fit
To answer from our home. The several messengers
From hence attend dispatch. Our good old friend,   125
Lay comforts to your bosom, and bestow
Your needful counsel to our business,
Which craves the instant use.

Gloucester   I serve you, madam.
Your Graces are right welcome.

[Exeunt. Flourish]

128.   *craves...use:* requires immediate action.

COMMENTARY

The threads of story introduced by Shakespeare in the exposition of Act I now begin to interweave in the development of Act II. The main plot that involves Lear and his daughters intersects with the subplot of Gloucester and his sons. In this act, one of the play's major themes—that of good versus evil—begins to solidify as lines are drawn clearly between these two oppositions. The parallels exposed in the previous act also become more fully elaborated and underscored.

of dissension between the two dukes, Lear's plan to prevent strife by dividing his kingdom clearly has been a failure as a preemptive strike.

As Edgar enters, Edmund assumes again his role as brother's keeper and protector. Edmund masterfully uses the information just gained from Curan to convince Edgar that he has been maligned. Supposedly, Edgar

Edmund continues his deceit

From the courtier Curan, Edmund receives two important pieces of information. First, Regan and her husband, the Duke of Cornwall, are en route to Gloucester's home. Edmund receives this news gladly, because he feels that his campaign against his brother Edgar may be assisted by the involvement of Cornwall. Second, Edmund learns of trouble between Cornwall and Albany, and though this is the first definite indication

A scene from the 1971 Soviet film version of King Lear, *directed by Grigori Kozintsev. Everett Collection*

has been overheard voicing favour for or opposition to the Dukes of Cornwall and Albany; Edmund is quick to use this information as a means toward his personal ends. Hearing Gloucester approach, Edmund suggests that the two brothers stage a mock sword duel. Edmund's stated reason for this false fight is to assist his brother by running interference between Edgar and Gloucester. We see, however, that Edmund's real plan is to place his brother in the worst possible light—as a disloyal son who attacks his own brother. Edmund wounds himself with his own sword just before Gloucester enters the scene.

Once again, Edmund plays on Gloucester's belief in the gods and superstition. In relating his supposed conversation with Edgar, Edmund claims to have made comments about "revenging gods" and their thunders, fully aware that by seeming to profess sentiments similar to those of his father, Edmund can further his case against Edgar and continue to pull Gloucester in (45). The success of Edmund's maneuvers is evident. Gloucester now declares that Edgar is unnatural and dubs Edmund a "[l]oyal and natural" boy (84). Gloucester promises to make Edmund the legitimate heir of the earldom.

Hasty judgment

Here again the parallel between Gloucester and Lear is apparent. Gloucester asks Edmund if Edgar would "deny his letter" (78). Without waiting for a response from Edmund, Gloucester draws his own conclusion and remarks, "I never got him" (78). Notice how, with this remark, Gloucester essentially disinherits Edgar. Gloucester attempts to sever the bond of blood by claiming no responsibility for the fathering of his legitimate son. Following in Lear's path, Gloucester seems to misunderstand the nature of the parent-child bond; each father is cleverly duped by his evil child (or children) and renounces the good.

Additionally, Gloucester makes his distrust and woes known to the Duke and Duchess of Cornwall. Some parents might seek to hide a child's transgression or to protect the wayward son, but Gloucester feels obligated to make public his grievance with Edgar and to accept Cornwall's promise to aid in the capture and punishment of the errant Edgar. (Notice that Gloucester does nothing to stop Edmund from discussing this matter and makes only a brief remark on the shame of doing so.)

Evidence mounts against Edgar

Regan is quick to draw a connection between Edgar's disloyalty and the "riotous knights" about which she has already received a communication from her sister (94). Edmund is equally quick to verify that Edgar was, indeed, "of that consort" (97). Edmund, then, immediately allies himself with Regan, and her reaction to Edmund's attention is soon to become apparent.

Note also that Regan refers to Edgar as her "father's godson" (91). This relationship is scarcely noted in the play, but the mention of it here has the peculiar quality of making Edgar appear even more evil. For Edgar to plot against his own father contradicts the proper and natural laws of obedience toward one's parent. When Edgar is seen as Lear's godson, however, all of Edgar's supposed plots can also be viewed as treasonous actions toward the king.

As the scene closes, Gloucester turns against Edgar, Edmund joins league with Cornwall, and Regan is intent upon drawing Gloucester in against the king. Having fled their own home to avoid Lear's visit, Cornwall and Regan descend upon Gloucester, fully anticipating his assistance and compliance. A veritable nest of evil seems situated at Gloucester's castle in the "dark-eyed" night—a night that is soon to witness an array of outrages.

Act II, Scene 2

Kent lets his tongue get the better of him; he insults Oswald at the home of Gloucester and instigates a sword fight. Consequently, the visiting Cornwall puts Kent in the stocks for fighting with Oswald.

ACT II, SCENE 2
Before Gloucester's castle.

[Enter KENT, and OSWALD, severally]

Oswald Good dawning to thee, friend. Art of this
   house?

Kent Ay.

Oswald Where may we set our horses?

Kent I' th' mire.   5

Oswald Prithee, if thou lov'st me, tell me.

Kent I love thee not.

Oswald Why then, I care not for thee.

Kent If I had thee in Lipsbury Pinfold, I would make
   thee care for me.   10

Oswald Why dost thou use me thus? I know thee not.

Kent Fellow, I know thee.

Oswald What dost thou know me for?

Kent A knave, a rascal, an eater of broken meats;   15
   a base, proud, shallow, beggarly, three-suited,
   hundred-pound, filthy worsted-stocking knave; a lily-
   livered, action-taking, whoreson, glass-gazing, super-
   serviceable, finical rogue; one-trunk-inheriting

NOTES

9. *Lipsbury Pinfold:* an enclosure where strayed animals are kept until reclaimed by owners; a good place to fight because neither opponent could escape.

15. *broken meats:* remains of food sent from the table of the nobles.

16. *three-suited:* a servant was provided with three suits of clothing per year.

17. *worsted-stocking:* knit stockings, as opposed to the silk stockings worn by gentlemen.

18. *glass-gazing:* always looking at himself in the mirror; feminine.

18-19. *super-serviceable:* too eager to do what his master wishes.

   finical: picky.

19. *one-trunk-inheriting:* one's whole inheritance from one's father will fit into one trunk.

slave; one that wouldst be a bawd in way of good   20
service, and art nothing but the composition of a
knave, beggar, coward, pander, and the son and
heir of a mongrel bitch; one whom I will beat into
clamorous whining if thou deny'st the least syllable
of thy addition.   25

Oswald Why, what a monstrous fellow art thou,
thus to rail on one that is neither known of thee
nor knows thee!

Kent What a brazen-faced varlet art thou to deny
thou knowest me! Is it two days ago since I tripped   30
up thy heels and beat thee before the King? *[Draws
his sword]* Draw, you rogue, for though it be night,
yet the moon shines. I'll make a sop o' th' moonshine
of you. You whoreson cullionly barbermonger,
draw!   35

Oswald Away, I have nothing to do with thee.

Kent Draw, you rascal. You come with letters
against the King, and take Vanity the puppet's part
against the royalty of her father. Draw, you rogue,
or I'll so carbonado your shanks. Draw, you rascal.   40
Come your ways!

Oswald Help, ho! Murder! Help!

Kent Strike, you slave! Stand, rogue! Stand, you
neat slave! Strike! *[Beats him]*

Oswald Help, ho! Murder, murder!   45

*[Enter EDMUND, with his rapier drawn, CORNWALL,
REGAN, GLOUCESTER, Servants]*

Edmund How now? What's the matter? Part!

Kent With you, goodman boy, if you please! Come,
I'll flesh ye; come on, young master.

Gloucester Weapons? Arms? What's the matter
here?   50

Cornwall Keep peace, upon your lives.
He dies that strikes again. What is the matter?

Regan The messengers from our sister and the
King.

20–21. *bawd...service:* ready to be his master's sexual partner if requested to do so.

21. *composition:* combination.

22. *pander:* pimp.

25. *addition:* title of honor.

29. *varlet:* rascal.

33. *sop o' th' moonshine:* A sop is something floating in one's drink. Kent will pierce Oswald enough to soak up the moonlight.

34. *cullionly:* rascal-like.

barbermonger: one who is always in the barbershop, the Elizabethan counterpart to beauty shop.

38. *Vanity the puppet's part:* Vanity appeared as an evil character in old morality plays and still survived in puppet shows in the Elizabethan period; refers here also to Goneril.

40. *carbonado:* to slice, as a steak may be sliced for cooking.

44. *neat:* prim and prissy.

48. *flesh ye:* give you your first real fight.

Cornwall What is your difference? Speak.   55

Oswald I am scarce in breath, my lord.

Kent No marvel, you have so bestirred your valour.
You cowardly rascal, nature disclaims in thee. A
tailor made thee.

Cornwall Thou art a strange fellow. A tailor   60
make a man?

Kent A tailor, sir. A stonecutter or a painter could
not have made him so ill, though they had been but
two years o' th' trade.

Cornwall Speak yet, how grew your quarrel?   65

Oswald This ancient ruffian, sir, whose life I have
spared at suit of his gray beard—

Kent Thou whoreson zed, thou unnecessary letter!
My lord, if you will give me leave, I will tread this
unbolted villain into mortar and daub the wall of a   70
jakes with him. Spare my gray beard? you wagtail.

Cornwall Peace, sirrah!
You beastly knave, know you no reverence?

Kent Yes, sir, but anger hath a privilege.

Cornwall Why art thou angry?   75

Kent That such a slave as this should wear a sword,
Who wears no honesty. Such smiling rogues as these
Like rats oft bite the holy cords atwain
Which are too intrinse t' unloose; smooth every passion
That in the natures of their lords rebel,   80
Bring oil to fire, snow to the colder moods;
Renege, affirm, and turn their halcyon beaks

58.   *nature...thee:* Nature refuses to acknowledge you.

67.   *at suit:* at the request.

68.   *zed...letter:* the letter "z" doesn't exist in Latin and can usually be replaced by "s" in English.

70.   *unbolted:* coarse or rough in temperament.

71.   *jakes:* an outhouse.

wagtail: a small bird that wags its tail up and down as it walks.

78.   *bite...atwain:* cause the bonds of holy matrimony to be broken.

79.   *smooth:* help to gratify or fulfill.

82.   *Renege, affirm:* deny or agree; a yes-man.

halcyon: the kingfisher bird that, if hung by the neck, was supposed to turn its bill into the prevailing wind.

Kent connects Oswald's behaviour with the halcyon's.

With every gale and vary of their masters,
Knowing naught, like dogs, but following.
A plague upon your epileptic visage!   85
Smile you my speeches, as I were a fool?
Goose, if I had you upon Sarum Plain,
I'ld drive ye cackling home to Camelot.

Cornwall What, art thou mad, old fellow?

Gloucester How fell you out? Say that.   90

Kent No contraries hold more antipathy
  Than I and such a knave.

Cornwall Why dost thou call him knave? What is his fault?

Kent His countenance likes me not.

Cornwall No more perchance does mine, nor his, nor hers. 95

Kent Sir, 'tis my occupation to be plain:
  I have seen better faces in my time
  Than stands on any shoulder that I see
  Before me at this instant.

Cornwall   This is some fellow
  Who, having been praised for bluntness, doth affect   100
  A saucy roughness, and constrains the garb
  Quite from his nature. He cannot flatter, he;
  An honest mind and plain—he must speak truth.
  An they will take it, so; if not, he's plain.
  These kind of knaves I know which in this plainness   105
  Harbour more craft and more corrupter ends
  Than twenty silly-ducking observants
  That stretch their duties nicely.

Kent Sir, in good faith, in sincere verity,
  Under th' allowance of your great aspect,   110
  Whose influence, like the wreath of radiant fire
  On flick'ring Phoebus' front—

Cornwall   What mean'st by this?

Kent To go out of my dialect, which you discommend
  so much. I know, sir, I am no flatterer. He
  that beguiled you in a plain accent was a plain   115
  knave, which, for my part, I will not be, though I
  should win your displeasure to entreat me to't.

83.	*gale and vary:* change of the wind.
85.	*epileptic:* twisted.
87–88.	*Goose...Camelot:* Sarum is Salisbury Plain in the south of England. Camelot is the home of King Arthur and the knights of the Round Table.
91.	*antipathy:* intense dislike.
94.	*His...not:* I don't like his face.
101.	*constrains the garb:* assumes a plain manner of speech.
104.	*so:* well and good.
107.	*observants:* flattering attendants.
112.	*Phoebus:* the sun god; note Kent has now adopted court speech.

Cornwall What was th' offence you gave him?

Oswald I never gave him any.
It pleased the King his master very late   120
To strike at me, upon his misconstruction;
When he, compact, and flattering his displeasure,
Tripped me behind; being down, insulted, railed,
And put upon him such a deal of man
That worthied him, got praises of the King   125
For him attempting who was self-subdued;
And, in the fleshment of this dread exploit,
Drew on me here again.

Kent   None of these rogues and cowards
But Ajax is their fool.

Cornwall   Fetch forth the stocks!
You stubborn ancient knave, you reverent braggart,   130
We'll teach you.

Kent   Sir, I am too old to learn.
Call not your stocks for me, I serve the King—
On whose employment I was sent to you;
You shall do small respect, show too bold malice
Against the grace and person of my master,   135
Stocking his messenger.

Cornwall Fetch forth the stocks. As I have life and honour,
There shall he sit till noon.

Regan Till noon? Till night, my lord, and all night too.

Kent Why, madam, if I were your father's dog,   140
You should not use me so.

Regan   Sir, being his knave, I will.

Cornwall This is a fellow of the selfsame colour
Our sister speaks of. Come, bring away the stocks.

[Stocks brought out]

Gloucester Let me beseech your Grace not to do so.
His fault is much, and the good King his master   145
Will check him for't. Your purposed low correction
Is such as basest and contemned'st wretches
For pilf'rings and most common trespasses
Are punished with.

---

127. *fleshment:* excitement.

129. *Ajax:* Ajax was a tremendous Greek braggart; also a synonym for an outhouse.

134–136. *You...messenger:* It would be an incredible insult to Lear to put the king's messenger in the stocks.

147. *contemned'st:* contemptible.

The King his master needs must take it ill   150
That he, so slightly valued in his messenger,
Should have him thus restrained.

Cornwall   I'll answer that.

Regan My sister may receive it much more worse,
To have her gentleman abused, assaulted,
For following her affairs. Put in his legs.   155

[KENT is put in the stocks]

Cornwall Come, my lord, away!

[Exit with all but GLOUCESTER and KENT]

Gloucester I am sorry for thee, friend. 'Tis the Duke's
    pleasure,
Whose disposition all the world well knows
Will not be rubbed nor stopped. I'll entreat for thee.

Kent Pray do not, sir. I have watched and travelled hard.   160
Some time I shall sleep out, the rest I'll whistle.
A good man's fortune may grow out at heels.
Give you good morrow.

Gloucester The Duke's to blame in this. 'Twill be ill taken.
    [Exit]

Kent Good King, that must approve the common saw,   165
Thou out of heaven's benediction com'st
To the warm sun.
Approach, thou beacon to this under globe,
That by thy comfortable beams I may
Peruse this letter. Nothing almost sees miracles   170
But misery. I know 'tis from Cordelia,
Who hath most fortunately been informed
Of my obscured course. And shall find time
From this enormous state, seeking to give
Losses their remedies.—All weary and o'erwatched,   175
Take vantage, heavy eyes, not to behold
This shameful lodging. Fortune, good night;
Smile once more, turn thy wheel. *[Sleeps]*

---

159.   *rubbed:* changed.

160.   *watched:* gone sleepless.

162.   *A good...heels:* Even a good man sometimes has
bad things happen to him.

165.   *approve...saw:* emphasize the truth of the common proverb.

170–171.   *Nothing...misery:* The miserable people are
almost always the ones to see miracles.

177.   *shameful lodging:* the stocks.

178.   *wheel:* medieval image of Fate or Fortune that
turns continually.

COMMENTARY

King Lear presents worlds in opposition: the world of good and the world of evil. The play revolves around two types of Nature: the Nature of Lear, which assumes a higher order of creation, and the Nature of Edmund, which emphasizes the animalistic. An established world of the "old" is evident in the tradition and sometimes questionable morality of Lear, Gloucester, and Kent. Also alive in the drama is the world of the young—the realm of violence, deceit, and self-serving ambition. In this scene, yet another pair of worlds are set in opposition: the worlds of the upper class and the servant.

Kent confronts Oswald

Arriving at Gloucester's castle at the same time, Kent and Oswald both bear letters that their respective masters have bidden be promptly delivered. Accordingly, a sort of race or competition is established between these two messengers. Kent is quick to unleash his anger on Oswald who, apparently somewhat slow-witted, fails to recognize Kent as the man who tripped him in the house of Goneril. Kent, careless in his zeal, verbally attacks Oswald in a classic barrage of insults, which at first bewilders the steward. Once reminded by Kent, however, of the time when these two servants previously met, Oswald wants to go about his business and have nothing more to do with Kent. Characteristically, Kent pushes this quarrel, drawing his sword against Oswald with the intent to vanquish the steward completely. The result is a negative one for Kent.

Just as Lear let his pride and temper get the better of him in the play's opening scene, ultimately causing Lear's suffering in the home of Goneril, so does Kent's tendency to fly off the handle now land him in difficulty. While Shakespeare's Elizabethan audience would have enjoyed hearing Kent rail at Oswald, the characters in the play do not enjoy it. After questioning the two servants about their brawl, Cornwall finds little to commend in Kent. (Though in Cornwall's defense, note that the Duke did, at least, question Oswald as to what offense he had given Kent.) If Kent at this point would calm his temper and behave somewhat reasonably, Cornwall may be willing to listen to Kent's side of the story. But Kent appears to have no side to tell; what Kent utters ranges from the plain speech of a seeming ruffian to the flowery but nonsensical flourishes of a courtier.

Kent has unwittingly played into the hands of Regan and Goneril. Both women have discovered, through long experience with their father, that an outburst of temper is likely to erupt from Lear with sometimes little provocation. The sisters expect their father to respond to insults against the king's messenger by living up to Lear's reputation, raging loud and long. These cunning daughters realize that in those moments when their father is angry, upset, and hurt in his pride, he is also at his weakest and is therefore more susceptible to control.

Lear's messenger in stocks

The insult to Oswald is deemed serious enough for Kent to be set in the stocks. Cornwall's reasoning is difficult to determine; to insult Kent this way is a terrible affront to Lear. Yet later, during moments when his own pride or anger is peaked, Cornwall is quite capable of bending either the law or the social amenities in order to serve his purpose.

Also important here is Regan's uncanny ability to take an evil proposition and make it even worse. Cornwall orders Kent be set in the stocks, and Cornwall designates that Kent sit there until noon. Regan, however, states that Kent shall sit "[t]ill night, my lord, and all night too" (139). Whatever Regan lacks in original thought she makes up for tenfold in cruel enhancement.

Gloucester is caught unawares in this situation; he finds himself uncomfortably placed. Cornwall and Regan have already solicited his aid; now, however, Gloucester finds that he has little stomach for putting Lear's messenger in stocks. Despite Gloucester's protests, Kent is set in the stocks, and Cornwall claims full responsibility for the action. Gloucester, left alone with Kent, commiserates with the captive, revealing a clue about the general public reception of the Duke of Cornwall. Gloucester comments upon the Duke's disposition, which "all the world well knows / Will not be rubbed nor stopped" (158–159). Apparently, Regan's husband has a reputation for inflexibility, if not for outright meanness.

Later, Gloucester will be made painfully aware of just how deep the evil streak in Cornwall runs.

News from Cordelia

As Kent sits stocked, alone and weary, he ruminates about some matters of importance. First, Kent wishes for the beacon of the sun to provide light enough to read by. What Kent wants to read is a letter from Cordelia. Cordelia obviously is not only alive and well but also in contact with Kent. Presumably Cordelia also knows that Kent has been disguised and in service to her father. Some hope glimmers here as the audience recognizes that the lost daughter is not truly lost.

Kent also makes reference to a concept well-known to Elizabethan audiences. "Fortune, good night," says Kent (177). "Smile once more, turn thy wheel" (178). Fortune or Fate has long been compared to a wheel whose revolutions bring humanity sometimes into shadow and despair but inevitably again into some measure of sunshine and good times. Dante referred to this wheel as "our lady of Permutations." The idea that "what goes around, comes around" is somewhat similar to this vision of life moving in a circular fashion and balancing out the evil with the good. As the play progresses, Shakespeare's audience likely wonders exactly when that wheel of fate is due to turn for the better, so gloomy and pessimistic is much of the drama.

Act II, Scene 3

Edgar assumes a new identity as a Bedlam beggar, portraying himself as Poor Tom. As this beggar, Edgar adopts the speech and actions of a lunatic and wears a blanket as his sole item of clothing.

ACT II, SCENE 3
A wood.

[Enter EDGAR]

Edgar I heard myself proclaimed,
  And by the happy hollow of a tree
  Escaped the hunt. No port is free, no place
  That guard and most unusual vigilance
  Does not attend my taking. Whiles I may 'scape,   5
  I will preserve myself; and am bethought
  To take the basest and most poorest shape
  That ever penury, in contempt of man,
  Brought near to beast: my face I'll grime with filth,
  Blanket my loins, elf all my hairs in knots,   10
  And with presented nakedness outface
  The winds and persecutions of the sky.
  The country gives me proof and precedent
  Of Bedlam beggars, who, with roaring voices,
  Strike in their numbed and mortified bare arms   15
  Pins, wooden pricks, nails, sprigs of rosemary;
  And with this horrible object, from low farms,
  Poor pelting villages, sheepcotes, and mills,
  Sometimes with lunatic bans, sometime with prayers,
  Enforce their charity. Poor Turlygod, poor Tom,   20
  That's something yet: Edgar I nothing am. *[Exit]*

NOTES

2.   *happy:* lucky.

10.   *elf:* mat. Matted hair was believed to be caused by elves.

14.   *Bedlam beggars:* lunatics discharged from Bedlam or Bethlehem Hospital, the London madhouse. This reference is anachronistic, because London did not exist in the time of Lear.

15.   *strike:* stick.

      mortified: deadened.

18.   *pelting:* paltry or poor.

19.   *bans:* curses.

20.   *poor Tom:* Bedlam beggars were known as Poor Toms.

21.   *That's...am:* There is still a chance for me, but as Edgar I am a dead man.

COMMENTARY

Edgar's treason has been publicly announced. He is an outlaw who must disguise himself to avoid capture and stay alive. Another facet of the good versus evil opposition becomes clear; in every case, evil shows its face in the sun while good is forced to hide.

The disguise that Edgar assumes is that of a Bedlam beggar, or Poor Tom. According to critic Alexander Leggatt, "[T]he stage lunatic was one of the popular figures in the drawer of Shakespeare's time; whatever else they thought of madness, Shakespeare's contemporaries saw it as good theatre." Edgar, begrimed and nearly naked, struck a familiar chord with Elizabethan theatregoers, and Edgar's rantings about striking wooden pricks into his "numbed" arms corresponds to actual reported activities of lunatics in Shakespeare's day (15).

The elaboration of a parallel is also notable here. When Tom remarks, "Edgar I nothing am," he mirrors Cordelia, who became nothing in the eyes of her father (21). Both of these honest and loyal children have now become outcasts while their evil siblings have come to power. Surely here Kent's wheel of fortune is at a very low point.

Act II, Scene 4

Lear finds Kent in stocks at Gloucester's castle. Regan and Goneril team up to deprive Lear of all his attendants. Cornwall orders Lear locked out of Gloucester's home during a windy, stormy night.

ACT II, SCENE 4
Before Gloucester's castle. Kent in the stocks.

[Enter LEAR, FOOL, and Gentleman]

Lear 'Tis strange that they should so depart from home,
And not send back my messenger.

Gentleman   As I learned,
The night before there was no purpose in them
Of this remove.

Kent Hail to thee, noble master.   5

Lear Ha! Mak'st thou this shame thy pastime?

Kent   No, my lord.

Fool Ha, ha! he wears cruel garters. Horses
are tied by the heads, dogs and bears by th' neck,
monkeys by th' loins, and men by th' legs. When a
man's over-lusty at legs, then he wears wooden   10
nether-stocks.

Lear What's he that hath so much thy place mistook
To set thee here?

Kent   It is both he and she,
Your son and daughter.

Lear No.   15

Kent Yes.

Lear No, I say.

Kent I say yea.

Lear No, no, they would not.

Kent Yes, they have.   20

Lear By Jupiter, I swear no!

Kent By Juno, I swear ay!

NOTES

10.   *over-lusty at legs:* a vagabond or aimless wanderer.

11.   *nether-stocks:* stockings for the lower leg; sarcastically refers to stocks as well.

Lear   They durst not do't;
They could not, would not do't. 'Tis worse than murder
To do upon respect such violent outrage.
Resolve me with all modest haste which way   25
Thou mightst deserve or they impose this usage,
Coming from us.

Kent   My lord, when at their home
I did commend your Highness' letters to them,
Ere I was risen from the place that showed
My duty kneeling, came there a reeking post,   30
Stewed in his haste, half breathless, panting forth
From Goneril his mistress salutations;
Delivered letters, spite of intermission,
Which presently they read; on whose contents
They summoned up their meiny, straight took horse,   35
Commanded me to follow and attend
The leisure of their answer, gave me cold looks;
And meeting here the other messenger,
Whose welcome I perceived had poisoned mine,
Being the very fellow which of late   40
Displayed so saucily against your Highness,
Having more man than wit about me, drew;
He raised the house with loud and coward cries.
Your son and daughter found this trespass worth
The shame which here it suffers.   45

Fool Winter's not gone yet, if the wild geese fly that way.
Fathers that wear rags
Do make their children blind,
But fathers that bear bags
Shall see their children kind.   50
Fortune, that arrant whore,
Ne'er turns the key to th' poor.
But for all this, thou shalt have as many dolours for thy
daughters as thou canst tell in a year.

Lear O, how this mother swells up toward my heart!   55
Hysterica passio, down, thou climbing sorrow;
Thy element's below. Where is this daughter?

Kent With the Earl, sir, here within.

Lear   Follow me not;
Stay here. *[Exit]*

---

30.   *reeking post:* sweating messenger.

33.   *spite of intermission:* despite the delay in reading my letter, which should have come first.

35.   *meiny:* followers.

46.   *Winter's...yet:* There are more cold, bad times to come.

49.   *bear bags:* have money.

53.   *dolours:* sadnesses, as well as a pun on dollars.
54.   *tell:* count.
55.   *mother:* hysteria.
56.   *Hysterica passio:* An overwhelming feeling of physical distress and suffocation.
57.   *element:* natural or normal location.

Gentleman Made you no more offence but what you
    speak of?   60

Kent None.
  How chance the King comes with so small a number?

Fool An thou hadst been set i' th' stocks for that
  question, thou'dst well deserved it.

Kent Why, fool?   65

Fool We'll set thee to school to an ant, to teach thee
  there's no labouring i' th' winter. All that follow their
  noses are led by their eyes but blind men, and
  there's not a nose among twenty but can smell him
  that's stinking. Let go thy hold when a great wheel   70
  runs down a hill, lest it break thy neck with following.
  But the great one that goes upward, let him
  draw thee after. When a wise man gives thee better
  counsel, give me mine again. I would have none but
  knaves follow it since a fool gives it.   75
  That sir which serves and seeks for gain,
  And follows but for form,
  Will pack when it begins to rain
  And leave thee in the storm.
  But I will tarry; the fool will stay,   80
  And let the wise man fly.
  The knave turns fool that runs away;
  The fool no knave, perdy.

Kent Where learned you this, fool?

Fool Not i' th' stocks, fool.   85

[Enter LEAR and GLOUCESTER]

Lear Deny to speak with me? They are sick, they are weary?
  They have travelled all the night? Mere fetches,
  The images of revolt and flying off!
  Fetch me a better answer.

66–75. *We'll...gives it:* The Fool utters a string of wise sayings to show how clearly he understand Lear's present condition.

67. *follow...noses:* go straight ahead.

78. *pack:* clear out.

83. *perdy:* by God.

87. *fetches:* excuses.

Gloucester   My dear lord,
You know the fiery quality of the Duke,   90
How unremovable and fixed he is
In his own course.

Lear   Vengeance, plague, death, confusion!
Fiery? What quality? Why, Gloucester, Gloucester,
I'ld speak with the Duke of Cornwall and his wife.

Gloucester Well, my good lord, I have informed them so. 95

Lear Informed them? Dost thou understand me, man?

Gloucester Ay, my good lord.

Lear The King would speak with Cornwall. The dear father
Would with his daughter speak, commands—tends—
          service.
Are they informed of this? My breath and blood!   100
Fiery? The fiery Duke, tell the hot Duke that—
No, but not yet. May be he is not well.
Infirmity doth still neglect all office
Whereto our health is bound. We are not ourselves
When nature, being oppressed, commands the mind   105
To suffer with the body. I'll forbear;
And am fallen out with my more headier will
To take the indisposed and sickly fit
For the sound man.—Death on my state. Wherefore
Should he sit here? This act persuades me   110
That this remotion of the Duke and her
Is practice only. Give me my servant forth.
Go tell the Duke and's wife I'ld speak with them!
Now, presently! Bid them come forth and hear me,
Or at their chamber door I'll beat the drum   115
Till it cry sleep to death.

Gloucester I would have all well betwixt you.

[Exit]

Lear O me, my heart, my rising heart! But down!

Fool Cry to it, nuncle, as the cockney did to the eels
when she put 'em i' th' paste alive. She knapped 'em   120
o' th' coxcombs with a stick and cried, 'Down,
wantons, down!' 'Twas her brother that, in pure
kindness to his horse, buttered his hay.

103–104. *Infirmity...bound:* When one is sick, one neglects one's proper duty.

106. *forbear:* be patient.

107. *am...will:* regret my hastiness.

109. *Wherefore:* why.

111. *remotion:* removal.

120. *knapped:* cracked.

[Enter CORNWALL, REGAN, GLOUCESTER, Servants]

Lear Good morrow to you both.

Cornwall   Hail to your Grace.

[KENT here set at liberty]

Regan I am glad to see your Highness.   125

Lear Regan, I think you are. I know what reason
I have to think so. If thou shouldst not be glad,
I would divorce me from thy mother's womb,
Sepulchring an adultress. *[to Kent]* O, are you free?
Some other time for that.—Beloved Regan,   130
Thy sister's naught. O Regan, she hath tied
Sharp-toothed unkindness, like a vulture, here.
I can scarce speak to thee. Thou'lt not believe
With how depraved a quality—O Regan!

Regan I pray you, sir, take patience. I have hope   135
You less know how to value her desert
Than she to scant her duty.

Lear   Say, how is that?

Regan I cannot think my sister in the least
Would fail her obligation. If, sir, perchance
She have restrained the riots of your followers,   140
'Tis on such ground, and to such wholesome end,
As clears her from all blame.

Lear My curses on her!

Regan   O, sir, you are old;
Nature in you stands on the very verge
Of his confine. You should be ruled, and led   145
By some discretion that discerns your state
Better than you yourself. Therefore I pray you
That to our sister you do make return;
Say you have wronged her.

Lear   Ask her forgiveness?
Do you but mark how this becomes the house: 150
"Dear daughter, I confess that I am old. *[Kneels]*
Age is unnecessary. On my knees I beg
That you'll vouchsafe me raiment, bed, and food."

128–129. *divorce...adultress:* I would suspect that your dead mother had been false to me.

131.   *naught:* wicked or worthless, as in zero.

150.   *becomes the house:* suits my dignity.

Regan Good sir, no more. These are unsightly tricks.
Return you to my sister.

Lear *[rises]*   Never, Regan   155
She hath abated me of half my train,
Looked black upon me, struck me with her tongue
Most serpent-like upon the very heart.
All the stored vengeances of heaven fall
On her ingrateful top! Strike her young bones,   160
You taking airs, with lameness.

Cornwall   Fie, sir, fie!

Lear You nimble lightnings, dart your blinding flames
Into her scornful eyes! Infect her beauty,
You fen-sucked fogs drawn by the pow'rful sun
To fall and blister.

Regan   O the blest gods!   165
So will you wish on me when the rash mood is on.

Lear No, Regan, thou shalt never have my curse.
Thy tender-hefted nature shall not give
Thee o'er to harshness. Her eyes are fierce, but thine
Do comfort, and not burn. 'Tis not in thee   170
To grudge my pleasures, to cut off my train,
To bandy hasty words, to scant my sizes,
And, in conclusion, to oppose the bolt
Against my coming in. Thou better know'st
The offices of nature, bond of childhood,   175
Effects of courtesy, dues of gratitude.
Thy half o' th' kingdom hast thou not forgot,
Wherein I thee endowed.

Regan   Good sir, to th' purpose.

[Tucket within]

Lear Who put my man i' th' stocks?

Cornwall   What trumpet's that?

Regan I know't—my sister's. This approves her letter,   180
That she would soon be here.
[Enter OSWALD]
          Is your lady come?

---

160. *top:* head.

164. *fen-sucked:* arising out of the swamp.

168. *tender-hefted:* gently framed, here in reference to personality.

172. *scant my sizes:* reduce what is allowed to me.

173–174. *oppose...in:* not allow me to come in.

178. *to the purpose:* please talk sense.

Lear This is a slave, whose easy-borrowed pride
  Dwells in the fickle grace of her he follows.
  Out, varlet, from my sight.

Cornwall   What means your Grace?

Lear Who stocked my servant? Regan, I have good hope   185
  Thou didst not know on't.
  [Enter GONERIL]
                        Who comes here? O heavens!
  If you do love old men, if your sweet sway
  Allow obedience, if you yourselves are old,
  Make it your cause. Send down, and take my part.
  [To Goneril] Art not ashamed to look upon this beard?   190
  O Regan, will you take her by the hand?

Goneril Why not by th' hand, sir? How have I offended?
  All's not offence that indiscretion finds
  And dotage terms so.

Lear   O sides, you are too tough!
  Will you yet hold? How came my man i' th' stocks?   195

Cornwall I set him there, sir; but his own disorders
  Deserved much less advancement.

Lear   You? Did you?

Regan I pray you, father, being weak, seem so.
  If till the expiration of your month
  You will return and sojourn with my sister,
  Dismissing half your train, come then to me.   200
  I am now from home, and out of that provision
  Which shall be needful for your entertainment.

Lear Return to her, and fifty men dismissed?
  No, rather I abjure all roofs, and choose   205
  To wage against the enmity o' th' air,
  To be a comrade with the wolf and owl,
  Necessity's sharp pinch. Return with her?
  Why, the hot-blooded France, that dowerless took
  Our youngest born, I could as well be brought   210
  To knee his throne, and, squire-like, pension beg
  To keep base life afoot. Return with her?
  Persuade me rather to be slave and sumpter
  To this detested groom.

182. *easy-borrowed:* assumed with no justification.

194. *dotage:* old age.

197. *advancement:* promotion.

198. *seem so:* behave suitably.

213. *sumpter:* beast of burden; packhorse.

Goneril   At your choice, sir.

Lear I prithee, daughter, do not make me mad.   215
I will not trouble thee, my child; farewell.
We'll no more meet, no more see one another.
But yet thou art my flesh, my blood, my daughter;
Or rather a disease that's in my flesh,
Which I must needs call mine. Thou art a boil,   220
A plague-sore, or embossed carbuncle
In my corrupted blood. But I'll not chide thee.
Let shame come when it will, I do not call it.
I do not bid the thunder-bearer shoot,
Nor tell tales of thee to high-judging Jove.   225
Mend when thou canst, be better at thy leisure;
I can be patient, I can stay with Regan,
I and my hundred knights.

Regan   Not altogether so.
I looked not for you yet, nor am provided
For your fit welcome. Give ear, sir, to my sister;   230
For those that mingle reason with your passion
Must be content to think you old, and so—
But she knows what she does.

Lear   Is this well spoken?

Regan I dare avouch it, sir. What, fifty followers?
Is it not well? What should you need of more?   235
Yea, or so many, sith that both charge and danger
Speak 'gainst so great a number? How in one house
Should many people, under two commands,
Hold amity? 'Tis hard, almost impossible.

Goneril Why might not you, my lord, receive attendance   240
From those that she calls servants, or from mine?

Regan Why not, my lord? If then they chanced to slack ye,
We could control them. If you will come to me
(For now I spy a danger), I entreat you
To bring but five-and-twenty. To no more   245
Will I give place or notice.

Lear I gave you all.

Regan   And in good time you gave it.

---

221. *embossed carbuncle:* swollen boil.

224. *thunder-bearer:* Jupiter.

231–232. *those...old:* Those who think reasonably about your passion know that you are old.

236. *sith:* since.

242. *slack:* neglect.

247. *in good time:* just in time; suggests that Regan considers Lear senile.

Lear Made you my guardians, my depositaries,
But kept a reservation to be followed
With such a number. What, must I come to you   250
With five-and-twenty? Regan, said you so?

Regan And speak't again, my lord. No more with me.

Lear Those wicked creatures yet do look well-favoured
When others are more wicked; not being the worst
Stands in some rank of praise. *[to Goneril]* I'll go
        with thee.   255
Thy fifty·yet doth double five-and-twenty,
And thou art twice her love.

Goneril   Hear me, my lord.
What need you five-and-twenty? ten? or five?
To follow in a house where twice so many
Have a command to tend you?

Regan   What need one?   260

Lear O reason not the need! Our basest beggars
Are in the poorest thing superfluous.
Allow not nature more than nature needs,
Man's life is cheap as beast's. Thou art a lady:
If only to go warm were gorgeous,   265
Why, nature needs not what thou gorgeous wear'st,
Which scarcely keeps thee warm. But, for true need—
You heavens, give me that patience, patience I need.
You see me here, you gods, a poor old man,
As full of grief as age, wretched in both.   270
If it be you that stirs these daughters' hearts
Against their father, fool me not so much
To bear it tamely; touch me with noble anger,
And let not women's weapons, water drops,
Stain my man's cheeks. No, you unnatural hags!   275
I will have such revenges on you both
That all the world shall—I will do such things—
What they are, yet I know not; but they shall be
The terrors of the earth. You think I'll weep.
No, I'll not weep. *[Storm and tempest]*   280
I have full cause of weeping, but this heart
Shall break into a hundred thousand flaws
Or ere I'll weep. O fool, I shall go mad!

[Exeunt LEAR, FOOL, KENT, and GLOUCESTER]

---

248.   *depositaries:* trustees.

262.   *Are...superfluous:* have some unnecessary belongings.

263.   *Allow not:* if you do not allow.

282.   *flaws:* broken pieces.

Cornwall Let us withdraw; 'twill be a storm.

Regan This house is little; the old man and 's people   285
Cannot be well bestowed.

Goneril 'Tis his own blame; hath put himself from rest
And must needs taste his folly.

Regan For his particular, I'll receive him gladly,
But not one follower.

Goneril   So am I purposed.   290
Where is my Lord of Gloucester?

Cornwall Followed the old man forth. *[Enter GLOUCESTER]*
He is returned.

Gloucester The King is in high rage.

Cornwall   Whither is he going?

Gloucester He calls to horse, but will I know not whither.

Cornwall 'Tis best to give him way; he leads himself.   295

Goneril My lord, entreat him by no means to stay.

Gloucester Alack, the night comes on, and the bleak winds
Do sorely ruffle. For many miles about
There's scarce a bush.

Regan   O, sir, to willful men
The injuries that they themselves procure   300
Must be their schoolmasters. Shut up your doors.
He is attended with a desperate train,
And what they may incense him to, being apt
To have his ear abused, wisdom bids fear.

Cornwall Shut up your doors, my lord; 'tis a wild night.   305
My Regan counsels well. Come out o' th' storm.

[Exeunt]

---

286. *bestowed:* lodged.

289. *his particular:* himself personally.

298. *ruffle:* blow heartily.

304. *abused:* deceived.

COMMENTARY

This scene is one of the longest in the play and also one of the most important, because here the vixen daughters of Lear come together as a formidable opposition to their aging father. The extent of the sisters' cruelty toward Lear becomes evident, and Lear takes another step on the road toward madness.

The daughters' full disrespect

The scene opens as Lear and his Fool, attended by an unnamed gentleman, arrive at Gloucester's castle to find Kent sitting in the stocks. Lear is already at a loss to explain why Cornwall and Regan were not at their home; consequently, when Lear arrives to discover his messenger in the stocks, his already kindled suspicions fire rapidly—precisely as his daughters had anticipated.

Kent sits in the stocks at Gloucester's castle.

Lear does not want to believe that Regan and Cornwall could be so disrespectful as to punish the king's messenger; Lear's argument with Kent on this matter goes a long way to highlight Lear's stubborn streak. But perhaps more than proving Lear stubborn, the interchange with Kent causes a rising passion in Lear—a soul-searching that the old king feels as it "swells up toward [his] heart" (55). Interestingly, Lear recognizes that this passion is not a virtue; neither is it the manner in which a sane man feels or responds. Lear fights against this unnatural emotion: "Hysterica passio, down, thou climbing sorrow; / Thy element's below" (56–57). Lear is plenty sane enough at this point to realize that losing control of himself can pave the way to madness, and he struggles to restrain his temper as he storms off in search of Regan.

The Fool, then, is left with Kent, and a dialogue arises between the two of them that is at once comical and deadly serious. Having heard Kent explain to Lear the circumstances that resulted in stocking, the Fool insightfully finds Kent to be something of a fool—a fool in need of instruction. With Cornwall and Oswald, Kent has attempted the type of honesty that court fools often pronounce. Kent, though, does not have the fool's occupation and thus has no license or permission to behave in such a disorderly—albeit honest—fashion.

Again, the issue of truth surfaces: When should one proclaim it honestly, and when should one speak the truth as it is preferred? The two truths are not always the same, and the Fool well understands this while Kent apparently does not—or will not. When Kent asks, "Where learned you this, fool?" the Fool replies, "Not i' th' stocks, fool" (84–85). Lear's Fool has learned to walk a fine line; Kent has learned only to rush the door.

Lear, already angered at Cornwall's treatment of Kent, becomes even more incensed when Gloucester, sent to inform the duke of the king's presence, returns to say that Cornwall and Regan refuse to speak with Lear. Surely another calculated move on the part of Regan, this refusal infuriates Lear further, and Lear has difficulty again with his "unconstant starts." Actors portraying Lear often stutter in anger here, as lines 98 and 99 suggest: "The dear father / Would with his daughter speak, commands—tends—service."

Lear rants on, catching himself at the end of line 101, as he attempts to apply reason and find some truly acceptable, rational excuse for the Duke's refusal to appear. Indeed, Lear almost convinces himself that all will eventually be well. "I'll forbear," he says (106). But another glance at Kent, still seated in the stocks, inflames the king again: "Bid them come forth and hear me, / Or . . . I'll beat the drum / Till it cry sleep to death" (114–116).

The last hope dashed

At long last Regan and Cornwall appear, and Lear loses no time in expounding to Regan about the insults and failings of Goneril. Lear quickly discovers, however, that Regan seems already to know what complaints her father is going to make. Further, Regan—the "Beloved Regan"—sides with her sister rather than Lear (130). "O, sir, you are old," says Regan (143). "Nature in you stands on the very verge / Of his confine. You should be ruled, and led" (144–145). Her words are saturated with cruelty and disrespect.

Critic Stephen Greenblatt writes that Early Modern England had a "strong official regard for the rights and privileges of age. By the will of God and the natural order of things, authority gravitated to old men." Regan, however, seeks to deprive her father of his authority. Still Lear fails to see the cruelty that is Regan, promising "Regan, thou shalt never have my curse. / Thy tender-hefted nature shall not give / Thee o'er to harshness" (167–169). Lear will shortly learn about the true nature of Regan, and he shall not find it "tender-hefted" (gentle).

With the arrival of Goneril, Lear's faith in Regan is destined to be short-lived. The argument about Lear's knights escalates, and finally Lear becomes exasperated, crying "I gave you all" (246). Lear's disgruntlement here is not merely disappointment about the number of knights his daughters will accept as Lear's companions. The issue here is again love—love treated as a bartered good. The large number of knights could easily instigate some sort of household revolution in either daughter's house, but Lear bargains neither for the knights nor for a compromise that better ensures household security. Lear says to Goneril, "I'll go with thee. / Thy fifty yet doth double five-and-twenty, / And thou art twice her love" (255–257). Again, Lear attempts to treat love as a marketable commodity. What a horror, then, when Lear sees his daughters' love reduced to the equivalent of a single servant.

In one of the more moving speeches of the play, Lear expresses a myriad of emotions in lines 261–283; some would argue that Lear gets part of his comeuppance here. When Lear as king devalued the true affection of Cordelia during the love trial, Lear set up a sort of chain reaction.

The struggle for sanity

Now that Lear—father as well as king—seeks honest affection from his older daughters, he finds that request denied. For all his practicality in attempting to find a measure for affection, Lear now bemoans the practical daughters who reason that Lear has no need for even one attendant to call his own. Lear's argument turns to pure pathos and desire. Even "[o]ur basest beggars / Are in the poorest thing superfluous," cries Lear. "Allow not nature more than nature needs, / Man's life is cheap as beast's" (261–263). Lear, in his growing passion, touches very closely here upon the ultimate lesson: In the long run, the life of a bare and unadorned human being is indeed little more than that of an animal. This lesson is one that Lear has yet to learn, but he is well on the way to his education.

Lear's lack of judgment and understanding should never, of course, be taken as any sort of excuse for the behavior of Regan and Goneril. These women, both examples of supreme self-interest, turn out to be two of the coldest creatures in all of literature. Hard-hearted and cruel, the two sisters are guilty of two crimes, according to critic Edwin Muir. One is the crime of filial ingratitude—Lear himself has said as much. The other crime is a public crime, a crime against the state. As royal princesses, Goneril and Regan are regents, representatives of the crown. Their actions certainly constitute what military personnel call "behavior unbecoming." Further, the sisters' involvement in and encouragement of factions against the king amounts to treason even though the kingdom has been divided between them, because Lear retains the name of king.

The struggle Lear undertakes now is to retain his sanity; by his words, he fears he may well lose the struggle. Lear calls upon the gods to grant him a noble anger; indeed, Lear's anger and hurt is such that tears threaten, and Lear does not care to weep in the presence of these vulture daughters. The old king finds himself unable to utter what "revenges" he shall have upon the sisters; he can say only that his redresses shall be "[t]he terrors of the earth" (276, 279). Valiantly struggling against tears, Lear finally departs with the Fool, Kent, and Gloucester, expressing loudly his deepest fear as he goes: "O fool, I shall go mad!" (283). What Lear cannot reconcile is more than just the unkindness of his daughters. Lear cannot see himself in that same light in which his daughters now see him: a powerless, weak old man given to eccentricities and volatile eruptions of temper.

Masterful language and imagery

Both Shakespeare and his audience were familiar with complex images, poetic phrases, and the mixing of the aristocratic with the commonplace. In this scene we can observe Shakespeare, the master of language, at work. The imagery of the wheel and its relationship to fate and destiny continues to be prevalent. We may notice the mixed metaphors and witticisms of the Fool. Passion is assuredly not lacking in the speeches of Lear, and in this single scene we watch both the grand manner of kings and the ordinary attitudes of the subject as both struggle to accommodate their spiritual natures to the cold, material world.

Observe also how Shakespeare has developed his characters in preparation for the forthcoming climactic act. Goneril, Cornwall, and Regan are sovereigns whose sense of their own worth leads them to defy morality. Lear, initially blind to the hypocrisy of his older daughters, begins to develop from a somewhat childishly-behaving king into a man beset by vicious offspring and mental turmoil. Edmund is showing himself to be a classic Machiavellian hero, replete with political savvy and a cold, evil nature. Of the "good faction" present at this time, perhaps the most profound description of their joint character is that they offer, regardless of their circumstances, sincere devotion and unhesitating loyalty.

Into the storm

As the scene closes, Lear goes out into the now stormy night, and his daughters remain within the walls of Gloucester's castle. Forbidden to allow Lear reentry, Gloucester must obey Cornwall's edict to "[s]hut up your doors" (305). The closing of those gates signifies the establishment of a new order. The cruel sisters are now in power; the aged king is locked out in the "wild night" (305). The audience recognizes the scenario as preparatory for some sort of climax, and how devastating that climax will be remains to be discovered in the third act.

Notes

KING LEAR
ACT III

Scene 1 103

Scene 2 106

Scene 3 110

Scene 4 112

Scene 5 120

Scene 6 122

Scene 7 127

Edgar *When we our betters see bearing our woes,*
We scarcely think our miseries our foes.
Who alone suffers suffers most i' th' mind,
Leaving free things and happy shows behind;
But then the mind much sufferance doth o'erskip
When grief hath mates, and bearing fellowship.
How light and portable my pain seems now,
When that which makes me bend makes the King bow.

Act III, Scene 1

Kent and a gentleman discuss Lear's subjection to the storm, commenting upon the king's raving and wandering upon the heath. The two men also discuss the arrival of French troops, implying that war will soon erupt in Britain.

ACT III, SCENE 1
A heath.

[Storm still. Enter KENT and a Gentleman severally]

Kent Who's there besides foul weather?

Gentleman One minded like the weather, most
 unquietly.

Kent I know you. Where's the King?

Gentleman Contending with the fretful elements;
 Bids the wind blow the earth into the sea,   5
 Or swell the curled waters 'bove the main,
 That things might change or cease; tears his white hair,
 Which the impetuous blasts, with eyeless rage,
 Catch in their fury and make nothing of;
 Strives in his little world of man to outscorn   10
 The to-and-fro-conflicting wind and rain.
 This night, wherein the cub-drawn bear would couch,
 The lion and the belly-pinched wolf
 Keep their fur dry, unbonneted he runs,
 And bids what will take all.

Kent   But who is with him?   15

Gentleman None but the fool, who labours to outjest
 His heart-struck injuries.

Kent   Sir, I do know you,
 And dare upon the warrant of my note
 Commend a dear thing to you. There is division,
 Although as yet the face of it is covered   20
 With mutual cunning, 'twixt Albany and Cornwall;
 Who have—as who have not, that their great stars
 Throned and set high?—servants, who seem no less,

NOTES

s.d.   *Storm still:* storm continues.

6.   *main:* mainland.

10.   *little...man:* It was a common Elizabethan idea that each individual man was a microcosm and reproduced within himself the entire universe.

12.   *cub-drawn bear:* mother bear drained of her milk by her young.

18.   *upon...note:* because I trust my positive evaluation of you.

Which are to France the spies and speculations
Intelligent of our state. What hath been seen,   25
Either in snuffs and packings of the Dukes,
Or the hard rein which both of them have borne
Against the old kind King, or something deeper,
Whereof, perchance, these are but furnishings—
But, true it is, from France there comes a power   30
Into this scattered kingdom, who already,
Wise in our negligence, have secret feet
In some of our best ports and are at point
To show their open banner. Now to you:
If on my credit you dare build so far   35
To make your speed to Dover, you shall find
Some that will thank you, making just report
Of how unnatural and bemadding sorrow
The King hath cause to plain.
I am a gentleman of blood and breeding,   40
And from some knowledge and assurance offer
This office to you.

Gentleman I will talk further with you.

Kent   No, do not.
For confirmation that I am much more
Than my out-wall, open this purse and take   45
What it contains. If you shall see Cordelia,
As fear not but you shall, show her this ring,
And she will tell you who that fellow is
That yet you do not know. Fie on this storm!
I will go seek the King.   50

Gentleman Give me your hand. Have you no more to say?

Kent Few words, but, to effect, more than all yet:
That when we have found the King—in which your pain
That way, I'll this—he that first lights on him
Holla the other.

[Exeunt]

24–25.	*spies...state:* reporters of the condition of our local affairs.
26.	*snuffs and packings:* resentments and plots against each other.
29.	*furnishings:* excuses.
39.	*plain:* complain.
40.	*blood:* noble family.
45.	*out-wall:* outer appearances.
52.	*to effect:* in importance.
53-54.	*in which. . . I'll this:* You go that way, I'll go this way.

COMMENTARY

The third act of this play presents the climax of the plot. In *King Lear,* the horrors presented in Act III provide plural turning points. A conversation between Kent and an unnamed gentleman in this first scene serves mainly to provide information to the audience about the political state of affairs in Lear's kingdom and to give additional news of Cordelia.

As discussed in the "Introduction to Early Modern England" and the "Introduction to *King Lear,*" Shakespearean plays appear in two different versions: quartos and folios. The quarto texts are editions of a single play, while the folio texts are collections of several plays. Interestingly, the Quarto version and the Folio version of *Lear* differ significantly in this scene. In the Quarto we learn of trouble brewing between Albany and Cornwall; we also learn that France has landed a military force upon British soil. In the Folio text, however, there is no specific mention of a French force. Only by recalling that Cordelia has wed the King of France do we have an inkling that because Cordelia is in the vicinity, French troops are likely present as well. The text in this book combines both versions, so we are aware that both civil war as well as conflict with a foreign state are possibilities in the near future.

The kingdom, both internally and externally, appears to be in a state of unrest. The storm on the heath—churning through this and subsequent scenes—is a reflection of that unrest. The unrest in the mind of the king and the fusion of various upheavals in Act III underscore how the Elizabethan world viewed its rulers: as appointees of the divine whose personal well-being—or lack thereof—was directly connected with the condition of the kingdom.

In this scene, Kent becomes separated from Lear—a significant development. Kent cannot help but feel chagrined and ineffectual; he is the point of contact between Lear and Cordelia, but at this moment Kent's master is lost to him. All Kent can do is commiserate with a gentleman of the realm, exchanging comments about Lear's current condition and about the entry of French troops into Britain. Though Kent does not reveal his identity, he does offer the gentleman a ring, probably a signet ring. This piece of jewelry is to serve as a calling card of sorts; if the gentleman encounters Cordelia, the ring will let her know that Kent is indeed still working for the advancement of the kingdom and for the reunion of Lear and his youngest daughter. It seems incredibly ironic that even in this time of unrest and separation, the good (in this case, Kent) must still keep itself in disguise.

Act III, Scene 2

Accompanied by his Fool, Lear sinks into madness and rages at the storm. The Fool provides a sounding board for the growing lunacies of his king.

ACT III, SCENE 2
Another part of the heath.

[Storm still. Enter LEAR and Fool]

Lear Blow, winds, and crack your checks. Rage, blow.
  You cataracts and hurricanoes, spout
  Till you have drenched our steeples, drowned the cocks
  You sulph'rous and thought-executing fires,
  Vaunt-couriers to oak-cleaving thunderbolts,   5
  Singe my white head. And thou, all-shaking thunder,
  Strike flat the thick rotundity o' th' world.
  Crack Nature's moulds, all germains spill at once,
  That makes ingrateful man.

Fool O nuncle, court holy-water in a dry house is   10
  better than this rain water out o' door. Good nuncle,
  in; ask thy daughters' blessing. Here's a night pities
  neither wise men nor fools.

Lear Rumble thy bellyful. Spit, fire. Spout, rain.
  Nor rain, wind, thunder, fire are my daughters.   15
  I tax not you, you elements, with unkindness.
  I never gave you kingdom, called you children;
  You owe me no subscription. Then let fall
  Your horrible pleasure. Here I stand your slave,
  A poor, infirm, weak, and despised old man.   20
  But yet I call you servile ministers,
  That will with two pernicious daughters join
  Your high-engendered battles 'gainst a head
  So old and white as this. O, ho! 'tis foul.

Fool He that has a house to put 's head in has a   25
  good headpiece.
  The codpiece that will house
  Before the head has any,

NOTES

2.   *cataracts:* downpours of rain.

     hurricanoes: waterspouts.

3.   *cocks:* weathervanes.

5.   *Vaunt-couriers:* forerunners.

8.   *germains:* seeds of life.

10.   *court holy-water:* politically correct court behaviour that compares with using holy water in church.

16.   *tax:* accuse.

27.   *codpiece:* often slang for phallus; a codpiece is cloth stitched onto the crotch area.

The head and he shall louse:
So beggars marry many.   30
The man that makes his toe
What he his heart should make
Shall of a corn cry woe,
And turn his sleep to wake.
For there was never yet fair woman but she made   35
mouths in a glass.

[Enter KENT]

Lear No, I will be the pattern of all patience;
I will say nothing.

Kent Who's there?

Fool Marry, here's grace and a codpiece; that's a   40
wise man and a fool.

Kent Alas, sir, are you here? Things that love night
Love not such nights as these. The wrathful skies
Gallow the very wanderers of the dark
And make them keep their eaves. Since I was man,   45
Such sheets of fire, such bursts of horrid thunder,
Such groans of roaring wind and rain, I never
Remember to have heard. Man's nature cannot carry
Th' affliction nor the fear.

Lear   Let the great gods
That keep this dreadful pudder o'er our heads   50
Find out their enemies now. Tremble, thou wretch,
That hast within thee undivulged crimes
Unwhipped of justice. Hide thee, thou bloody hand,
Thou perjured, and thou simular of virtue
That art incestuous. Caitiff, to pieces shake,   55
That under covert and convenient seeming
Has practiced on man's life. Close pent-up guilts,
Rive your concealing continents and cry
These dreadful summoners grace. I am a man
More sinned against than sinning.

Kent   Alack, bareheaded?   60
Gracious my lord, hard by here is a hovel;
Some friendship will it lend you 'gainst the tempest.
Repose you there, while I to this hard house

29.	*he:* it
31–34.	*toe...wake:* He who prefers a less honorable body part will regret that preference.
36.	*glass:* mirror.
40.	*Marry:* indeed.
44.	*Gallow:* terrify.
50.	*pudder:* turmoil.
54.	*simular of virtue:* one who pretends to be virtuous.
55.	*Caitiff:* wretched person.
58.	*Rive...continents:* split open that which hides you.
59.	*summoners:* Summoners were officers of the church who brought people up on charges of immorality.
63.	*hard house:* cruel household.

(More harder than the stones whereof 'tis raised,
Which even but now, demanding after you,   65
Denied me to come in) return, and force
Their scanted courtesy.

Lear   My wits begin to turn.
Come on, my boy. How dost, my boy? Art cold?
I am cold myself. Where is this straw, my fellow?
The art of our necessities is strange,   70
And can make vile things precious. Come, your hovel,
Poor fool and knave, I have one part in my heart
That's sorry yet for thee.

Fool [*sings*]
He that has and a little tiny wit,
With, heigh-ho, the wind and the rain,   75
Must make content with his fortunes fit
Though the rain it raineth every day.

Lear True, boy. Come, bring us to this hovel.

[*Exit with KENT*]

Fool This is a brave night to cool a courtesan. I'll
speak a prophecy ere I go: 80
When priests are more in word than matter;
When brewers mar their malt with water;
When nobles are their tailors' tutors,
No heretics burned, but wenches' suitors;
When every case in law is right,   85
No squire in debt nor no poor knight;
When slanders do not live in tongues,
Nor cutpurses come not to throngs;
When usurers tell their gold i' th' field,
And bawds and whores do churches build—   90
Then shall the realm of Albion
Come to great confusion.
Then comes the time, who lives to see't,
That going shall be used with feet.
This prophecy Merlin shall make, for I live before   95
his time.

[*Exit*]

---

67. *scanted:* stingy.

74–77. *He...day:* a stanza of the song sung by the Clown in *Twelfth Night.*

80–94. *prophecy...feet:* a list of common events that the Fool pretends are never likely to happen.

88. *cutpurses:* pickpockets.

89. *tell:* count.

91. *Albion:* England.

94. *going...feet:* feet will be used for walking.

COMMENTARY

One of the great directorial challenges inherent in a performance of *King Lear* involves the staging of the storm scenes on the heath. In particular, Lear's raging back at the storm here in Scene 2 presents special problems. Although the most profound storm exists in Lear's mind, most directors nevertheless feel obliged to provide something of an external storm for realism's sake. The storm, then, has been produced in various ways, with effects ranging from electronically synthesized sounds and deluges of water to very minimalistic sets with more subdued torrents.

The overall success of the scene, however, depends entirely upon Lear himself. Despite the commentary of the Fool and Kent, the power of Lear's towering personality must carry the scene. Defiant in his rage, Lear embraces the fury of the storm, daring the fullest ire of nature to "[s]trike flat the thick rotundity o' th' world" (7). Implicit in Lear's taunt is his vision of himself as world; as all else in Lear's life has just crumbled around him, Lear's view here is that he now stands open to assault from every angle.

Battling the tempest

As Lear shouts at the storm, addressing the winds and rains almost as if they were human, both we and Lear recognize that a new view of reality is appearing here. In his power and glory, Lear has been accustomed to seeing life and nature as predictable, reasonable, and controllable. Now, however, all of Lear's expectations are being challenged. That which he has considered predictable has been proven unruly, that which has appeared reasonable now appears fanciful, and that which has been restrained and disciplined now rages uncontrolled. When what Lear expects is overthrown by the new reality, we see what is called *dramatic irony*.

For Lear, this dramatic irony—the disparity between what he felt was the truth about his daughters and what he has discovered the truth to be—plunges him into fury that leads directly to the unhinging of his mind. Lear envisions the storm as a cohort of his "two pernicious daughters," and he declares that the gods who cause the storm are bent upon discovering the deep-held secrets of their enemies (22). "My wits begin to turn," admits Lear to the Fool as Kent arrives and entreats Lear to come along and seek the shelter of a nearby hovel (68).

The bare essentials

A new concern for the essentials of survival begins to grow now in Lear; he discovers that "[t]he art of our necessities . . . can make vile things precious" (70–71). Lear also finds it in his heart to pity his Fool: "Poor fool and knave," says Lear. "I have one part in my heart / That's sorry yet for thee" (72–73). The tables surely turn, for the Fool previously has expressed concern and pity for his king. Now Lear worries about his Fool being cold. And with something of a revelation—as though the concept is quite new to him—Lear states, "I am cold myself" (69).

Note the Fool's song in response to Lear's pity. Lear feels sorry that the Fool is exposed to the storm, and the Fool sings a four-line song reminiscent of Feste's concluding song in Shakespeare's *Twelfth Night*. The action in this scene of *King Lear* somewhat resembles that of the other play; likely, Shakespeare noted the similarity in plot and emotion and intended for the audience to make the connection as well.

In addition to singing, the Fool also utters a prophecy. The gist of the prophecy deals with the unnaturalness in the world and how that unnaturalness can sometimes appear to be the normal order. In *Shakespeare, Our Contemporary*, critic Jan Kott says about this inversion, "The Fool knows that the only true madness is to regard this world as rational. . . . The world stands upside down." Lear's world is indeed topsy-turvy, and the king is just beginning to realize that fact.

Lear has not had a complete change of heart, however. For perhaps the first time in his life, Lear is taking note of the miseries of others, but the king has not yet recognized that his own current sufferings are at least in part of his own making. The staging of the love test, the shunning of Cordelia, and the bickering over the retinue of 100 knights were all within Lear's capability of control. Lear, however, stubbornly forges along his own path, and he affirms in this scene that he is "a man / More sinned against than sinning" (59–60). Lear has yet to realize and accept his own responsibility for the wretched state of affairs in which he finds himself.

Act III, Scene 3

Gloucester, having received a letter that speaks of divisions between Albany and Cornwall and of French invaders, plans to aid Lear. Edmund, trusted by his father and told of this news, sees an opportunity to betray Gloucester.

ACT III, SCENE 3
A room in Gloucester's castle.

[Enter GLOUCESTER and EDMUND]

Gloucester Alack, alack, Edmund, I like not this unnatural dealing. When I desired their leave that I might pity him, they took from me the use of mine own house, charged me on pain of perpetual displeasure neither to speak of him, entreat for him, or any way sustain him.   5

Edmund Most savage and unnatural.

Gloucester Go to; say you nothing. There is division between the Dukes, and a worse matter than that. I have received a letter this night—'tis dangerous to be spoken—I have locked the letter in my closet. These injuries the King now bears will be revenged home; there is part of a power already footed; we must incline to the King. I will look him and privily relieve him. Go you and maintain talk with the Duke, that my charity be not of him perceived. If he ask for me, I am ill and gone to bed. If I die for it, as no less is threatened me, the King my old master must be relieved. There is strange things toward, Edmund; pray you be careful.   20

[Exit]

Edmund This courtesy forbid thee shall the Duke
Instantly know, and of that letter too.
This seems a fair deserving, and must draw me
That which my father loses—no less than all.   25
The younger rises when the old doth fall. *[Exit]*

NOTES

14. *footed:* landed on our shores.

15. *privily relieve:* secretly aid.

24. *This...deserving:* I should be well-rewarded for this betrayal.

COMMENTARY

This scene inspires the question: How can two such persons as Gloucester and Edmund share the same blood? Gloucester, full of pity for the king, pledges to aid Lear secretly. Edmund receives this news with malevolent joy, seeing in this mercy mission a ripe opportunity to forward his own designs. Some critics have questioned whether this malice on the part of Edmund is a comment by Shakespeare on the evil of illegitimacy. Such a theory, however, hardly holds water when applied to the cruelty of the legitimate children of the king.

In addition to expecting praise for informing upon his father, Edmund also envisions reward for his political endeavors. Gloucester tells Edmund of the plan to help Lear and of a letter describing a foreign "power already footed" (14). How Gloucester came by this letter is a mystery, yet it is plain that the letter contains the same information to which Kent is privy in Scene 1 of this act.

The chance to divulge treasonous news fills Edmund with delight. Edmund expects the ultimate recompense for his betrayal: "This seems a fair deserving, and must draw me / That which my father loses—no less than all" (24–25). Edmund's closing line—"The younger rises when the old doth fall"—provides a chilling view of a world in which the older generation is overthrown by the wicked new (26).

Act III, Scene 4

Lear, struggling against the madness that he perceives is growing within him, acknowledges the general woes of the poor and meets Edgar who's posing as Tom o' Bedlam. Gloucester offers aid to Lear and his party.

ACT III, SCENE 4
The heath, before a hovel.

[Enter LEAR, KENT, and Fool]

Kent Here is the place, my lord. Good my lord, enter.
 The tyranny of the open night's too rough
 For nature to endure. *[Storm still]*

Lear   Let me alone.

Kent Good my lord, enter here.

Lear   Wilt break my heart?

Kent I had rather break mine own. Good my lord,
          enter.   5

Lear Thou think'st 'tis much that this contentious storm
 Invades us to the skin. So 'tis to thee,
 But where the greater malady is fixed
 The lesser is scarce felt. Thou'dst shun a bear;
 But if thy flight lay toward the roaring sea,   10
 Thou'dst meet the bear i' th' mouth. When the mind's free,
 The body's delicate. The tempest in my mind
 Doth from my senses take all feeling else
 Save what beats there. Filial ingratitude,
 Is it not as this mouth should tear this hand   15
 For lifting food to't? But I will punish home.
 No, I will weep no more. In such a night
 To shut me out! Pour on; I will endure.
 In such a night as this! O Regan, Goneril,
 Your old kind father, whose frank heart gave all—   20
 O, that way madness lies; let me shun that.
 No more of that.

Kent   Good my lord, enter here.

NOTES

8.   *fixed:* rooted deeply.

11. *i' th' mouth:* head-on.

     free: unworried.

14. *Filial ingratitude:* unthankfulness from a child.

Lear Prithee go in thyself; seek thine own ease.
  This tempest will not give me leave to ponder
  On things would hurt me more, but I'll go in.   25
  [To the Fool] In, boy; go first. You houseless poverty—
  Nay, get thee in. I'll pray, and then I'll sleep.
  [Exit Fool]
  Poor naked wretches, wheresoe'er you are,
  That bide the pelting of this pitiless storm,
  How shall your houseless heads and unfed sides,   30
  Your looped and windowed raggedness, defend you
  From seasons such as these? O, I have ta'en
  Too little care of this! Take physic, pomp;
  Expose thyself to feel what wretches feel,
  That thou mayst shake the superflux to them   35
  And show the heavens more just.

Edgar *[within]* Fathom and half, fathom and half!
  Poor Tom!
  [Enter Fool]

Fool Come not in here, nuncle; here's a spirit.
  Help me, help me!   40

Kent Give me thy hand. Who's there?

Fool A spirit, a spirit. He says his name's poor Tom.

Kent What art thou that dost grumble there i' th' straw?
  Come forth.
  [Enter EDGAR as Tom o' Bedlam]

Edgar Away! the foul fiend follows me. Through   45
  the sharp hawthorn blow the winds. Humh! go to
  thy cold bed, and warm thee.

Lear Didst thou give all to thy daughters? And art
  thou come to this?

Edgar Who gives anything to poor Tom? whom the   50
  foul fiend hath led through fire and through flame,
  through ford and whirlpool, o'er bog and quagmire;
  that hath laid knives under his pillow and halters
  in his pew, set ratsbane by his porridge, made him
  proud of heart, to ride on a bay trotting horse over   55

31.   *looped and windowed:* full of holes.

33.   *Take physic, pomp:* be instructed/cured, great ones.

35.   *superflux:* surplus.

37.   *Fathom and half:* sailor's cry when checking depth of sea.

53–54.   *knives, halters, ratsbane:* various means to suicide.

four-inched bridges, to course his own shadow for
a traitor. Bless thy five wits, Tom's acold. O, do, de,
do, de, do, de. Bless thee from whirlwinds, star-
blasting, and taking. Do poor Tom some charity,
whom the foul fiend vexes. There could I have him   60
now—and there—and there again—and there—

[Storm still]

Lear Have his daughters brought him to this pass?
Couldst thou save nothing? Wouldst thou give 'em all?

Fool Nay, he reserved a blanket, else we had been
all shamed.   65

Lear Now all the plagues that in the pendulous air
Hang fated o'er men's faults light on thy daughters!

Kent He hath no daughters, sir.

Lear Death, traitor; nothing could have subdued nature
To such a lowness but his unkind daughters.   70
Is it the fashion that discarded fathers
Should have thus little mercy on their flesh?
Judicious punishment—'twas this flesh begot
Those pelican daughters.

Edgar Pillicock sat on Pillicock Hill. Alow, alow,   75
loo, loo!

Fool This cold night will turn us all to fools and madmen.

Edgar Take heed o' th' foul fiend; obey thy parents; keep thy words' justice; swear not; commit
not with man's sworn spouse; set not thy sweet   80
heart on proud array. Tom's acold.

Lear What hast thou been?

Edgar A servingman, proud in heart and mind;
that curled my hair, wore gloves in my cap; served
the lust of my mistress' heart, and did the act of   85
darkness with her; swore as many oaths as I spake
words, and broke them in the sweet face of heaven.
One that slept in the contriving of lust, and waked

56. *course:* hunt after.

57. *five wits:* common sense, imagination, fantasy, reason, memory.

59. *taking:* evil influence of fairies.

74. *pelican:* Pelicans feed their young on their own blood, but when the young grow older, they turn on the parent bird.

75. *Pilicock. . . loo!:* A fragment from a nursery rhyme.

78-81. *obey...array:* a rendering of the Ten Commandments.

84. *gloves:* as presents from a mistress.

to do it. Wine loved I deeply, dice dearly; and in
woman out-paramoured the Turk. False of heart,   90
light of ear, bloody of hand; hog in sloth, fox in
stealth, wolf in greediness, dog in madness, lion in
prey. Let not the creaking of shoes nor the rustling
of silks betray thy poor heart to woman. Keep thy
foot out of brothels, thy hand out of plackets, thy   95
pen from lenders' books, and defy the foul fiend.
Still through the hawthorn blows the cold wind; says
suum, mun, nonny. Dolphin my boy, boy, sessa! let
him trot by. *[Storm still]*

Lear Thou wert better in a grave than to answer   100
with thy uncovered body this extremity of the skies.
Is man no more than this? Consider him well.
Thou ow'st the worm no silk, the beast no hide, the
sheep no wool, the cat no perfume. Ha! here's three
on's are sophisticated. Thou art the thing itself; un-   105
accommodated man is no more but such a poor, bare,
forked animal as thou art. Off, off, you lendings!
Come, unbutton here.

[Begins to disrobe]

Fool Prithee, nuncle, be contented; 'tis a naughty night
to swim in. Now a little fire in a wild field   110
were like an old lecher's heart—a small spark, all
the rest on's body cold. Look, here comes a walking fire.

[Enter GLOUCESTER with a torch]

Edgar This is the foul Flibbertigibbet. He begins
at curfew, and walks till the first cock. He gives the
web and the pin, squints the eye, and makes the hare-   115
lip; mildews the white wheat, and hurts the poor
creature of earth.
Swithold footed thrice the 'old;
He met the nightmare, and her nine fold
Bid her alight   120
And her troth plight,
And aroint thee, witch, aroint thee!

Kent How fares your Grace?

Lear What's he?

Kent Who's there? What is't you seek?   125

90. *out-paramoured:* had more mistresses than.

95. *plackets:* openings in a petticoat.

105. *on's:* of us.

107. *lendings:* borrowed things, in this case Lear's clothes.

113. *Flibbertigibbet:* a name for the devil, taken from a 1603 book by Samuel Harsnett.

114. *curfew:* at 9 p.m. in those days.

114. *web...pin:* cataracts of the eyes.

118–122. *Swithold...thee:* Saint Withold was an Anglo-Saxon saint. Edgar's rhyme is a charm to prevent horses from having nightmares.

119. *nine fold:* nine offspring.

121. *her troth plight:* promise to do no harm.

122. *aroint:* be gone.

Gloucester What are you there? Your names?

Edgar Poor Tom, that eats the swimming frog, the
toad, the todpole, the wall-newt and the water; that
in the fury of his heart, when the foul fiend rages,
eats cow-dung for sallets, swallows the old rat and   130
the ditch-dog, drinks the green mantle of the standing pool; who is whipped from tithing to tithing, and
stock-punished and imprisoned; who hath had three
suits to his back, six shirts to his body.
Horse to ride, and weapon to wear,   135
But mice and rats, and such small deer,
Have been Tom's food for seven long year.
Beware my follower! Peace, Smulkin, peace, thou fiend!

Gloucester What, hath your Grace no better company?

Edgar The prince of darkness is a gentleman.   140
  Modo he's called, and Mahu.

Gloucester Our flesh and blood, my lord, is grown so vile
  That it doth hate what gets it.

Edgar Poor Tom's acold.

Gloucester Go in with me. My duty cannot suffer   145
  T'obey in all your daughter's hard commands.
  Though their injunction be to bar my doors
  And let this tyrannous night take hold upon you,
  Yet have I ventured to come seek you out
  And bring you where both fire and food is ready.   150

Lear First let me talk with this philosopher.
  What is the cause of thunder?

Kent Good my lord, take his offer; go into th' house.

Lear I'll talk a word with this same learned Theban.
  What is your study?   155

Edgar How to prevent the fiend, and to kill vermin.

Lear Let me ask you one word in private.

---

128.   *water:* water-newt.

130.   *sallets:* salads.

131.   *mantle:* scum.

132.   *tithing:* parish or church district; also a tenth of
one's earnings given to the church.

135–137. These lines are adapted from the romance *Bevis
of Hampton.*

138–141. *Smulkin...Mahu:* spirits.

154.   *Theban:* scholar, in association with Greek city of
Thebes.

Kent Importune him once more to go, my lord.
  His wits begin t' unsettle.

Gloucester   Canst thou blame him?
  [Storm still]
  His daughters seek his death. Ah, that good Kent,   160
  He said it would be thus, poor banished man!
  Thou say'st the King grows mad—I'll tell thee, friend,
  I am almost mad myself. I had a son,
  Now outlawed from my blood; he sought my life
  But lately, very late. I loved him, friend,   165
  No father his son dearer. True to tell thee,
  The grief hath crazed my wits. What a night 's this!
  I do beseech your Grace—

Lear   O, cry you mercy, sir.
  Noble philosopher, your company.

168 *cry you mercy:* excuse me.

Edgar Tom's acold.   170

Gloucester In, fellow, there, into th' hovel; keep thee warm.

Lear Come, let's in all.

Kent   This way, my lord.

Lear   With him!
  I will keep still with my philosopher.

Kent Good my lord, soothe him; let him take the fellow.

Gloucester Take him you on.   175

Kent Sirrah, come on; go along with us.

Lear Come, good Athenian.

177. *Athenian:* philosopher.

Gloucester No words, no words! Hush.

Edgar Child Rowland to the dark tower came;
  His word was still, 'Fie, foh, and fum,   180
  I smell the blood of a British man.'

179. *Child:* a young warrior who has not yet achieved knighthood.

[Exeunt]

COMMENTARY

A play's climax is the ultimate moment that serves as a turning point in the action. Most see Scene 4 as that climactic moment, at least for Lear. Here on the heath, still battered by the exterior storm of nature and hounded by the internal storm in his mind, Lear finds himself situated before a lowly hut that offers but scant protection from the elements. Here the unsettled mind of the king begins to reach a fever pitch, and Lear and his Fool meet another form of madness in the disguised Edgar.

Just as Shakespeare plays on the imagery of the body in Act II when Lear calls Goneril a "boil, a plague-sore, an embossed carbuncle," so does Shakespeare here call upon the medical theories prevalent in his day. Lear responds to Kent's entreaties to take shelter with a mournful "Wilt break my heart?" (4). Indeed, Lear has good reason for his query, for the king is aware that respite from the storm will allow his ravaging emotions to be more acutely felt. "But where the greater malady is fixed," cries Lear, "[t]he lesser is scarce felt" (8–9). The notion that a more acute pain, once alleviated, will give way to suffering from lesser pains was a familiar one to Shakespeare and his audiences.

Losing the battle against madness

Lear continues to fight his madness here. To this point, Lear has struggled against it valiantly. Yet here we see that Lear is beginning to lose this battle; note that he feels he has the power to place curses upon his daughters. Further, Lear is becoming obsessed by his own failings, and though the Fool tries desperately to draw Lear's mind away from these depressing thoughts, the king's errors and the wrongs done to him now loom utmost in his mind.

More evidence of Lear's internal struggle surfaces. His remarks wander back and forth. He promises vengeance for his daughters' "[f]ilial ingratitude," yet he also pledges to "weep no more" (14, 17). Immediately thereafter, Lear rails at the storm and at the cruel daughters who would shut him out "[i]n such a night as this" (19). By line 21, Lear has recognized that "O, that way madness lies; let me shun that." Finally convinced to take shelter, Lear decides to pray, and here the king becomes the first of three characters to discover that certain important things in his life have heretofore gone untended. In his sympathy for the "[p]oor naked wretches," Lear admits "O, I have ta'en / Too little care of this!" (28, 32–33).

The Bedlam beggar

From the depths of the hovel, having terrified Lear's Fool, Edgar appears disguised as Bedlam beggar and fully enacting his assumed role. The beggar character was well-known to Shakespeare's audience, and playgoers saw the stereotypical Bedlam as something to be despised. Numerous Elizabethan accounts relate the descriptions of Poor Tom figures who roamed the English countryside, sticking pins and twigs in their skin, terrifying young maidens into offering money, and more often than not only pretending to be mad.

Though some of these souls were truly unhinged—escaped or released men from the Bethlehem (or Bedlam) Hospital—many were simply wanderers and vagabonds whose lack of good fortune or initiative placed them on the lowest rungs of society's ladder. If Elizabethans felt any pity at all for Edgar disguised as Poor Tom, they felt that sympathy because they saw the good character of Edgar shining through the blanket costume of the lunatic.

Lear battles the storm both internally and externally.

Such, then, is the vision that rises before Elizabethan eyes at the entry of Tom, the lunatic whose nakedness is scarcely covered because "he reserved a blanket, else we had been all shamed" (64). Tom is a vision of contradictions, in many ways uttering in his feigned madness such paradoxes as Lear utters out of a true illness: "[G]o to thy cold bed," rasps Tom, "and warm thee" (46–47). Edgar's performance as the Bedlam beggar becomes even more convincing when, in combination with his wandering speech, he jousts and jabs at the unseen demons who torment him: "There I could have him now—and there—and there again—and there" (60–61).

Lear is certain that Tom's desperate plight has been brought about through the conniving of Tom's daughters. Lear's mind is obviously dominated by this obsession: "[N]othing," cries Lear, "could have subdued nature / To such a lowness but his unkind daughters" (69–70). Lear even curses Tom's fictitious daughters in lines 66–67, just as Lear has already cursed Goneril and Regan. Lear's cursing creates a bizarre picture when coupled with Tom's peculiar version of biblical commandments in lines 79–82, and again in lines 94 and 95.

The picture that Tom paints of himself in response to Lear's "What hast thou been?" is as base a view as one could imagine and is in some respects perhaps reminiscent of Edmund (83). According to Poor Tom, he has been a servant who satisfied the sexual wishes of his mistress. He has been given to swearing falsely and breaking promises. He drank, he gambled, he "out-paramoured the Turk"; he has been lazy, sneaky, greedy, and mad (90). All the rules and instructions Tom recites in lines 94 through 96 he has apparently broken, and he presents himself to Lear as the picture of utter depravity.

"Unaccommodated man"

Moved not by the recitation of the Bedlam beggar's misconduct but rather by Tom's present, near-naked condition, Lear has another revelation. He sees Tom as "the thing itself" and recognizes that "unaccommodated man is no more but such a poor, bare, forked animal" (105–107). This is an important realization for the distraught king, for in the past Lear has assumed that respectability went hand-in-hand with appearance. Now, however, Lear sees that though circumstances

may strip a human of all outward show of strength, the basic humanity remains and is worthy of respect and care. When Lear tears at his own clothing, he recognizes that his own situation in life is not so very different after all from that of the beggar.

Note the significance of names with respect to Edgar as Tom. As Gloucester arrives carrying a torch, Tom calls Gloucester "the foul Flibbertigibbet" (113). (The Notes mention Shakespeare's source for this and other demon names.) The emphasis is not so much upon the name as it is upon the behaviours associated with the fiend or person named. For Tom, the defining features of the demon are its actions: the night stalks, the purposed deformities, the uncaring injuries. Tom even identifies himself mainly by his characteristics; he elaborates upon his accustomed menu, describes his reception in the community, and details the pieces of his wardrobe. This lack of emphasis upon the importance of name alone is not new for Shakespeare. Recall those famous lines from *Romeo and Juliet:* "What's in a name? That which we call a rose by any other word would smell as sweet."

Shakespeare's word choices open up multiple meanings here. When Tom mentions that he is customarily "whipped from tithing to tithing," the general sense of the word "tithing" to Elizabethans was that of a parish or district; Tom, therefore, was whipped wherever he went (132). A more contemporary connotation of "tithing," however, relates to the tenth of one's salary given to the church. Read in this sense, Tom's line also means he was whipped from Sunday (the day of tithing) to Sunday: hence, he was whipped continually.

Near the end of the scene, Lear has elevated Tom to the position of philosopher, Theban, and Athenian. To Lear, Tom's words are wise ones, yet they seem wise only because Lear's true madness is escalating. Remarks that others would see as bemused ramblings, Lear believes are sane pronouncements. Aristotle once said that "no excellent soul is exempt from a mixture of madness," and Taine wrote, "Insanity is not a distinct and separate empire; our ordinary life borders upon it, and we cross the frontier in some part of our nature." There is a ring of truth, then, in the Fool's description of the world as a place where the "upside-down" is normal. But the mystery remains regarding how everything that seems wrong can ultimately be right.

Act III, Scene 5

Edmund informs Cornwall of Gloucester's aid to Lear. As a reward for this revelation and loyalty, Cornwall promises to strip Gloucester of his estate and title and bestow these upon Edmund.

ACT III, SCENE 5
A room in Gloucester's castle.

[Enter CORNWALL and EDMUND]

Cornwall I will have my revenge ere I depart his
   house.

Edmund How, my lord, I may be censured, that nature thus gives way to loyalty, sometimes fears me to
   think of.   5

Cornwall I now perceive it was not altogether your
   brother's evil disposition made him seek his death;
   but a provoking merit, set awork by a reproveable
   badness in himself.

Edmund How malicious is my fortune that I must   10
   repent to be just! This is the letter which he spoke
   of, which approves him an intelligent party to the
   advantages of France. O heavens, that this treason
   were not! or not I the detector!

Cornwall Go with me to the Duchess.   15

Edmund If the matter of this paper be certain,
   you have mighty business in hand.

Cornwall True or false, it hath made thee Earl of
   Gloucester. Seek out where thy father is, that he
   may be ready for our apprehension.   20

Edmund *[aside]* If I find him comforting the
   King, it will stuff his suspicion more fully.—I will
   persevere in my course of loyalty, though the conflict
   be sore between that and my blood.

Cornwall I will lay trust upon thee, and thou shalt   25
   find a dearer father in my love. *[Exeunt]*

NOTES

4.   *loyalty:* loyalty to Cornwall.

    sometimes fears me: makes me somewhat afraid.

9.   *badness in himself:* untrustworthiness in Gloucester.

11. *repent...just:* be sorry that I acted correctly in betraying my father.

22. *stuff his suspicion:* increase suspicion of him.

COMMENTARY

Shakespeare has two purposes in this scene between Cornwall and Edmund. First is a very practical purpose. Recall that the last scene featured appearances by Gloucester, Lear, Edgar, Kent, and the Fool. According to an unwritten rule of Elizabethan theatre called the "law of reentry," it was bad drama for the characters at the end of one scene to enter the stage immediately in the following scene. Because Act III, Scene 6 will return the audience to Lear and his followers, Shakespeare needed to create this intervening scene to avoid breaking the reentry convention.

The second purpose of the scene is to bring Edmund's endeavors to their culmination. When he informs Cornwall of the supposed treason of Gloucester, Cornwall awards Edmund with the title of "Earl of Gloucester" (18–19). Edmund hopes to push his advantage yet more; he feels that though "the conflict be sore between [his course of loyalty] and [his] blood," he will be able to enhance his position with Cornwall further if he can actually catch Gloucester giving assistance to Lear (23–24). Note the irony in Edmund's concern about loyalty and blood. To Cornwall, Edmund's remark sounds like that of a child bemoaning the need to betray his father. For Edmund—and for the audience—the remark reveals only Edmund's loyalty to his own plans.

Act III, Scene 6

Lear puts his older daughters "on trial." During this mock trial, Edgar, Kent, and the Fool serve as jurors. Gloucester urges a change of location that deprives Lear of much-needed and potentially healing sleep.

ACT III, SCENE 6
A farmhouse adjoining the castle.

[Enter KENT and GLOUCESTER]

Gloucester Here is better than the open air; take it
thankfully. I will piece out the comfort with what
addition I can. I will not be long from you.

Kent All the power of his wits have given way to
his impatience. The gods reward your kindness.   5

[Exit GLOUCESTER]

[Enter LEAR, EDGAR, and FOOL]

Edgar Frateretto calls me, and tells me Nero is an
angler in the lake of darkness. Pray, innocent, and
beware the foul fiend.

Fool Prithee, nuncle, tell me whether a madman
be a gentleman or a yeoman.   10

Lear A king, a king.

Fool No, he's a yeoman that has a gentleman to
his son; for he's a mad yeoman that sees his son a
gentleman before him.

Lear To have a thousand with red burning spits   15
Come hizzing in upon 'em—

Edgar The foul fiend bites my back.

Fool He's mad that trusts in the tameness of a
wolf, a horse's health, a boy's love, or a whore's oath.

Lear It shall be done; I will arraign them straight.   20
[To Edgar] Come, sit thou here, most learned justice.
[To the Fool] Thou, sapient sir, sit here. Now, you
she-foxes—

Edgar Look, where he stands and glares. Want'st
thou eyes at trial, madam?
Come o'er the bourn, Bessy, to me.   25

NOTES

6.   *Frateretto:* another fiend from Samuel Harsnett's 1603 book.

Nero: Roman emperor of deplorable morals.

10.   *yeoman:* property owner below rank of gentleman.

22.   *sapient:* wise.

24.   *eyes:* an audience.

madam: Regan or Goneril

25.   *bourn:* brook.

Fool Her boat hath a leak,
And she must not speak
Why she dares not come over to thee.

Edgar The foul fiend haunts poor Tom in the voice
of a nightingale. Hoppedance cries in Tom's belly   30
for two white herring. Croak not, black angel; I
have no food for thee.

Kent How do you, sir? Stand you not so amazed.
Will you lie down and rest upon the cushions?

Lear I'll see their trial first. Bring in their evidence.   35
[To Edgar] Thou, robed man of justice, take thy place.
[To the Fool] And thou, his yokefellow of equity,
Bench by his side. *[to Kent]* You are o' th' commission;
Sit you too.

Edgar Let us deal justly   40
Sleepest or wakest thou, jolly shepherd?
Thy sheep be in the corn;
And for one blast of thy minikin mouth
Thy sheep shall take no harm
Purr, the cat is gray.   45

Lear Arraign her first. 'Tis Goneril, I here take my
oath before this honourable assembly, kicked the
poor King her father.

Fool Come hither mistress. Is your name Goneril?

Lear She cannot deny it.   50

Fool Cry you mercy, I took you for a joint-stool.

Lear And here's another, whose warped looks proclaim
What store her heart is made on. Stop her there!
Arms, arms, sword, fire! Corruption in the place!
False justicer, why hast thou let her 'scape?   55

Edgar Bless thy five wits!

Kent O pity! Sir, where is the patience now
That you so oft have boasted to retain?

Edgar *[aside]* My tears begin to take his part so much
They mar my counterfeiting.   60

30.   *Hoppedance:* Samuel Harsnett, Shakespeare's source for various names for devils, uses Hoberdidance.

31.   *Croak:* the low term for a stomach growling.

37.   *yokefellow of equity:* law partner.

43.   *minikin:* dainty.

51.   *joint-stool:* a wooden, three-legged stool.

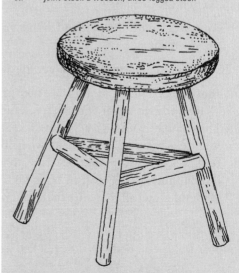

Lear's mock trial uses joint-stools in place of his daughters.

Lear The little dogs and all,
　Tray, Blanch, and Sweetheart—see, they bark at me.

Edgar Tom will throw his head at them. Avaunt, you curs.
　Be thy mouth or black or white,
　Tooth that poisons if it bite;   65
　Mastiff, greyhound, mongrel grim,
　Hound or spaniel, brach or lym,
　Or bobtail tike, or trundle-tail—
　Torn will make him weep and wail;
　For, with throwing thus my head,   70
　Dogs leaped the hatch, and all are fled.
　Do, de, de, de. Sessa! Come, march to wakes and
　fairs and market towns. Poor Tom, thy horn is dry.

Lear Then let them anatomize Regan. See what
　breeds about her heart. Is there any cause in nature   75
　that makes these hard hearts? *[to Edgar]* You, sir,
　I entertain for one of my hundred; only I do not like
　the fashion of your garments. You will say they are
　Persian; but let them be changed.

Kent Now, good my lord, lie here and rest awhile.   80

Lear Make no noise, make no noise; draw the curtains.
　So, so. We'll go to supper i' th' morning.

Fool And I'll go to bed at noon.

[Enter GLOUCESTER]

Gloucester Come hither, friend. Where is the King
　my master?

Kent Here, sir, but trouble him not; his wits are gone.   85

Gloucester Good friend, I prithee take him in thy arms.
　I have o'erheard a plot of death upon him.
　There is a litter ready; lay him in't
　And drive toward Dover, friend, where thou shalt meet
　Both welcome and protection. Take up thy master.   90
　If thou shouldst dally half an hour, his life,
　With thine and all that offer to defend him,

63.　*throw:* shake.

　　Avaunt: Go away.

67.　*lym:* bloodhound.

68.　*bobtail tike:* short-tailed mutt.

　　trundle-tail: curly-tailed dog.

71.　*hatch:* lower half of a divided, or Dutch, door.

73.　*horn:* bottle carried by beggars full of drink given by charitable persons.

74.　*anatomize:* dissect.

79.　*Persian:* very ornate or fancy.

88.　*litter:* stretcher.

Stand in assured loss. Take up, take up,
And follow me, that will to some provision
Give thee quick conduct.

Kent   Oppressed nature sleeps.   95
This rest might yet have balmed thy broken sinews,
Which, if convenience will not allow,
Stand in hard cure. *[to the Fool]* Come, help to bear
     thy master.
Thou must not stay behind.

Gloucester   Come, come, away!

[Exeunt all but EDGAR]

Edgar When we our betters see bearing our woes,   100
We scarcely think our miseries our foes.
Who alone suffers suffers most i' th' mind,
Leaving free things and happy shows behind;
But then the mind much sufferance doth o'erskip
When grief hath mates, and bearing fellowship.   105
How light and portable my pain seems now,
When that which makes me bend makes the King bow.
He childed as I fathered. Tom, away.
Mark the high noises, and thyself bewray
When false opinion, whose wrong thoughts defile thee,   110
In thy just proof repeals and reconciles thee.
What will hap more to-night, safe 'scape the King!
Lurk, lurk. *[Exit]*

98.   *Stand...cure:* will hardly be cured.

109.   *high noises:* rumours of great events.

109–111.   *thyself...thee:* keep your identity secret until you are proven innocent.

113.   *Lurk:* hide.

COMMENTARY

We have to admire Shakespeare's creativity and sense of stagecraft in this third act. Note how many aspects of human personality are presented to us here—how many fine distinctions of madness. We observe Lear's insanity, listen to the Fool's wit, and admire the accuracy of Edgar's portrayal of the Bedlam. What a student of human nature Shakespeare was to have created for us these moving characters who at times almost seem fragments of a single personality. Each action and each utterance seem wholly appropriate for the particular dramatic situation.

This sense of rightness pervades Scene 6, not so much because we agree with what happens but because truth itself permeates the action. Lear's mind is dominated by the thought of wicked daughters—both his own and the fictional ones of Poor Tom. But Lear is also quite deranged at this point, and his ramblings and antics are viewed by many literary-minded psychiatrists as highly apropos to his condition.

The daughters on trial

Settled now in the somewhat more amenable surroundings of a farmhouse, Lear and his entourage engage in an apparently disconnected series of words and phrases that perhaps only Shakespeare could have devised. Edgar rants about his demons, the Fool offers jokes and riddles, and Lear organizes a judicial investigation of Goneril and Regan.

Lear holds a mock trial of Goneril and Regan. Appointed as judges and jury, Edgar, Kent, and the Fool observe as Lear arraigns his daughters, who are represented by three-legged stools. Lear's reason in madness and madness in reason is clearly exhibited, and the fact that the others in Lear's party offer no real objection to these events gives the whole scene an air of absurdity.

Note the animal imagery that is rife in this scene; the characters allude to wolves, horses, she-foxes, nightingales, herrings, sheep, cats, and dogs—nine varieties of dog, in fact. The concept to grasp here is the very elemental "nature" of this farmhouse drama—the enactment of Lear's "Man's life is cheap as beast's." The deadly seriousness of that thought is offset by the ludicrous action of the scene, especially as Tom now seems to usurp the Fool's position as poet. Along with the rhymed list of canines he presents, Poor Tom shares a ditty in lines 41–44 that resembles the old nursery rhyme: "Little Boy Blue, come blow your horn. The sheep's in the meadow; the cow's in the corn."

In a poignant moment, Lear suggests that Tom's kennel "anatomize Regan" (74). Lear's supposed reasoning here is that perhaps some "cause in nature" has hardened the hearts of his daughters (75). Lear immediately links this thought with that bone of contention, the 100 knights his daughters refuse to host. Lear announces to Edgar, "You, sir, / I entertain for one of my hundred" (76–77). In some ways this invitation is superbly moving; remember that Lear speaks here, albeit unknowingly, to his own godson. Though Edgar plays the role of Bedlam beggar throughout this scene, he yet remains Edgar. The betrayed son of Gloucester, not a rambling madman, is watching Lear's descent.

No time to rest

Edgar somewhat parrots the earlier remarks of his godfather about pain and suffering: "How light and portable my pain seems now, / When that which makes me bend, makes the King bow" (106–107). His comment echoes Lear's earlier statement that "where the greater malady is fixed / The lesser is scarce felt" (III.4.8–9). Edgar voices his recognition of the parallel between his filial relationship to Gloucester and that of Lear to his daughters, saying, "He childed as I fathered" (108).

This scene presents a poignant picture of suffering. The long-loyal Kent realizes that Lear's nature is greatly weighed down with depression, and Kent suggests that had Lear been given the opportunity to sleep, some measure of comfort and reason might have returned. The immediate disturbance of Lear's much-needed rest has much to do with his continued suffering and frenzy. Rest and closure are needed at this point by all concerned; note how Tom's lines, all but the last two words of which are spoken not from the personality of the beggar but in the more elegant speech of Edgar, lend a sense of closure to the scene.

As Kent urges him to rest, Lear clearly evidences his mental exhaustion, urging his fellows to "make no noise; draw the curtains. / So, so. We'll go to supper i' th' morning" (81–82). Lear's tirade is slowing in pace, but his mind is far from healed. Indeed, healing sleep will not come to Lear until much later. Instead, Gloucester arrives with news that it is no longer safe for Lear and his mismatched entourage to remain at this farmhouse; immediate relocation is necessary to escape a plot against Lear's life. What should have been a rest and relief from strain and tension for all concerned, therefore, becomes a flight in the night.

Act III, Scene 7

Gloucester is Cornwall's captive. The deepest cruelty of Regan and Cornwall is revealed as Cornwall plucks out the eyes of Gloucester. Servants prove their loyalty; one is killed by Regan because he attacks and mortally wounds Cornwall, and others assist Gloucester after he has been blinded.

ACT III, SCENE 7
A room in Gloucester's castle.

[Enter CORNWALL, REGAN, GONERIL, EDMUND, and Servants]

Cornwall *[to Goneril]* Post speedily to my lord
your husband; show him this letter. The army of
France is landed. *[to Servants]* Seek out the traitor
Gloucester. *[Exeunt some Servants]*

Regan Hang him instantly.   5

Goneril Pluck out his eyes.

Cornwall Leave him to my displeasure. Edmund,
keep you our sister company. The revenges we are
bound to take upon your traitorous father are not fit
for your beholding. Advise the Duke where you are   10
going, to a most festinate preparation. We are bound
to the like. Our posts shall be swift and intelligent
betwixt us. Farewell, dear sister; farewell, my Lord
of Gloucester.
[Enter OSWALD]
How now? Where's the King?   15

Oswald My Lord of Gloucester hath conveyed him hence.
Some five or six and thirty of his knights,
Hot questrists after him, met him at gate;
Who, with some other of the lord's dependants,
Are gone with him toward Dover, where they boast   20
To have well-armed friends.

Cornwall   Get horses for your mistress.
[Exit OSWALD]

Goneril Farewell, sweet lord, and sister.

Cornwall Edmund, farewell.
[Exeunt GONERIL and EDMUND]
                              Go seek the traitor Gloucester,

NOTES

1.   *Post:* ride quickly.

11.   *festinate:* rapid.

18.   *questrists:* seekers.

Pinion him like a thief, bring him before us.
[Exeunt other Servants]
Though well we may not pass upon his life   25
Without the form of justice, yet our power
Shall do a court'sy to our wrath, which men
May blame, but not control.
[Enter GLOUCESTER and Servants]
                              Who's there, the traitor?

Regan Ingrateful fox, 'tis he.

Cornwall Bind fast his corky arms.   30

Gloucester What means your Graces? Good my
          friends, consider
You are my guests. Do me no foul play, friends.

Cornwall Bind him, I say. *[Servants bind him]*

Regan   Hard, hard! O filthy traitor.

Gloucester Unmerciful lady as you are, I'm none.

Cornwall To this chair bind him. Villain, thou shalt find— 35
[Regan plucks his beard]

Gloucester By the kind gods, 'tis, most ignobly done
To pluck me by the beard.

Regan So white, and such a traitor?

Gloucester   Naughty lady,
These hairs which thou dost ravish from my chin
Will quicken and accuse thee. I am your host.   40
With robber's hands my hospitable favours
You should not ruffle thus. What will you do?

Cornwall Come, sir, what letters had you late from
          France?

Regan Be simple-answered, for we know the truth.

Cornwall And what confederacy have you with the traitors 45
Late footed in the kingdom?

Regan To whose hands you have sent the lunatic King.
Speak.

---

24.   *pinion:* tie his arms.

25.   *pass:* pronounce judgment.

26–27. *yet...wrath:* While we lack the power (to pass judgment on his life), our anger will propel us.

30.   *corky:* dry and withered.

s.d. *Regan plucks his beard:* an act of extreme contempt, roughly equivalent to contemporary spitting in someone's face.

38.   *Naughty:* wicked, for Elizabethans.

40.   *quicken:* come to life.

Gloucester I have a letter guessingly set down,
Which came from one that's of a neutral heart,   50
And not from one opposed.

Cornwall   Cunning.

Regan   And false.

Cornwall Where has thou sent the King?

Gloucester To Dover.

Regan Wherefore to Dover? Wast thou not charged
at peril—

Cornwall Wherefore to Dover? Let him answer that.   55

Gloucester I am tied to th' stake, and I must stand
the course.

Regan Wherefore to Dover?

Gloucester Because I would not see thy cruel nails
Pluck out his poor old eyes; nor thy fierce sister
In his anointed flesh stick boarish fangs.   60
The sea, with such a storm as his bare head
In hell-black night endured, would have buoyed up
And quenched the stelled fires.
Yet, poor old heart, he holp the heavens to rain
If wolves had at thy gate howled that stern time,   65
Thou should'st have said, 'Good porter, turn the key'.
All cruels else subscribe. But I shall see
The winged vengeance overtake such children.

Cornwall See't shalt thou never. Fellows, hold the chair.
Upon these eyes of thine I'll set my foot.   70

Gloucester He that will think to live till he be old,
Give me some help.—O cruel! O ye gods!

[*Cornwall puts out Gloucester's eye*]

Regan One side will mock another. Th' other too.

Cornwall If you see vengeance—

First Servant   Hold your hand, my lord
I have served you ever since I was a child;   75
But better service have I never done you
Than now to bid you hold.

Regan   How now, you dog?

56. *course:* attack of the dogs, as in bear-baiting.

63. *stelled fires:* starlight.
64. *holp:* helped.

67. *All...subscribe:* All other cruel beings would yield to pity.

First Servant If you did wear a beard upon your chin,
 I'd shake it on this quarrel. What do you mean!

Cornwall My villain! *[Draw and fight]*   80

First Servant Nay, then, come on, and take the chance
 of anger.

Regan Give me thy sword. A peasant stand up thus?

*[She takes a sword and runs at him behind,
 kills him]*

First Servant O, I am slain! My lord, you have one eye left
 To see some mischief on him. O! *[Dies]*

Cornwall Lest it see more, prevent it. Out, vile jelly.   85
 Where is thy lustre now?

[GLOUCESTER'S other eye put out]

Gloucester All dark and comfortless. Where's my
      son Edmund?
 Edmund, enkindle all the sparks of nature
 To quit this horrid act.

Regan   Out, treacherous villain;
 Thou call'st on him that hates thee. It was he   90
 That made the overture of thy treasons to us;
 Who is too good to pity thee.

Gloucester O my follies! Then Edgar was abused.
 Kind gods, forgive me that, and prosper him.

Regan Go thrust him out at gates, and let him smell   95
 His way to Dover. *[Exit one with GLOUCESTER]*
           How is't, my lord? How look you?

Cornwall I have received a hurt. Follow me, lady.
 Turn out that eyeless villain. Throw this slave
 Upon the dunghill. Regan, I bleed apace.
 Untimely comes this hurt. Give me your arm.   100
 [Exeunt]

Second Servant I'll never care what wickedness I do,
 If this man come to good.

79. *What...mean!:* how dare you.

88. *enkindle...nature:* let your natural love blaze strong.

89. *quit:* revenge.

99. *apace:* quickly.

Third Servant   If she live long,
And in the end meet the old course of death,
Women will all turn monsters.

Second Servant Let's follow the old Earl, and get the bedlam₁₀₅
To lead him where he would. His roguish madness
Allows itself to anything. *[Exit]*

Third Servant Go thou. I'll fetch some flax and whites
of eggs
To apply to his bleeding face. Now heaven help him.   110
[Exit]

105.   *bedlam:* Edgar as Poor Tom.

COMMENTARY

This scene presents a controversial scenario. In it, Shakespeare violates one of the rules of classical theatre. If you have read Sophocles's *Oedipus*, recall that Jocasta's death and Oedipus's blinding occur offstage. These events become apparent after the fact; the violence itself is not perpetrated onstage. Here in Gloucester's castle, however, the horrible violence effected upon Gloucester is performed before the audience's eyes.

The Gloucester subplot comes into direct contact with the main story line as Gloucester is brought before Cornwall. Note that before Gloucester is even apprehended, both sisters offer suggestions about how to punish him. Regan suggests hanging; characteristically, Goneril suggests an even more vicious punishment: "Pluck out his eyes" (6).

Cornwall's true nature

In the brief interim before Gloucester is actually ushered in, Cornwall's irascible nature surfaces. Inflamed with thoughts of the war that is likely to come because French troops have now landed at Dover, Cornwall is ready to enlarge upon his previous cruelty. Earlier, remember, Cornwall placed Kent in the stocks, irreverently insulting the messenger of the king. Now, Cornwall coldly reasons, "Though well we may not pass upon his life / Without the form of justice, yet our power / Shall do a court'sy to our wrath, which men / May blame, but

not control" (25–28). Gloucester has previously referred to Cornwall's disposition as one that "will not be rubbed or stopped." In this scene, Cornwall blatantly places himself above the law.

The difference in general attitude between Gloucester and Cornwall is striking. Gloucester hails from the old regime. His set of values entertains no place for insult and discourtesy. As host to the duke and duchess, Gloucester assumes a general respect and decency observed by all. With bewilderment, then, Gloucester comments upon crass treatment by his guests. "Good my friends," remarks Gloucester, "consider / You are my guests. Do me no foul play, friends" (31–32).

Derailed justice

Gloucester's plea, of course, goes unheeded. Bound to a chair at the command of Cornwall, Gloucester's interrogation is accompanied by the insolent Regan's plucking of his beard. Nothing Gloucester says concerning information about the French forces is believed, and his revelation that Lear is now safely at Dover provides Cornwall and Regan with valuable information with which to forward their plots against the king. Gloucester is no more effective in defending himself while tied to the chair than were the joint-stools that served for Lear's evil daughters during the mock trial. An overwhelming sense of derailed justice persists. The injustice began in the first scene with Cordelia's disinheritance, continues here, and remains an issue through the rest of the play.

The common conception of justice revolves around perpetrators being appropriately punished for their crimes. Most democratic nations also hold, however, that such justice is applied according to certain statutes and procedures that clearly indicate the guilt of the accused. *Poetic justice,* on the other hand, connotes something a bit different. This type of justice is a logical and direct result of events and actions—a retribution that is swift and that sometimes seems to benefit the evildoer. Poetic justice often means that a good man who has erred, even though he has seemingly learned from his mistake, will generally reap the punishment for his past bad actions.

Gloucester falls victim to Cornwall's cruelty.

Bearing these ideas of justice in mind, it seems inconceivable that Gloucester, regardless of his faults and errors, deserves what befalls him here in his own home at the hands of his guests, especially when we consider how truly compassionate he has been to the slighted king. One of the major arguments concerning this tragedy of *King Lear* is that neither poetic justice nor legal justice is well-served, as further evidenced later in the drama.

Incessant cruelty

One of the ironies in this scene is Gloucester's prophetic statement when he bravely tells Regan that he "would not see thy cruel nails / Pluck out [Lear's] poor old eyes" (58–59). That precise punishment is instead levied against Gloucester. Further, Cornwall announces to Gloucester that "[u]pon these eyes of thine I'll set my foot" (70). The viciousness of Cornwall seems to know no bounds.

After Gloucester is blinded, note how the cruelty of the scene continues. Gloucester's hopes of being avenged by Edmund are viciously shattered, for he learns that it was Edmund who betrayed him to Cornwall. Regan, enraged at the audacity of a servant who dares to intercede, kills the intercessor. (In many performances, the actress portraying Regan simply turns away with a cold stare when the injured Cornwall asks for her arm.)

Despite the punishment that awaits them if Regan should discover their actions, two servants not only comment upon how monstrous her behaviour is but also offer their help to the "old Earl" (105). Without the final lines and actions of these servants, Act III would close with an almost unbearable pathos. Because of their inclusion, however, we know that Gloucester will eventually be reunited with Edgar as "the bedlam," so a glimpse of hope remains (105).

Notes

Notes

COLES NOTES TOTAL STUDY EDITION

KING LEAR
ACT IV

Scene 1 137

Scene 2 142

Scene 3 147

Scene 4 150

Scene 5 152

Scene 6 155

Scene 7 168

Lear *Be your tears wet? Yes, faith. I pray weep not.*
If you have poison for me, I will drink it.
I know you do not love me; for your sisters
Have, as I do remember, done me wrong.
You have some cause, they have not.

Cordelia *No cause, no cause.*

Act IV, Scene 1

The disguised Edgar now becomes the guide for his blinded father, who has been led to the countryside by a loyal Old Man.

ACT IV, SCENE 1
The heath.

[Enter EDGAR]

Edgar Yet better thus, and known to be contemned,
Than still contemned and flattered. To be worst,
The lowest and most dejected thing of fortune,
Stands still in esperance, lives not in fear.
The lamentable change is from the best;   5
The worse returns to laughter. Welcome then
Thou unsubstantial air that I embrace:
The wretch that thou hast blown unto the worst
Owes nothing to thy blasts.
[Enter GLOUCESTER and an Old Man]
      But who comes here?
My father, poorly led? World, world, O world!   10
But that thy strange mutations make us hate thee,
Life would not yield to age.

Old Man   O my good lord,
I have been your tenant, and your father's tenant,
These fourscore years.

Gloucester Away, get thee away. Good friend, be gone.   15
Thy comforts can do me no good at all;
Thee they may hurt.

Old Man   You cannot see your way.

Gloucester I have no way, and therefore want no eyes;
I stumbled when I saw. Full oft 'tis seen
Our means secure us, and our mere defects   20
Prove our commodities. O dear son Edgar,
The food of thy abused father's wrath,
Might I but live to see thee in my touch
I'ld say I had eyes again!

NOTES

1. *contemned:* despised.

2. *still:* always.

4. *esperance:* hope.

6. *worse...laughter:* A change from the worst must be for the better.

11-12. *But that...age:* If the world were not so irrational, we might never be reconciled to age and death.

20. *Our means secure us:* Our wealth makes us confident.

Old Man   How now? Who's there?

Edgar *[aside]* O gods! who is't can say 'I am at   25
    the worst'?
I am worse than e'er I was.

Old Man   'Tis poor mad Tom.

Edgar *[aside]* And worse I may be yet. The worst is not
So long as we can say 'This is the worst.'

Old Man Fellow, where goest?

Gloucester   Is it a beggerman?

Old Man Madman and beggar too.   30

Gloucester He has some reason, else he could not beg. | **31.**   *reason:* ability to reason.
I' th' last night's storm I such a fellow saw,
Which made me think a man a worm. My son
Came then into my mind, and yet my mind
Was then scarce friends with him. I have heard more
    since.   35
As flies to wanton boys are we to th' gods;
They kill us for their sport.

Edgar *[aside]*   How should this be?
Bad is the trade that must play fool to sorrow,
Ang'ring itself and others.—Bless thee, master.

Gloucester Is that the naked fellow?

Old Man   Ay, my lord.   40

Gloucester Get thee away. If for my sake
Thou wilt o'ertake us hence a mile or twain
I' th' way toward Dover, do it for ancient love; | **43.**   *ancient love:* the sort of love that used to exist between men.
And bring some covering for this naked soul,
Which I'll entreat to lead me.

Old Man   Alack, sir, he is mad.   45

Gloucester 'Tis the time's plague when madmen lead the
    blind.
Do as I bid thee, or rather do thy pleasure.
Above the rest, be gone.

Old Man I'll bring him the best 'parel that I have, | **49.**   *'parel:* apparel.
Come on't what will.   50

Gloucester Sirrah naked fellow—

Edgar Poor Tom's acold. *[aside]* I cannot daub it further.

Gloucester Come hither, fellow.

Edgar *[aside]* And yet I must.—Bless thy sweet
    eyes, they bleed.

Gloucester Know'st thou the way to Dover?   55

Edgar Both stile and gate, horseway and footpath.
  Poor Tom hath been scared out of his good wits.
  Bless thee, good man's son, from the foul fiend. Five
  fiends have been in poor Tom at once: of lust, as
  Obidicut; Hobbididence, prince of dumbness; Mahu,   60
  of stealing; Modo, of murder; Flibbertigibbet, of
  mopping and mowing, who since possesses chamber-
  maids and waiting women. So, bless thee, master.

Gloucester Here, take this purse, thou whom the
    heavens' plagues
  Have humbled to all strokes. That I am wretched   65
  Makes thee the happier. Heavens, deal so still!
  Let the superfluous and lust-dieted man,
  That slaves your ordinance, that will not see
  Because he does not feel, feel your pow'r quickly;
  So distribution should undo excess,   70
  And each man have enough. Dost thou know Dover?

Edgar Ay, master.

Gloucester There is a cliff, whose high and
    bending head
  Looks fearfully in the confined deep.
  Bring me but to the very brim of it,   75
  And I'll repair the misery thou dost bear
  With something rich about me. From that place
  I shall no leading need.

Edgar Give me thy arm.
  Poor Tom shall lead thee. *[Exeunt]*

---

52.   *daub:* pretend.

60.   *Obidicut...Flibbertigibbet:* fiends and demons named in a 1603 book by Samuel Harsnett.

62.   *mopping and mowing:* making faces or grimacing.

65.   *humbled...strokes:* made humble enough to withstand anything.

67.   *superfluous:* having excessive riches.
    lust-dieted: whose lusts are satisfied.

68.   *slaves your ordinance:* suppresses your command (to share).

77.   *something rich:* a gift.

COMMENTARY

After the horrendous vision offered at the close of Act III, viewers need some relief for their battered sensitivities. In contrast with the violence just witnessed in Gloucester's castle, this scene is poignant in its depiction of the blinded Gloucester being guided by the still-disguised Edgar. The scene also underscores the pessimism that continues to abound.

As the scene opens, Edgar speaks words containing a hint of optimism. Because he is "[t]he lowest and most dejected thing of fortune," he believes his situation can only improve—it cannot worsen (3). No sooner does he utter these words than an Old Man

The blinded Gloucester in a 1997 Old Vic production.
Billie Rafaeli/ PAL

enters leading the blinded Gloucester. The kindness of this Old Man, who is one of Gloucester's tenants, has been somewhat slighted by critics; he is, after all, not a major character. Yet what he does is important, for he not only brings Gloucester to Edgar but also agrees to bring clothing to Poor Tom. Such loyalty from Gloucester's tenant contrasts sharply with the disloyalty of Gloucester's bastard son.

Gloucester speaks and philosophizes without knowing that his disguised son Edgar now joins him. Gloucester's most famous lines—"As flies to wanton boys are we to th' gods; / They kill us for their sport"—stand in stark opposition to the hopeful words spoken by Edgar at the beginning of the scene (36–37). In addition, Gloucester's reference to the gods reminds Edgar of his father's peculiar weakness with respect to the supernatural—a weakness upon which Edgar will shortly play.

Edgar is clearly distressed by the visible evidence of his father's suffering, and we might think that he should now reveal himself to his father. But he does not do so, difficult as it is for him to maintain his beggar's role. Remember that Edgar is still an outlaw, and while no mention is made at present of further injury planned for Gloucester, the possibility of pursuit nevertheless exists. Gloucester, in his present condition, is not likely to keep Edgar's identity secret. Further, Gloucester has another lesson to learn. He desires that Edgar guide the way to the cliffs of Dover; Edgar's dramatic task as Poor Tom, then, is to help Gloucester not only find the cliffs he seeks but to learn an important lesson about life as well.

Gloucester becomes the second man in the play to recognize how little care he has taken in the past for those less fortunate than he. Mirroring Lear's earlier remarks, Gloucester cries, "Let the superfluous and lust-dieted man, / That slaves your ordinance, that will not see / Because he does not feel, feel your pow'r quickly; / So distribution should undo excess, / And each man have enough" (67–71). Gloucester, the "lust-dieted man, " realizes now something of the basic suffering of humanity and the roots common to all.

But Gloucester has not yet come to terms with the fact that each person is ultimately responsible for his own life. Gloucester's purgatory yet awaits him. He must experience it before he can develop into a greater man than the naive person who, according to Jan Kott, initially has "nothing about him" that "hints at the tragic old man whose eyes will be gouged out."

Act IV, Scene 2

Goneril seeks to gain favor with Edmund and derides Albany's manhood. Albany berates Goneril for her treatment of Lear and learns of Edmund's betrayal of Gloucester.

ACT IV, SCENE 2
Before the Duke of Albany's palace.

[Enter GONERIL, EDMUND, and OSWALD]

Goneril Welcome, my lord. I marvel our mild husband
Not met us on the way.
                    [to Oswald] Now, where's your master?

Oswald Madam, within, but never man so changed.
I told him of the army that was landed:
He smiled at it. I told him you were coming: 5
His answer was, 'The worse.' Of Gloucester's treachery
And of the loyal service of his son
When I informed him, then he called me sot
And told me I had turned the wrong side out.
What most he should dislike seems pleasant to him;   10
What like, offensive.

Goneril   *[to Edmund]* Then shall you go no further.
It is the cowish terror of his spirit,
That dares not undertake. He'll not feel wrongs
Which tie him to an answer. Our wishes on the way
May prove effects. Back, Edmund, to my brother.   15
Hasten his musters and conduct his pow'rs.
I must change names at home, and give the distaff
Into my husband's hands. This trusty servant
Shall pass between us. Ere long you are like to hear
(If you dare venture in your own behalf)   20
A mistress's command. Wear this. Spare speech.
[Gives a favour]
Decline your head. This kiss, if it durst speak,
Would stretch thy spirits up into the air.
Conceive, and fare thee well.

NOTES

8.   *sot:* fool.

9.   *turned the wrong side out:* taken the wrong side.

12.   *cowish:* cowardly.

15.   *prove effects:* be fulfilled.

16.   *musters:* gathered troops.

17.   *names:* roles.

        distaff: stick used for spinning wool yarn.

24.   *Conceive:* understand.

Edmund Yours in the ranks of death. *[Exit]*

Goneril   My most dear Gloucester. 25
O, the difference of man and man:
To thee a woman's services are due;
My fool usurps my body.

Oswald   Madam, here comes my lord.
[Exit. Enter ALBANY]

Goneril I have been worth the whistle.

Albany   O Goneril,
You are not worth the dust which the rude wind   30
Blows in your face. I fear your disposition:
That nature which contemns its origin
Cannot be bordered certain in itself.
She that herself will sliver and disbranch
From her material sap, perforce must wither   35
And come to deadly use.

Goneril No more; the text is foolish.

Albany Wisdom and goodness to the vile seem vile;
Filths savour but themselves. What have you done?
Tigers not daughters, what have you performed?   40
A father, and a gracious aged man,
Whose reverence even the head-lugged bear would lick,
Most barbarous, most degenerate, have you madded.
Could my good brother suffer you to do it?
A man, a prince, by him so benefited!   45
If that the heavens do not their visible spirits
Send quickly down to tame these vile offences,
It will come,
Humanity must perforce prey on itself,
Like monsters of the deep.

Goneril   Milk-livered man,   50
That bear'st a cheek for blows, a head for wrongs;
Who hast not in thy brows an eye discerning
Thine honour from thy suffering; that not know'st
Fools do those villains pity who are punished
Ere they have done their mischief. Where's thy drum? 55

28.   *My fool:* She refers to her husband Albany.

29.   *worth...whistle:* Goneril parodies the proverb "'Tis a poor dog that is not worth the whistle."

33.   *bordered certain:* predictable.

34.   *sliver and disbranch:* cut off.

37.   *text:* subject.

42.   *head-lugged bear:* bear with its head torn by hunting dogs.

43.   *madded:* driven mad.

45.   *him:* Lear.

48.   *It:* chaos.

52.   *discerning:* able to distinguish.

55.   *Where's thy drum?:* Why aren't you raising an army?

France spreads his banners in our noiseless land,
With plumed helm thy state begins to threat,
Whilst thou, a moral fool, sits still and cries
'Alack, why does he so?'

Albany   See thyself, devil:,
Proper deformity seems not in the fiend   60
So horrid as in woman.

Goneril   O vain fool!

Albany Thou changed and self-covered thing, for shame
Bemonster not thy feature. Were't my fitness
To let these hands obey my blood,
They are apt enough to dislocate and tear   65
Thy flesh and bones. Howe'er thou art a fiend,
A woman's shape doth shield thee.

Goneril Marry, your manhood—mew!

[Enter a Messenger]

Albany What news?

Messenger O, my good lord, the Duke of Cornwall's dead, 70
Slain by his servant, going to put out
The other eye of Gloucester.

Albany   Gloucester's eyes?

Messenger A servant that he bred, thrilled with remorse,
Opposed against the act, bending his sword
To his great master; who, thereat enraged,   75
Flew on him, and amongst them felled him dead;
But not without that harmful stroke which since
Hath plucked him after.

Albany   This shows you are above,
You justicers, that these our nether crimes
So speedily can venge. But, O poor Gloucester,   80
Lost he his other eye?

Messenger   Both, both, my lord.
This letter, madam, craves a speedy answer.
'Tis from your sister.

56.   *noiseless*: not on military alert.

62.   *self-covered*: keeping your true nature hidden.

64.   *blood*: anger.

66.   *Howe'er*: although.

68.   *Marry...mew!*: Goneril makes fun of Albany's manhood or virility; mew is a term from falconry meaning to keep under restraint; often interpreted here as a derisive sound or catcall as well.

73.   *thrilled*: excited by.

76.   *felled him dead*: killed the servant.

79.   *nether crimes*: crimes done on earth, beneath the realm of the gods.

Goneril   *[aside]* One way I like this well;
But being widow, and my Gloucester with her,
May all the building in my fancy pluck   85
Upon my hateful life. Another way
The news is not so tart.—I'll read, and answer.

[Exit]

Albany Where was his son when they did take his eyes?

Messenger Come with my lady hither.

Albany   He is not here.

Messenger No, my good lord; I met him back again.   90

Albany Knows he the wickedness?

Messenger Ay, my good lord. 'Twas he informed
     against him,
And quit the house on purpose, that their punishment
Might have the freer course.

Albany   Gloucester, I live
To thank thee for the love thou showed'st the King,   95
And to revenge thine eyes. Come hither, friend.
Tell me what more thou know'st. *[Exeunt]*

85-86. *May all. . . life:* may make my life hateful by destroying my plans.

87. *tart:* unpleasant.

COMMENTARY

As Scene 2 opens, a new twist in the plot presents itself. Previously, Goneril has spoken with something less than affection to her husband Albany. Now she issues outright derision. Again talking in an unusually familiar fashion with her steward Oswald, Goneril remarks on the "cowish" nature of her husband (12). She feels obliged to become the man of the house, so to speak. Obviously, there is no love lost in this marital relationship—at least not on Goneril's part.

Goneril's infidelity

Goneril also is clearly not above disloyalty and unfaithfulness. Her father Lear is not the only one to be fleeced by Goneril; Albany stands to become a classic cuckold. Goneril's hints to Edmund—"Ere long you are like to hear / (If you dare venture in your own behalf) / A mistress's command"—are thinly veiled at best (19–21). Plainly, she intends a romantic interlude, and

she presents Edmund with a love token in earnest of that affair.

Her thoughts still anticipating future involvement with Edmund, Goneril comments to her entering husband about the cold reception she receives. His response is to tell her, "You are not worth the dust which the rude wind / Blows in your face" (30–31). This is the first evidence in the play of Albany standing up to his wife, and we learn that he does so out of disgust at the treatment of Lear.

Quickly brought down to earth by Albany's cutting slight, Goneril ridicules her husband, calling his words foolish and his personality "[m]ilk-livered" (50). Despite the fact that Albany is showing his spine for the first time, Goneril refuses to credit him with any strength of character. But we can imagine that if Goneril's treatment of the king causes Albany to have to restrain himself lest he "dislocate and tear / [her] flesh and bones," his response would be no less furious if he knew of his wife's plans for Edmund (65–66).

Albany's dilemma

Note the position in which Albany finds himself at this point. He knows that Cornwall is dead; consequently, the enmity between these two noblemen, hinted at and rumoured already in the play, now shifts to a conflict between Albany and the merry widow Regan. The entrance of French troops into the realm adds yet another twist, and while Albany has not entered into any treasonous alliance with the French, it is clear that his allegiance rests with the mistreated Lear.

Additionally, Albany now mistrusts his wife and is fast discovering how unstable his domestic life has become. This series of events, coupled with Albany's realization that a human being can harbour much that is unpleasant, plays into the theme of nature threaded through the play. Albany compares Goneril and her sister with beastly creatures. The women are "[t]igers," and in their actions Albany sees humanity preying upon itself "[l]ike monsters of the deep" (40, 50).

Act IV, Scene 3

Kent and a Gentleman discuss Cordelia's emotional state and remark upon the anticipated reunion of Cordelia and Lear.

ACT IV, SCENE 3
The French camp near Dover.

[Enter KENT and a Gentleman]

Kent Why the King of France is so suddenly gone
back know you no reason?

Gentleman Something he left imperfect in the state,
which since his coming forth is thought of, which
imports to the kingdom so much fear and danger   5
that his personal return was most required and
necessary.

Kent Who hath he left behind him general?

Gentleman The Marshal of France, Monsieur La Far.

Kent Did your letters pierce the Queen to any   10
demonstration of grief?

Gentleman Ay, sir. She took them, read them in
my presence,
And now and then an ample tear trilled down
Her delicate cheek. It seemed she was a queen
Over her passion, who, most rebel-like,   15
Sought to be king o'er her.

Kent   O, then it moved her?

Gentleman Not to a rage. Patience and sorrow strove
Who should express her goodliest. You have seen
Sunshine and rain at once—her smiles and tears
Were like a better way: those happy smilets   20
That played on her ripe lip seem not to know
What guests were in her eyes, which parted thence
As pearls from diamonds dropped. In brief,
Sorrow would be a rarity most beloved,
If all could so become it.

NOTES

3. *imperfect:* undone.

13. *trilled:* trickled.

18. *goodliest:* most fittingly.

20. *smilets:* little smiles.

25. *If...it:* If everyone looked as beautiful in sadness.

Kent   Made she no verbal question?   25

Gentleman Faith, once or twice she heaved the
    name of father
Pantingly forth, as if it pressed her heart;
Cried 'Sisters; sisters, shame of ladies, sisters!
Kent, father, sisters? What, i' th' storm i' th' night?
Let pity not be believed!' There she shook   30
The holy water from her heavenly eyes,
And clamour moistened; then away she started
To deal with grief alone.

Kent   It is the stars,
The stars above us govern our conditions;
Else one self mate and make could not beget
Such different issues. You spoke not with her since?

Gentleman No.

Kent Was this before the King returned?

Gentleman   No, since.

Kent Well, sir, the poor distressed Lear's i' th' town;
Who sometime, in his better tune, remembers   40
What we are come about, and by no means
Will yield to see his daughter.

Gentleman   Why, good sir?

Kent A sovereign shame so elbows him; his own
    unkindness,
That stripped her from his benediction, turned her
To foreign casualties, gave her dear rights   45
To his dog-hearted daughters—these things sting
His mind so venomously that burning shame
Detains him from Cordelia.

Gentleman   Alack, poor Gentleman.

Kent Of Albany's and Cornwall's powers you heard not?

Gentleman 'Tis so; they are afoot.   50

Kent Well, sir, I'll bring you to our master Lear
And leave you to attend him. Some dear cause
Will in concealment wrap me up awhile.

32. *clamour moistened:* eased her pain with tears.

35. *one self . . . make:* one couple.

40. *better tune:* more rational state.

43. *sovereign:* overpowering.

    elbows him: reminds him of the past.

52. *dear cause:* important reason.

When I am known aright, you shall not grieve
Lending me this acquaintance. I pray you go   55
Along with me. *[Exeunt]*

COMMENTARY

A meeting between Kent and a gentleman at the French camp near Dover prepares the audience for what will transpire shortly between Lear and Cordelia. Although we learned earlier that Kent has been in contact with Lear's youngest daughter, her presence in the kingdom now becomes clearer.

Cordelia has come, with her husband the King of France, at the head of the French invading army. For reasons of security to his own state, the French king has returned to France, leaving Cordelia behind with the marshal and troops. Imminent danger to Cordelia is not directly addressed, but the fact that she is here without her husband-king can be thought to foreshadow some disaster. Note also that as the French are camped near Dover, the troops—and Lear—are situated in close proximity to the location where Gloucester has asked Poor Tom to lead him.

The gentleman's moving description of Cordelia's grief serves to further the contrast between this abandoned yet loyal daughter and the vixens who are her sisters. With every right in the world to turn her back on the father who has done the same to her, Cordelia yet stands steadfast in her "ill-spoken" love and decries the actions of Goneril and Regan. Yet Cordelia's grief is not immediately to be alleviated or her loyalty rewarded because Lear, encompassed by a "sovereign shame [that] so elbows him," will not go to see Cordelia (43). Lear, ridden with guilt, remains a mad roamer on the heath, and what little kingdom he has there among the weeds and rushes, he intends to retain. Consequently, Kent must not only effect the reunion of Lear and Cordelia but also monitor the proceedings of the civil and international unrest.

Act IV, Scene 4

Cordelia describes the mad condition of her father and indicates preparedness for forthcoming military conflict with Britain.

ACT IV, SCENE 4
The same.

[Enter, with Drum and Colours, CORDELIA, Doctor, and Soldiers]

Cordelia Alack, 'tis he! Why, he was met even now
As mad as the vexed sea, singing aloud,
Crowned with rank fumiter and furrow weeds,
With hardocks, hemlock, nettles, cuckoo flow'rs,
Darnel, and all the idle weeds that grow   5
In our sustaining corn. A century send forth!
Search every acre in the high-grown field
And bring him to our eye. *[Exit an Officer]*
                              What can man's wisdom
In the restoring his bereaved sense?
He that helps him take all my outward worth.   10

Doctor There is means, madam.
Our foster nurse of nature is repose,
The which he lacks. That to provoke in him
Are many simples operative, whose power
Will close the eye of anguish.

Cordelia   All blest secrets,   15
All you unpublished virtues of the earth,
Spring with my tears; be aidant and remediate
In the good man's distress. Seek, seek for him,
Lest his ungoverned rage dissolve the life
That wants the means to lead it.

[Enter Messenger]

Messenger   News, madam.   20
The British pow'rs are marching hitherward.

Cordelia 'Tis known before. Our preparation stands

NOTES

s.d.   *Drum...Colours:* generally a drummer and a soldier carrying a flag.

3–5.   *fumiter...Darnel:* English weeds, wildflowers, and grasses.

6.   *century:* a group of 100 soldiers.

14.   *simples operative:* helpful medicinal herbs.

16.   *unpublished virtues:* unknown healing powers.

20.   *wants...it:* lacks the reason to guide it.

22.   *our preparation:* the troops we have ready.

In expectation of them. O dear father,
It is thy business that I go about.
Therefore great France   25
My mourning, and importuned tears hath pitied.
No blown ambition doth our arms incite,
But love, dear love, and our aged father's right.
Soon may I hear and see him! *[Exeunt]*

27.   *blown:* puffed up.

COMMENTARY

In his madness, Lear has indeed concocted a little kingdom for himself in the fields near Dover. Cordelia has received a report that Lear was spied close to the French encampment wearing a crown fashioned from "all the idle weeds that grow / In our sustaining corn" (5–6). This news about her bemused and bedraggled father is almost more than a loving daughter can bear, and Cordelia pledges any price to see her father improved.

Note also the additional demands placed on Cordelia in the absence of her sovereign husband. News is brought that "[t]he British pow'rs are marching hitherward," and Cordelia has already attended to preparing for an inevitable battle (21). In this pre-Christian setting, it is remarkable that the seemingly overwhelming duties Cordelia must fulfill seem suspiciously similar to those placed before Jesus. Because *King Lear* was performed for a Christian audience, such comparisons would be easily perceived by Elizabethan playgoers. For example, when referring to her father, Cordelia says, "It is thy business that I go about" (24). Her words bring to mind the biblical phrase "I go about my Father's business."

Act IV, Scene 5

Oswald remains a loyal steward to Goneril yet willingly accepts Regan's commission to murder Gloucester.

ACT IV, SCENE 5
Gloucester's castle.

[Enter REGAN and OSWALD]

Regan But are my brother's pow'rs set forth?

Oswald   Ay, madam.

Regan Himself in person there?

Oswald   Madam, with much ado.
  Your sister is the better soldier.

Regan Lord Edmund spoke not with your lord at home?

Oswald No, madam.   5

Regan What might import my sister's letter to him?

Oswald I know not, lady.

Regan Faith, he is posted hence on serious matter.
  It was great ignorance, Gloucester's eyes being out,
  To let him live. Where he arrives he moves   10
  All hearts against us. Edmund, I think, is gone,
  In pity of his misery, to dispatch
  His nighted life; moreover, to descry
  The strength o' th' enemy.

Oswald I must needs after him, madam, with my letter.   15

Regan Our troops set forth to-morrow. Stay with us.
  The ways are dangerous.

Oswald   I may not, madam.
  My lady charged my duty in this business.

Regan Why should she write to Edmund? Might not you

NOTES

2.   *with much ado:* after much persuasion.

8.   *posted:* gone.

13.   *nighted:* blinded.

       descry: discover.

Transport her purposes by word? Belike,   20
Some things—I know not what. I'll love thee much,
Let me unseal the letter.

Oswald   Madam, I had rather—

Regan I know your lady does not love her husband,
I am sure of that; and at her late being here
She gave strange eliads and most speaking looks   25
To noble Edmund. I know you are of her bosom.

Oswald I, madam?

Regan I speak in understanding—y'are, I know't—
Therefore I do advise you take this note:
My lord is dead; Edmund and I have talked,   30
And more convenient is he for my hand
Than for your lady's. You may gather more.
If you do find him, pray you give him this;
And when your mistress hears thus much from you,
I pray desire her call her wisdom to her.   35
So fare you well.
If you do chance to hear of that blind traitor,
Preferment falls on him that cuts him off.

Oswald Would I could meet him, madam! I should show
What party I do follow.   40

Regan Fare thee well. *[Exeunt]*

20.	*Belike:* perhaps.
21.	*love thee much:* make it worth your while.
25.	*strange eliads:* amorous glances.
26.	*of her bosom:* aware of her secret thoughts.
29.	*take this note:* note well.
31.	*convenient:* appropriate.
38.	*Preferment. . . off:* The person who kills Gloucester will be rewarded.

COMMENTARY

Immediately following a scene in which Cordelia's continued devotion to her father is a focal point, this scene presents another twist on the wheel of fate—this time, not nearly as optimistic. Three main functions are served here: the establishment of Oswald's loyalty to Goneril, the recognition by Regan that she has erred in allowing Gloucester to live, and the romantic entanglement of Gloucester's bastard son with Lear's opportunistic daughters. Of these three functions, the most important is the developing triangle now forming among Goneril, Regan, and Edmund.

Regan, in an incredibly familiar conversation with Goneril's servant Oswald, reveals her designs upon Edmund. "Edmund and I have talked," says Regan, "And more convenient is he for my hand / Than for your lady's. You may gather more" (30–32). Regan grows increasingly suspicious of Goneril as a potential rival for Edmund's affections, and she is chagrined when Oswald declines to let her read Goneril's letter to Edmund.

Oswald, in his refusal to be tempted into betraying his mistress, exhibits a loyalty that parallels that of Kent to Lear. Though Kent and Oswald are vastly different men, each nevertheless shares a bond with his master that cannot be compromised. Unfortunately, the minions of evil are often as adept and devoted as the ministers of good.

Finally, Regan's disposition reveals further evidence of darkness. She recognizes her poor judgment in allowing Gloucester to live, thus adding to that element of error already traced throughout the play. She indicates her belief that Edmund has gone in search of his father in order to kill him. Regan fears Gloucester's influence on those he meets: "Where he arrives," she says, "he moves / All hearts against us" (10–11).

Anxious to rectify her mistake, Regan commissions Oswald to remain on the lookout for the blinded earl, promising that "[p]referment falls on him that cuts him off" (38). Though Oswald refuses to betray his mistress Goneril, he is quite willing to perform evil service for Regan. In this way Oswald can be beloved of both women, a position in which Edmund is also situated.

Act IV, Scene 6

Edgar leads Gloucester to the Dover "cliffs," from which Gloucester "falls." We observe another identity change for Edgar as he and Gloucester encounter the mad Lear. Edgar kills Oswald and obtains a letter that reveals Goneril's planned adultery with Edmund.

ACT IV, SCENE 6
The country near Dover.

[Enter GLOUCESTER and EDGAR]

Gloucester When shall I come to th' top of that same hill?

Edgar You do climb up it now. Look how we labour.

Gloucester Methinks the ground is even.

Edgar   Horrible steep.
   Hark, do you hear the sea?

Gloucester   No, truly.

Edgar Why, then, your other senses grow imperfect   5
   By your eyes' anguish.

Gloucester   So may it be indeed.
   Methinks thy voice is altered, and thou speak'st
   In better phrase and matter than thou didst.

Edgar Y'are much deceived. In nothing am I changed
   But in my garments.

Gloucester   Methinks y'are better spoken.   10

Edgar Come on, Sir; here's the place. Stand still.
      How fearful
   And dizzy 'tis to cast one's eyes so low!
   The crows and choughs that wing the midway air
   Show scarce so gross as beetles. Halfway down
   Hangs one that gathers sampire—dreadful trade;   15
   Methinks he seems no bigger than his head.
   The fishermen that walk upon the beach
   Appear like mice; and yond tall anchoring bark,
   Diminished to her cock; her cock, a buoy
   Almost too small for sight. The murmuring surge   20

NOTES

13.   *choughs:* jackdaw birds.

14.   *gross:* large.

15.   *sampire:* a strongly scented plant growing on the Dover cliffs.

18.   *bark:* ship.

19.   *Diminished...cock:* as small as the landing boat.

That on th' unnumb'red idle pebble chafes
Cannot be heard so high. I'll look no more,
Lest my brain turn, and the deficient sight
Topple down headlong.

Gloucester   Set me where you stand.

Edgar Give me your hand. You are now within a foot   25
Of th' extreme verge. For all beneath the moon
Would I not leap upright.

Gloucester   Let go my hand.
Here friend, 's another purse; in it a jewel
Well worth a poor man's taking. Fairies and gods
Prosper it with thee. Go thou further off;   30
Bid me farewell, and let me hear thee going.

Edgar Now fare ye well, good sir.

Gloucester   With all my heart.

Edgar *[aside]* Why I do trifle thus with his despair
Is done to cure it.

Gloucester   O you mighty gods!
[He kneels]
This world I do renounce, and in your sights   35
Shake patiently my great affliction off.
If I could bear it longer and not fall
To quarrel with your great opposeless wills,
My snuff and loathed part of nature should
Burn itself out. If Edgar live, O bless him!   40
Now, fellow, fare thee well.

[He falls forward and swoons]

Edgar   Gone, sir—farewell.
And yet I know not how conceit may rob
The treasury of life when life itself
Yields to the theft. Had he been where he thought,
By this had thought been past. Alive or dead?   45
Ho you, sir! Friend! Hear you, sir? Speak!
Thus might he pass indeed. Yet he revives.
What are you, sir?

Gloucester   Away, and let me die.

Gloucester believes he is on the cliffs of Dover.

39.   *snuff:* Gloucester compares his life to a burnt-out candle.

42-43.   *conceit...of life:* imagination may kill him.

46.   *Ho you, sir!:* Edgar pretends they are at the bottom of the cliff.

Edgar Hadst thou been aught but gossamer, feathers, air,
So many fathom down precipitating,   50
Thou'dst shivered like an egg; but thou dost breathe,
Hast heavy substance, bleed'st not, speak'st, art sound.
Ten masts at each make not the altitude
Which thou hast perpendicularly fell.
Thy life 's a miracle. Speak yet again.   55

Gloucester But have I fall'n, or no?

Edgar From the dread summit of this chalky bourn.
Look up a-height. The shrill-gorged lark so far
Cannot be seen or heard. Do but look up.

Gloucester Alack, I have no eyes.   60
Is wretchedness deprived that benefit
To end itself by death? 'Twas yet some comfort
When misery could beguile the tyrant's rage
And frustrate his proud will.

Edgar   Give me your arm.
Up—so. How is't? Feel you your legs? you stand.   65

Gloucester Too well, too well.

Edgar   This is above all strangeness.
Upon the crown o' th' cliff what thing was that
Which parted from you?

Gloucester   A poor unfortunate beggar.

Edgar As I stood here below, methought his eyes
were two full moons; he had a thousand noses,   70
Horns whelked and waved like the enridged sea.
It was some fiend. Therefore, thou happy father,
Think that the clearest gods, who make them honours
Of men's impossibilities, have preserved thee.

Gloucester I do remember now. Henceforth I'll bear   75
Affliction till it do cry out itself
'Enough, enough, and die.' That thing you speak of,
I took it for a man. Often 'twould say
'The fiend, the fiend'—he led me to that place.

---

50. *precipitating:* falling.

53. *Ten...each:* ten ships' masts, one on top of the other.

57. *bourn:* boundary.

58. *gorged:* throated.

71. *whelked:* twisted into spirals.

73–74. *who...impossibilities:* who promote honour for themselves by performing miracles impossible for humans.

Edgar Bear free and patient thoughts.   80
[Enter LEAR mad, fantastically dressed with flowers]
                              But who comes here?
The safer sense will ne'er accommodate
His master thus.

Lear No, they cannot touch me for coining;
I am the King himself.

Edgar O thou side-piercing sight!   85

Lear Nature's above art in that respect. There's
your press money. That fellow handles his bow like
a crow-keeper. Draw me a clothier's yard. Look, look,
a mouse! Peace, peace; this piece of toasted cheese
will do't. There's my gauntlet; I'll prove it on a   90
giant. Bring up the brown bills.
O, well flown, bird. I' th' clout, i' th' clout—hewgh!
Give the word.

Edgar Sweet marjoram.

Lear Pass.   95

Gloucester I know that voice.

Lear Ha! Goneril with a white beard? They flattered me like a dog, and told me I had the white
hairs in my beard ere the black ones were there.
To say 'ay' and 'no' to everything that I said! 'Ay'   100
and 'no' was no good divinity. When the rain came
to wet me once, and the wind to make me chat-
ter; when the thunder would not peace at my bid-
ding; there I found 'em, there I smelt 'em out.
Go to, they are not men o' their words. They told me I   105
was everything. 'Tis a lie—I am not ague-proof.

Gloucester The trick of that voice I do well remember.
Is't not the King?

Lear   Ay, every inch a king.
When I do stare, see how the subject quakes.
I pardon that man's life. What was thy cause?   110
Adultery?
Thou shalt not die. Die for adultery? No.

81–82. *The safer...thus:* A man in his right mind would never dress this way.

83. *touch...coining:* arrest me for counterfeiting the king's image on a coin.

87. *press money:* money given to hired soldiers.

88. *clothier's yard:* Archers draw their arrows back one yard to reach the ear.

91. *brown bills:* foot soldiers.

92. *bird:* arrow.

clout: target made of canvas.

hewgh: imitates whizzing sound of arrow in flight.

93. *word:* password.

94. *Sweet marjoram:* herb associated with treatment of madness; here offered as the password.

101. *no...divinity:* false doctrine; James 5:12 says "let your yea be yea; and your nay, nay."

106. *ague-proof:* safe from chills and fever; in a larger sense, Lear is as susceptible to the worries of the common man as anyone.

107. *trick:* peculiar tone.

The wren goes to't, and the small gilded fly
Does lecher in my sight.
Let copulation thrive; for Gloucester's bastard son   115
Was kinder to his father than my daughters
Got 'tween the lawful sheets.
To't, luxury, pell-mell, for I lack soldiers.
Behold yond simp'ring dame,
Whose face between her forks presages snow,   120
That minces virtue, and does shake the head
To hear of pleasure's name.
The fitchew nor the soiled horse goes to't
With a more riotous appetite.
Down from the waist they are Centaurs,   125
Though women all above.
But to the girdle do the gods inherit,
Beneath is all the fiend's.
There's hell, there's darkness, there is the sulphur-
ous pit; burning, scalding, stench, consumption. Fie,   130
fie, fie! pah, pah! Give me an ounce of civet; good
apothecary, sweeten my imagination! There's money
for thee.

Gloucester O, let me kiss that hand.

Lear Let me wipe it first; it smells of mortality.   135

Gloucester O ruined piece of nature; this great world
  Shall so wear out to naught. Dost thou know me?

Lear I remember thine eyes well enough. Dost thou
  squiny at me? No, do thy worst, blind Cupid; I'll
        not love.
  Read thou this challenge; mark but the penning of it.   140

Gloucester Were all thy letters suns, I could not see.

Edgar *[aside]* I would not take this from report—it is,
  And my heart breaks at it.

Lear Read.

Gloucester What, with the case of eyes?   145

---

114. *lecher:* lust.

120. *forks:* legs.

  presages snow: suggests frigidity.

121. *minces:* walks with a light, prance-like step.

123. *fitchew:* a polecat.

125. *Centaurs:* mythological half-man, half-stallion creatures.

127. *girdle:* waist.

129. *hell:* traditional slang for female genitals.

131. *civet:* perfume.

139. *squiny:* look sideways, somewhat like a prostitute does.

  blind Cupid: a typical sign hung over the entrance to a whorehouse.

145. *case:* empty sockets.

Lear O, ho, are you there with me? No eyes in your
head, nor no money in your purse? Your eyes are in
a heavy case, your purse in a light; yet you see how
this world goes.

Gloucester I see it feelingly.   150

Lear What, art mad? A man may see how this world
goes with no eyes. Look with thine ears. See how yond
justice rails upon yond simple thief. Hark in thine
ear. Change places and, handy-dandy, which is the
justice, which is the thief? Thou hast seen a farmer's   155
dog bark at a beggar?

Gloucester Ay, sir.

Lear And the creature run from the cur. There
thou mightst behold the great image of authority—
a dog's obeyed in office.   160
Thou rascal beadle, hold thy bloody hand!
Why dost thou lash that whore? Strip thy own back.
Thou hotly lusts to use her in that kind
For which thou whip'st her. The usurer hangs the cozener.
Through tattered clothes small vices do appear;   165
Robes and furred gowns hide all. Plate sin with gold,
And the strong lance of justice hurtless breaks;
Arm it in rags, a pygmy's straw does pierce it.
None does offend, none—I say none! I'll able 'em.
Take that of me, my friend, who have the power   170
To seal th' accuser's lips. Get thee glass eyes
And, like a scurvy politician, seem
To see the things thou dost not. Now, now, now, now!
Pull off my boots. Harder, harder! So.

Edgar O, matter and impertinency mixed;   175
Reason in madness.

Lear If thou wilt weep my fortunes, take my eyes.
I know thee well enough; thy name is Gloucester.
Thou must be patient. We came crying hither;
Thou know'st, the first time that we smell the air   180
We wawl and cry. I will preach to thee. Mark.

---

146. *with me:* in my situation.

148. *case:* situation.

154. *handy-dandy:* a nursery game: Handy-dandy, sugar candy, which hand will you have?

160. *in office:* in a position of authority.

161. *beadle:* a church official.

164. *cozener:* one who cheats or deceives.

172. *scurvy politician:* vile opportunist.

175. *matter and impertinency:* sense and nonsense.

181. *wawl:* wail.

Gloucester Alack, alack the day.

Lear When we are born, we cry that we are come
To this great stage of fools.—This' a good block.
It were a delicate stratagem to shoe   185
A troop of horse with felt. I'll put't in proof,
And when I have stol'n upon these son-in-laws,
Then kill, kill, kill, kill, kill!

[Enter a Gentleman with Attendants]

Gentleman O, here he is! Lay hand upon him. Sir,
Your most dear daughter—   190

Lear No rescue? What, a prisoner? I am even
The natural fool of fortune. Use me well;
You shall have ransom. Let me have surgeons;
I am cut to th' brains.

Gentleman   You shall have anything.

Lear No seconds? All myself?   195
Why, this would make a man a man of salt,
To use his eyes for garden waterpots,
Ay, and laying autumn's dust. I will die bravely,
Like a smug bridegroom. What, I will be jovial!
Come, come, I am a king; masters, know you that?   200

Gentleman You are a royal one, and we obey you.

Lear Then there's life in't. Come, an you get it,
you shall get it by running. Sa, sa, sa, sa!

[Exit running, followed by Attendants]

Gentleman A sight most pitiful in the meanest wretch,
Past speaking of in a king. Thou hast one daughter   205
Who redeems nature from the general curse
Which twain have brought her to.

Edgar Hail, gentle sir.

Gentleman   Sir, speed you. What's your will?

Edgar Do you hear aught, sir, of a battle toward?

Gentleman Most sure and vulgar. Every one hears that   210
Which can distinguish sound.

186. *in proof:* to the test.

195. *No seconds?:* no one to help me.

199. *Like...bridegroom:* alludes to 1603 execution of Lord Grey of Wilton, who went to his death with the cheer of a young bridegroom.

202. *there's life in't:* All is not lost.

203. *Sa...sa:* cry sometimes used with sudden action or for hunting with hounds.

207. *twain:* Regan and Goneril.

210. *vulgar:* well-known to everyone.

Edgar   But, by your favour,
How near's the other army?

Gentleman Near and on speedy foot. The main descry   213.   *main descry:* the sight of the main body.
Stands on the hourly thought.

Edgar   I thank you, sir. That's all.

Gentleman Though that the Queen on special cause   215
is here,
Her army is moved on.

Edgar   I thank you, sir. *[Exit Gentleman]*

Gloucester You ever-gentle gods, take my breath from me;
Let not my worser spirit tempt me again
To die before you please.

Edgar   Well pray you, father.

Gloucester Now, good sir, what are you?   220

Edgar A most poor man, made tame to fortune's blows,
Who, by the art of known and feeling sorrows,
Am pregnant to good pity. Give me your hand;   223.   *pregnant:* able to conceive.
I'll lead you to some biding.   224.   *biding:* place where you can stay.

Gloucester   Hearty thanks.
The bounty and the benison of heaven   225
To boot, and boot.   226.   *To boot:* in addition.

[Enter OSWALD]   *and boot:* and may it help you.

Oswald   A proclaimed prize! Most happy;
That eyeless head of thine was first framed flesh
To raise my fortunes. Thou old unhappy traitor,
Briefly thyself remember. The sword is out
That must destroy thee.

Gloucester   Now let thy friendly hand   230
Put strength enough to't. *[EDGAR interposes]*

Oswald   Wherefore, bold peasant,
Dar'st thou support a published traitor? Hence,
Lest that th' infection of his fortune take
Like hold on thee. Let go his arm.

Edgar Chill not let go, zir, without vurther 'casion.   235

Oswald Let go, slave, or thou diest.

Edgar Good gentleman, go your gait, and let poor
voke pass. An chud ha' bin zwaggered out of my life,
'twould not ha' bin zo long as 'tis by a vortnight.
Nay, come not near th' old man. Keep out, che vore   240
ye, or Ise try whether your costard or my ballow be
the harder. Chill be plain with you.

Oswald Out, dunghill! *[They fight]*

Edgar Chill pick your teeth, zir. Come. No matter
vor your foins. *[OSWALD falls]*   245

Oswald Slave, thou hast slain me. Villain, take my purse.
If ever thou wilt thrive, bury my body,
And give the letters which thou find'st about me
To Edmund Earl of Gloucester. Seek him out
Upon the English party. O, untimely death!   250
Death! *[He dies]*

Edgar I know thee well. A serviceable villain,
As duteous to the vices of thy mistress
As badness would desire.

Gloucester   What, is he dead?

Edgar Sit you down, father; rest you.   255
Let's see these pockets; the letters that he speaks of
May be my friends. He's dead; I am only sorry
He had no other deathsman. Let us see.
Leave, gentle wax; and, manners, blame us not
To know our enemies' minds. We rip their hearts;   260
Their papers is more lawful. *[Reads the letter]*
'Let our reciprocal vows be remembered. You have
many opportunities to cut him off. If your will want
not, time and place will be fruitfully offered. There
is nothing done, if he return the conqueror. Then   265
am I the prisoner, and his bed my gaol; from the
loathed warmth wherof deliver me, and supply the
place for your labour.
'Your (wife, so I would say) affectionate servant,
'GONERIL.'   270

---

235.   *Chill... 'casion:* peasant dialect of Somerset, England:
I'll not let go without further reason.

237.   *go your gait:* go on your way.

238.   *voke:* folk.

          chud: if I could.

240–241.   *che vore ye:* I warn you.

241.   *costard:* head.

          ballow: club.

244.   *pick:* knock out.

245.   *foins:* thrusts.

258.   *deathsman:* executioner.

259.   *wax:* used to seal the letter.

263.   *him:* Albany.

O indistinguished space of woman's will—
A plot upon her virtuous husband's life,
And the exchange my brother! Here in the sands
Thee I'll rake up, the post unsanctified
Of murderous lechers; and in the mature time   275
With this ungracious paper strike the sight
Of the death-practiced Duke. For him 'tis well
That of thy death and business I can tell.

Gloucester The King is mad. How stiff is my vile sense,
That I stand up, and have ingenious feeling   280
Of my huge sorrows! Better I were distract;
So should my thoughts be severed from my griefs,
And woes by wrong imaginations lose
The knowledge of themselves. *[Drum afar off]*

Edgar   Give me your hand.
Far off methinks I hear the beaten drum.   285
Come, father, I'll bestow you with a friend.

[Exeunt]

274.   *rake up:* hide in the dirt.
       post: message.

277.   *death-practiced:* whose death has been plotted.

281.   *distract:* mad.

COMMENTARY

On the cliffs of Dover, Edgar appears in yet another role. He pretends to be a peasant, leading Gloucester on his journey to the cliffs. Even Gloucester notices the change from Edgar's earlier role, for he thinks that this man's speech is altogether better phrased than it was when they first met. Despite Edgar's comments to the contrary, an air of change is apparent, and that atmosphere foreshadows the changes soon to be seen in Gloucester and Lear.

The lesson of the cliff

The blinded Gloucester and his disguised son present vivid pictures of human suffering in this scene. Now dubbed a traitor and stripped of status, sight, and sons, Gloucester wants only to throw himself over the cliffs and drown in the sea. Edgar, too, has been in misery. Just as Lear has entered into the madness of lost identity, so has Edgar nearly lost himself in the role of Bedlam beggar. Falling from the upper echelons of society to the lowest, Edgar has engaged in a journey that stripped him of all life's acoutrements: his name, his reputation, his position, his family ties, his apparel, and (seemingly) his sanity.

Yet Edgar's determination to help his father teaches a vital lesson. It reminds us that humanity, when it operates with morality and a sense of values, is a great community in which individuals succeed by taking responsibility for one another's well-being. The good of the many is served through ensuring the good of the few and the one. Here on the Dover fields with his blinded father, Edgar is just one step away from hitting rock bottom. He holds on to the small advantage of that one step only so he can pull his father from the threatening abyss of suicidal depression.

In the midst of so much tragedy, the interaction between Gloucester and Edgar takes on a comical feel at times. Jan Kott explains that the comedy is effected through proper staging of the scene: "Edgar is supporting Gloucester; he lifts his feet high pretending to walk uphill. Gloucester, too, lifts his feet, as if expecting the ground to rise, but underneath his feet there is only air. The entire scene is written for a very definite type of theatre, namely pantomime. This pantomime only makes sense if enacted on a flat and level stage." Performances of *King Lear* staged with something resembling real cliffs or heights do a great injustice to Shakespeare's dramatic impetus here, for Gloucester's fall is meant to be comical, and anything tending toward realism destroys the intended effect.

A "somersault on an empty stage"

In lines 34–40, as Gloucester prepares to dive from the rocks, he once again calls upon the "mighty gods" who have ever held his attention. As Kott points out, his speech here tells us that "Gloucester's suicide has a meaning only if the gods exist. It is a protest against undeserved suffering and the world's injustice. But if the gods, and their moral order in the world, do not exist, Gloucester's suicide does not solve or alter anything. It is only a somersault on an empty stage." Of course, Gloucester's suicide attempt turns out to be just that— a "somersault on an empty stage." As a result, his high-sounding protest comes to "nothing," reiterating the emphasis upon nothingness that threads throughout the play.

Edgar is not yet finished with role-playing; he dons yet another personality after Gloucester's supposed fall. Now Edgar claims to be a passing countryman who witnessed Gloucester's plunge from the cliffs. Note how Edgar is in some respects similar to Edmund at this point. Edmund has repeatedly taken advantage of his father's gullibility; here, Edgar does the same.

Well aware of his father's tendency toward belief in the supernatural, Edgar leads Gloucester to believe it was a fiend whose "eyes were two full moons" that stood nearby as Gloucester fell (69–70). Just as Edgar plays on Gloucester's beliefs, Shakespeare played on his contemporary audiences' fascination with folk tales and legends. By placing Gloucester on a rocky cliff, the playwright was able to play upon common knowledge that boulders and mountainous areas were often thought to be the abodes of supernatural beings. Gloucester and playgoer alike are easily drawn into Edgar's tale of a cliff dweller with whelked horns and a thousand noses.

Surrendering to life

At least part of what Gloucester is doing in this scene is questioning—even challenging—the relationship between humanity and the gods. The interconnections of divinity and human life have always produced questions about the value of human life and our responsibility to maintain and nurture it. In the presence of a divinity, does humanity have jurisdiction over its own existence?

Jan Kott writes that "if there are no gods, suicide is impossible. There is only death. Suicide cannot alter human fate, but only accelerate it. . . . It is a surrender." Gloucester, having failed in his protest, begins to accept, with some forced stoicism, the dole of life: "Henceforth I'll bear / Affliction till it do cry out itself / 'Enough, enough and die'" (75–77). What Gloucester surrenders to here is not death but life, however cruel and cold it seems to be.

Lear transformed

The first major movement of this scene now complete, the stage is set for the entrance of that other mind-weary character, Lear himself. Just as Cordelia has heard, the maddened Lear is now roaming the fields "fantastically dressed with flowers." (In the film version of *Lear* starring Laurence Olivier, Lear even guts and eats an uncooked rabbit.)

Note the dramatic difference between the Lear we saw at the beginning of the play and the Lear we see now. The Lear who sat on the throne and disinherited Cordelia was a passionate monarch—regal, powerful, sure of himself, and confident in his ability to control the world around him. This new Lear, however, has been so dominated by his cruel daughters that little of the former tyrant remains visible. R. C. Bald remarks that "in no other play of Shakespeare's is the change in the principal characters during the course of the action so striking as in this."

Whereas earlier scenes showed Lear at least somewhat focused on the sources of his anger, the Lear of the flowers now rambles almost incoherently. Gloucester easily recognizes "[t]he trick of that voice" and identifies his king despite the loss of sight (107). But the voice of the king is all that Gloucester finds familiar, for the content of Lear's speeches is far from those powerful, sovereign commands Gloucester is accustomed to hearing.

Lear does not even recognize his Earl of Gloucester but rather dubs him "Goneril with a white beard" (97). The blind Gloucester and Lear converse; Lear questions Gloucester about his "cause" (110). Recall that in the first scene of the play, Gloucester bragged about having a bastard son. He boasted of the "good sport at his mak-

Laurence Olivier as Lear in a 1984 film of King Lear.
Everett Collection

ing" and the fact that Edmund's mother "grew round-wombed, and had indeed . . . a son for her cradle ere she had a husband for her bed" (I.1.23, 14–15). How ironic that in this scene Lear declares that Gloucester will not die for adultery.

In excusing an act engaged in by both the "wren . . . and the small gilded fly," Lear inadvertently twists the knife in Gloucester's heart (113). Lear cries that "Gloucester's bastard son / Was kinder to his father than my daughters / Got 'tween the lawful sheets" (115–117). Note

also how Lear's defense of adultery here parallels Edmund's defense of bastardy in Act I, Scene 2.

A thirst for revenge

Even in the extremes of his derangement, Lear express a desire for revenge. Lear denounces women, who from the waist down are all "Centaurs, / though women all above" (125–126). This venomous statement is followed by a fit of retching ("Fie, fie, fie! pah! pah!"), as though the very idea of femininity turns Lear's stomach and brings bile to his mouth (130–131). William Hazlitt writes that by this point in the play, "[T]he mind of Lear staggers between the weight of attachment and the hurried movements of passion . . . like a tall ship driven about by the winds." Indeed, most actors portray Lear in this scene as semifrantic and always in motion.

Yet for all his ravings, Lear evokes pity from Gloucester as well as from the audience. We don't agree with how Lear has treated Kent and Cordelia, and we don't find it wise that Lear gave away his kingdom. How, though, can we help but have sympathy for and empathy with this king whose passionate temperament and one-sided thinking has brought so much sadness and pain upon himself?

Note also the emphasis upon eyes, sight, and blindness in this scene. Lear remarks to Gloucester, "I remember thine eyes well enough. Dost thou / squiny at me?" (138–139). He commands Gloucester to "[r]ead thou this challenge" and makes further comments in lines 146–173 that hinge upon seeing, looking, and beholding (140). He even urges Gloucester to "[g]et thee glass eyes / And, like a scurvy politician, seem / To see the things thou dost not" (171–173). Lear doesn't admit to recognizing Gloucester until line 178.

As Lear continues in his flailings and musings, play-acting a scene in which he will "kill, kill" his sons-in-law, Cordelia's men enter (188). Even though the men are respectful to Lear and promise him comfort, Lear is so caught up in his fictions that he eludes those who would help him. Pursued by attendants, Lear leaves the stage to Edgar and Gloucester. The news they receive is both good and bad: Cordelia is indeed nearby. Her army, however, has moved on. Cordelia is left with precious few to protect her as she attempts to retrieve her father.

Goneril's letter to Edmund

The closing section of this scene brings the entry and demise of Oswald. Delighted to have found Gloucester and anticipating a fine reward for service, Oswald prepares to make short shrift of the blind earl. Edgar, of course, intervenes. He first attempts diplomacy, adopting a thick accent in his speech and urging Oswald to move along.

Edgar's nonviolence marks an important difference between his morality and that of Edmund and his followers. Violence is not in the forefront of Edgar's mind, and cruelty is not his first thought. But when his initial peaceful maneuver fails, Edgar is forced to fight, and Oswald is mortally wounded. True to the last, Oswald's last thoughts and dying remarks concern his mission. As an audience that knows the contents of Oswald's letter—"loving" remarks from Goneril to Edmund—we should sense immediately that Edgar will never deliver that letter to Edmund as Oswald has requested. Indeed, Edgar proves us right; he plans instead to deliver the letter in due time to Albany.

Edgar still does not identify himself to Gloucester, which is perplexing. Indeed, three times in the scene's closing lines he calls Gloucester "father," and once he acknowledges his brother. Yet Edgar's mission, like Oswald's, is not yet fulfilled. Armed with the letter taken from Oswald—the letter that will indict Goneril for her plans with Edmund—Edgar plans to further the cause of Lear and Gloucester "in the mature time" (275).

Act IV, Scene 7

Lear and Cordelia reunite as Lear's mind turns toward sanity again. Battle is imminent between France and Britain.

ACT IV, SCENE 7
The French camp.

[Enter CORDELIA, KENT, Doctor, and Gentleman]

Cordelia O thou good Kent, how shall I live and work
To match thy goodness? My life will be too short
And every measure fail me.

Kent To be acknowledged, madam, is o'erpaid.
All my reports go with the modest truth;   5
Nor more nor clipped, but so.

Cordelia   Be better suited.
These weeds are memories of those worser hours.
I prithee put them off.

Kent   Pardon, dear madam.
Yet to be known shortens my made intent.
My boon I make it that you know me not   10
Till time and I think meet.

Cordelia Then be't so, my good lord. *[to the Doctor]*
                          How does the King?

Doctor Madam, sleeps still.

Cordelia O you kind gods,
Cure this great breach in his abused nature!   15
Th' untuned and jarring senses, O, wind up
Of this child-changed father!

Doctor   So please your Majesty
That we may wake the King? He hath slept long.

Cordelia Be governed by your knowledge, and proceed
I th' sway of your own will. Is he arrayed?   20

[Enter LEAR in a chair carried by Servants]

NOTES

5.   *modest:* strictly accurate.

6.   *suited:* dressed.

7.   *weeds:* garments.

9.   *made intent:* plan.

10.   *boon:* favour.

16.   *wind:* tune.

17.   *child-changed:* changed by his children into a child.

Gentleman Ay, madam. In the heaviness of sleep
We put fresh garments on him.

Doctor Be by, good madam, when we do awake him.
I doubt not of his temperance.   24.   *temperence:* sanity.

Cordelia   Very well. *[Music]*

Doctor Please you draw near. Louder the music there.   25

Cordelia O my dear father, restoration hang
Thy medicine on my lips, and let this kiss
Repair those violent harms that my two sisters
Have in thy reverence made.   29.   *thy reverence:* your revered person.

Kent   Kind and dear princess.

Cordelia Had you not been their father, these white   30   30.   *white flakes:* hair and beard.
    flakes
Did challenge pity of them. Was this a face
To be opposed again the jarring winds?
To stand against the deep dread-bolted thunder?
In the most terrible and nimble stroke
Of quick cross lightning to watch, poor perdu,   35   35.   *poor perdu:* poor lost one; in military terms, a look-out in an exposed and unprotected position.
With this thin helm? Mine enemy's dog,   36.   *helm:* helmet of hair.
Though he had bit me, should have stood that night
Against my fire; and wast thou fain, poor father,   38.   *fain:* glad.
To hovel thee with swine and rogues forlorn
In short and musty straw? Alack, alack,   40
'Tis wonder that thy life and wits at once
Had not concluded all.—He wakes. Speak to him.

Doctor Madam, do you; 'tis fittest.

Cordelia How does my royal lord? How fares your
    Majesty?

Lear You do me wrong to take me out o' th' grave.   45
Thou art a soul in bliss; but I am bound
Upon a wheel of fire, that mine own tears
Do scald like molten lead.

Cordelia   Sir, do you know me?

Lear You are a spirit, I know. Where did you die?

Cordelia Still, still, far wide!   50   50.   *wide:* wide of the mark.

Doctor He's scarce awake. Let him alone awhile.

Lear Where have I been? Where am I? Fair daylight?
I am mightily abused. I should e'en die with pity
To see another thus. I know not what to say.
I will not swear these are my hands. Let's see—   55
I feel this pin prick. Would I were assured
Of my condition.

Cordelia   O look upon me, sir,
And hold your hand in benediction o'er me.
You must not kneel.

Lear   Pray, do not mock me.
I am a very foolish fond old man,   60
Fourscore and upward, not an hour more nor less;
And, to deal plainly,
I fear I am not in my perfect mind.
Methinks I should know you, and know this man;
Yet I am doubtful, for I am mainly ignorant   65
What place this is; and all the skill I have
Remembers not these garments; nor I know not
Where I did lodge last night. Do not laugh at me;
For, as I am a man, I think this lady
To be my child Cordelia.

Cordelia   And so I am! I am!   70

Lear Be your tears wet? Yes, faith. I pray weep not.
If you have poison for me, I will drink it.
I know you do not love me; for your sisters
Have, as I do remember, done me wrong.
You have some cause, they have not.

Cordelia   No cause, no cause.   75

Lear Am I in France?

Kent   In your own kingdom, sir.

Lear Do not abuse me.

Doctor Be comforted, good madam. The great rage
You see is killed in him; and yet it is danger
To make him even o'er the time he has lost.   80

61.   *Fourscore and upward:* a score being 20, Lear is over 80 years old.

78.   *rage:* frenzy.

Desire him to go in. Trouble him no more
Till further settling.

Cordelia Will't please your Highness walk?

Lear   You must bear with me.
Pray you now, forget and forgive. I am old and
    foolish.

[Exeunt all but KENT and Gentleman]

Gentleman Holds it true, sir, that the Duke of   85
Cornwall was so slain?

Kent Most certain, sir.

Gentleman Who is conductor of his people?

Kent As 'tis said, the bastard son of Gloucester.

Gentleman They say Edgar, his banished son, is   90
with the Earl of Kent in Germany.

Kent Report is changeable. 'Tis time to look
about; the powers of the kingdom approach apace.

Gentleman The arbitrement is like to be bloody.
Fare you well, sir. *[Exit]*   95

Kent My point and period will be throughly wrought,
Or well or ill, as this day's battle's fought.
    [Exit]

94.   *arbitrement:* result or conclusion.

96.   *point and period:* end of my chapter; end of my
            usefulness.

COMMENTARY

Critic A.C. Bradley remarks that throughout this play, "Lear follows an old man's whim, half generous, half selfish; and in a moment it looses all the powers of darkness upon him." Lear begins to emerge from the darkness in this scene, generally referred to as a scene of reconciliation. Lear finally obtains the sleep and rest that Kent much earlier said would ease Lear's "oppressed nature," and here Lear begins to retrieve something of his lost self.

Kent has done Cordelia a great service by restoring her father to her, and he deserves a reward commensurate with that service. Cordelia gratefully acknowledges this. Characteristically, however, Kent feels that "[t]o be acknowledged . . . is o'erpaid" (4). He refuses even the offer of new garments, certain that he can do further good by remaining disguised a little longer. While the loyal service of Oswald to Goneril has proven to be greedy, self-serving, and violent, the service of Kent to Lear and Cordelia is self-denying, modest, and honourable.

Notice here the use of music and the doctor's urging that the volume be increased. As well as helping establish the setting of harmony and calm for the audience, music is also part of Lear's therapy. From the bitter weather, harsh arguments, and deranged ravings of the past stormy times, Lear's mind is in desperate need of soothing, just as his body is in need of rest.

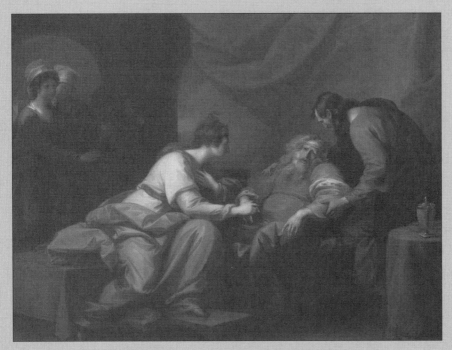

The Meeting of Lear and Cordelia, *ca. 1784, by Benjamin West.*
The Huntington Library/SuperStock

far cry from the maelstrom in body and spirit to which Lear has been subjected. Still "far wide" (not yet recovered), Lear initially mistakes Cordelia for a "soul in bliss" (50, 46). But ever so gently, Cordelia brings Lear around to an awareness not only of who she is but also of where he is. Cordelia assures Lear that he is in his own kingdom, not the subdivided land that Lear gave to Albany and Cornwall. Note also that Lear, after the simplest of Christian teachings, offers no long apologies, explanations, or wailings, but simply says to Cordelia, "Pray you now, forget and forgive, I am old and foolish" (85–86).

Cordelia in this scene clearly has much to share with her father. Her words are poetic and her thoughts sympathetic as she muses on what storms her father has suffered because of his other daughters. And how appropriate her use of "poor perdu" (lost one) in reference to Lear (35). The French phrase originates from the military. But when applied to her father, the words are doubly symbolic, for the mad and lonely Lear has been every bit as isolated as an endangered sentry.

As Lear awakens from his rest, he arrives at something like the end of purgatory. Just as Gloucester faced his moment of truth on the Dover cliffs, so now Lear faces Cordelia. Here at last is some peace and order, a

Some versions of this play text end the scene here, with the calm and peaceful reunion of Lear and Cordelia. Other versions, including ours, contain lines that place Kent in conversation with a gentleman. The two share news, comparing conflicting and changeable reports, and Kent closes the scene. His final words indicate suspense—a prophecy of Kent's destiny to be fulfilled this very day. Because the next act begins in a more hurried, military setting, this meeting of Kent and the Gentleman serves as a bridge for what would otherwise be a very abrupt shift from the peaceful tent of Cordelia to the war zone of Edmund.

Notes

Notes

COLES NOTES TOTAL STUDY EDITION

KING LEAR
ACT V

Scene 1 177

Scene 2 182

Scene 3 184

Lear *And my poor fool is hanged: no, no, no life?*
Why should a dog, a horse, a rat, have life,
And thou no breath at all? Thou'lt come no more,
Never, never, never, never, never.

Act V, Scene 1

Regan suspects Edmund of dalliance with Goneril. Edgar, still disguised, offers the dead Oswald's letter to Albany. Edmund intends further treason.

ACT V, SCENE 1
The British camp near Dover.

[Enter, with Drum and Colours, EDMUND, REGAN, Gentleman and Soldiers]

Edmund Know of the Duke if his last purpose hold,
Or whether since he is advised by aught
To change the course. He's full of alteration
And self-reproving. Bring his constant pleasure.

[Exit an Officer]

Regan Our sister's man is certainly miscarried.   5

Edmund 'Tis to be doubted, madam.

Regan   Now, sweet lord,
You know the goodness I intend upon you.
Tell me, but truly—but then speak the truth—
Do you not love my sister?

Edmund   In honoured love.

Regan But have you never found my brother's way   10
To the forfended place?

Edmund   That thought abuses you.

Regan I am doubtful that you have been conjunct
And bosomed with her, as far as we call hers.

Edmund No, by mine honour, madam.

Regan I never shall endure her. Dear my lord,   15
Be not familiar with her.

Edmund   Fear me not.
She and the Duke her husband!

NOTES

1. *Know:* find out.

4. *constant pleasure:* final decision.

5. *is...miscarried:* has met with some accident.

6. *doubted:* feared

11. *forfended:* forbidden.

    abuses you: is too dishonourable for you to think.

12-13. *I...hers:* I hear that you have been sexually intimate with her.

[Enter, with Drum and Colours, ALBANY,
GONERIL, Soldiers]

Goneril *[aside]* I had rather lose the battle than that sister
Should loosen him and me.

Albany Our very loving sister, well bemet.   20
Sir, this I heard: the King is come to his daughter
With others whom the rigour of our state
Forced to cry out. Where I could not be honest,
I never yet was valiant. For this business,
It touches us as France invades our land,   25
Not bolds the King with others, whom I fear
Most just and heavy causes make oppose.

Edmund Sir, you speak nobly.

Regan   Why is this reasoned?

Goneril Combine together 'gainst the enemy;
For these domestic and particular broils   30
Are not the question here.

Albany   Let's then determine
With th' ancient of war on our proceeding.

Edmund I shall attend you presently at your tent.

Regan Sister, you'll go with us?

Goneril No.   35

Regan 'Tis most convenient. Pray go with us.

Goneril O ho, I know the riddle.—I will go.

[Exeunt both the Armies]

[Enter EDGAR]

Edgar *[to Albany]* If e'er your Grace had speech
    with man so poor,
Hear me one word.

Albany   *[to those departing]* I'll overtake
    you. *[to Edgar]* Speak.

Edgar Before you fight the battle, ope this letter.   40
If you have victory, let the trumpet sound

19. *loosen:* separate

22. *rigour...state:* our formidable government.

24–27. *For...oppose:* We are concerned here because France invades us, not because France encourages Lear and others who rightly oppose us.

28. *reasoned:* argued in this way.

30. *domestic and particular:* family and personal.

32. *ancient of war:* veteran officers.

37. *O...riddle:* You don't want me to be with Edmund.

41. *sound:* sound a summons

For him that brought it. Wretched though I seem,
I can produce a champion that will prove
What is avouched there. If you miscarry,
Your business of the world hath so an end,   45
And machination ceases. Fortune love you.

Albany Stay till I have read the letter.

Edgar   I was forbid it.
When time shall serve, let but the herald cry,
And I'll appear again.

Albany Why, fare thee well. I will o'erlook thy   50
    paper. *[Exit EDGAR]*

[Enter EDMUND]

Edmund The enemy's in view; draw up your powers.
Here is the guess of their true strength and forces
By diligent discovery; but your haste
Is now urged on you.

Albany   We will greet the time. *[Exit]*

Edmund To both these sisters have I sworn my love;   55
Each jealous of the other, as the stung
Are of the adder. Which of them shall I take?
Both? One? Or neither? Neither can be enjoyed,
If both remain alive. To take the widow
Exasperates, makes mad her sister Goneril;   60
And hardly shall I carry out my side,
Her husband being alive. Now then, we'll use
His countenance for the battle, which being done,
Let her who would be rid of him devise
His speedy taking off. As for the mercy   65
Which he intends to Lear and to Cordelia—
The battle done, and they within our power,
Shall never see his pardon; for my state
Stands on me to defend, not to debate. *[Exit]*

---

44.   avouched: accused.

46.   machination: plotting.

53.   discovery: spying.

54.   *greet the time:* prepare to face our enemies.

61.   *carry out my side:* do what I plan to do.

63.   *countenance:* authority.

69.   *Stands on:* requires.

COMMENTARY

In this scene, the conflict between Goneril and Regan escalates. Both women have distinct designs upon Edmund, and Edmund apparently has no qualms about playing both sides of the field. Notice how he evades a direct response to Regan's questions about his relationship with Goneril. Regan's primary concern is whether or not Edmund and Goneril have been sexually intimate. Edmund sidesteps her questions, which does not ease Regan's doubts, and she feels obliged to issue a command: "Dear my lord, / Be not familiar with her" (15–16).

A tentative alliance

Goneril and Albany join Regan and Edmund in the British camp. Given Albany's opinion of Goneril and Regan, stated so clearly in Act IV, Scene 2, we suspect that his loyalty is divided between the sisters and the king. Albany states that he will fight against the French, but only because of the threat of foreign invasion; he does not want his actions interpreted as affronts to Lear. The others feign agreement, claiming (as Goneril states) that "these domestic and particular broils" should be ignored for the time being in order to focus on the French threat (30).

Despite having forged a tentative alliance, Regan and Goneril still extend their talons in this scene. Each clearly feels malice toward the other

British troops prepare to battle the French invaders.

because of their mutual designs on Edmund. Neither wants to allow the other to be alone with Edmund. Thus, both must exit simultaneously. When Goneril offers to linger, Regan insists that she leave. Goneril knows Regan's mind: "O ho, I know the riddle," she quips (37).

Edgar's proposal

Edgar's entrance shortly after the exit of the sisters poses an interesting situation for Albany. Albany's mind is still uneasy regarding the conflict with France, and Edgar's proposal does little to settle the duke's unrest.

Edgar brings with him the letter that Goneril wrote for Edmund, which Oswald was supposed to deliver. The letter reveals Goneril's intentions for Edmund. Edgar asks Albany to read the letter before going to battle with the French.

When Edgar asks Albany to have a trumpet sounded after the impending battle, he is offering a formal challenge to prove the contents of the letter. This trumpet call is part of a ritualistic formula; note that Edgar states in lines 43 and 44 that he can "produce a champion"— or knight—who can prove that what is said in the letter is indeed the truth.

What Edgar proposes is a traditional *trial by combat*. Normally, such an event required a certain amount of ceremony, including the proclamation of the participants' lineage and the announcement of the complaint. The person who won the battle was assumed vindicated; his cause was deemed just. In Act V, we will see the trial by combat take place. Here, Edgar simply makes the proposal; he does not want to be present when Albany reads the letter that explains the reason for the challenge.

Edgar's letter and request place Albany in a potentially compromising situation. Albany does not know Edgar or his allegiances, so he has no means of knowing the true reason for this challenge. At the same time, the audience knows the contents of the letter but does not yet understand the full nature of Edgar's challenge. What we have, then, is Albany faced with a formal challenge for an unknown reason, and an audience that knows the reason but not the precise form that the challenge will take. In this way, suspense is enhanced.

Edmund's indifference

Note that much of Edmund's closing soliloquy concerns Goneril and Regan. Edmund's relative indifference is apparent; he seems to have no preference for either duchess—much like their own father has no preference for either daughter in the opening scene of the play. Edmund's mercilessness also becomes clear; he determines that Cordelia and Lear shall never see Albany's pardon. Following on the heels of Edgar's mysterious visit, these lines by Edmund serve to heighten the contrast between the two brothers. They also indicate that perhaps it is Edmund who will be required to face the challenge that Edgar has issued.

Act V, Scene 2

The French troops lose the battle, and Edgar seeks safety for Gloucester.

ACT V, SCENE 2
A field between the two camps.

[Alarum within. Enter, with Drum and Colours, LEAR
held by the hand by CORDELIA; and Soldiers
of France, over the stage and exeunt]
[Enter EDGAR and GLOUCESTER]

Edgar Here, father, take the shadow of this tree
For your good host. Pray that the right may thrive.
If ever I return to you again,
I'll bring you comfort.

Gloucester   Grace go with you, sir.

[Exit EDGAR]

[Alarum and retreat within. Enter EDGAR]

Edgar Away, old man! Give me thy hand. Away!   5
King Lear hath lost, he and his daughter ta'en.
Give me thy hand. Come on.

Gloucester No further, sir. A man may rot even here.

Edgar What, in ill thoughts again? Men must endure
Their going hence, even as their coming hither;   10
Ripeness is all. Come on.

Gloucester And that's true too. *[Exeunt]*

NOTES

s.d. *Alarum:* trumpet signal for army to advance.

2. *host:* shelter.

11. *Ripeness:* perfect readiness for whatever life brings.

COMMENTARY

Shakespeare is able to accomplish a great deal here with a symbolic military march and corresponding retreat. He provides a concise representation of the battle between France and Britain—a battle that ends in defeat for the French and capture for Lear and Cordelia.

Edgar reports the news of Lear's defeat to Gloucester. Discouraged, Gloucester begs to be left alone. Edgar responds, "Men must endure / Their going hence, even as their coming hither; / Ripeness is all" (9–11). His words effectively paraphrase Ecclesiastes: "To everything there is a season, and a time to every purpose under the heavens." Gloucester has not yet reached his season of death, and Edgar seeks to remind his father of this.

Valentina Shendrikova and Yuri Jarvet in the 1971 Soviet film version of Lear. Everett Collection

Act V, Scene 3

Lear anticipates pleasant captivity with Cordelia, but Edmund's order for the deaths of Lear and his daughter hints that Lear's happiness is to be short-lived. Goneril poisons Regan. Edgar challenges, fights, and mortally wounds Edmund, revealing himself as Edmund's brother. Edmund's order to stop the murders of Lear and Cordelia is too late; we see the heart-rending entrance of Lear with the dead Cordelia. Goneril commits suicide, and Lear dies. Kent plans to take his own life.

ACT V, SCENE 3
The British camp.

[Enter, in conquest, with Drum and Colours, EDMUND;
LEAR and CORDELIA as prisoners; Soldiers, Captain]

Edmund Some officers take them away. Good guard
Until their greater pleasures first be known
That are to censure them.

Cordelia   We are not the first
Who with best meaning have incurred the worst.
For thee, oppressed king, I am cast down;   5
Myself could else outfrown false Fortune's frown.
Shall we not see these daughters and these sisters?

Lear No, no, no, no! Come, let's away to prison.
We two alone will sing like birds i' th' cage.
When thou dost ask me blessing, I'll kneel down   10
And ask of thee forgiveness. So we'll live,
And pray, and sing, and tell old tales, and laugh
At gilded butterflies, and hear poor rogues
Talk of court news; and we'll talk with them too—
Who loses and who wins; who's in, who's out—   15
And take upon 's the mystery of things
As if we were God's spies; and we'll wear out,
In a walled prison, packs and sects of great ones
That ebb and flow by th' moon.

Edmund   Take them away.

Lear Upon such sacrifices, my Cordelia,   20
The gods themselves throw incense. Have I caught thee?
He that parts us shall bring a brand from heaven

NOTES

2.   *their...pleasures:* the desire of my superiors.

3.   *censure:* pass judgment.

13.   *gilded butterflies:* fashionable people at court.

17.   *wear out:* outlast.

18–19.   *packs...moon:* court people whose luck changes every month.

And fire us hence like foxes. Wipe thine eyes.
The goodyears shall devour them, flesh and fell,
Ere they shall make us weep! We'll see 'em starved first.   25
Come. *[Exeunt LEAR and CORDELIA, guarded]*

Edmund Come hither, captain; hark.
Take thou this note. *[Gives a paper]* Go follow
    them to prison.
One step I have advanced thee. If thou dost
As this instructs thee, thou dost make thy way
To noble fortunes. Know thou this, that men   30
Are as the time is. To be tender-minded
Does not become a sword. Thy great employment
Will not bear question. Either say thou'lt do't,
Or thrive by other means.

Captain   I'll do't, my lord.

Edmund About it; and write happy when th' hast done.   35
Mark, I say instantly, and carry it so
As I have set it down.

Captain I cannot draw a cart, nor eat dried oats—
If it be man's work, I'll do't. *[Exit]*

[Flourish. Enter ALBANY, GONERIL, REGAN, Soldiers]

Albany Sir, you have showed to-day your valiant strain,   40
And fortune led you well. You have the captives
Who were the opposites of this day's strife.
I do require them of you, so to use them
As we shall find their merits and our safety
May equally determine.

Edmund   Sir, I thought it fit   45
To send the old and miserable King
To some retention and appointed guard;
Whose age had charms in it, whose title more,
To pluck the common bosom on his side
And turn our impressed lances in our eyes   50
Which do command them. With him I sent the Queen,
My reason all the same; and they are ready

24. *fell:* skin.

28. *advanced:* promoted.

31. *as the time is:* in wartime, without scruples.

47. *retention:* imprisonment.

49. *common bosom:* sympathy of our own soldiers.

50. *impressed lances:* soldiers we have drafted.

To-morrow, or at further space, t' appear
Where you shall hold your session. At this time
We sweat and bleed, the friend hath lost his friend,   55
And the best quarrels, in the heat, are cursed
By those that feel their sharpness.
The question of Cordelia and her father
Requires a fitter place.

Albany   Sir, by your patience,
I hold you but a subject of this war,   60
Not as a brother.

Regan   That's as we list to grace him.
Methinks our pleasure might have been demanded
Ere you had spoke so far. He led our powers,
Bore the commission of my place and person,
The which immediacy may well stand up   65
And call itself your brother.

Goneril   Not so hot!
In his own grace he doth exalt himself
More than in your addition.

Regan   In my rights
By me invested, he compeers the best.

Albany That were the most if he should husband you.   70

Regan Jesters do oft prove prophets.

Goneril   Holla, holla!
That eye that told you so looked but asquint.

Regan Lady, I am not well; else I should answer
From a full-flowing stomach. General,
Take thou my soldiers, prisoners, patrimony;   75
Dispose of them, of me; the walls is thine.
Witness the world that I create thee here
My lord and master.

Goneril   Mean you to enjoy him?

Albany The let-alone lies not in your good will.

Edmund Nor in thine, lord.

Albany   Half-blooded fellow, yes.   80

56.	*quarrels:* causes.
61.	*list to grace:* choose to honour.
69.	*compeers:* equals.
72.	*asquint:* falsely.
74.	*stomach:* capacity for anger.
79.	*let-alone:* power to prevent or permit.
80.	*Half-blooded:* bastard.

Regan *[to Edmund]* Let the drum strike, and
    prove my title thine.

Albany Stay yet; hear reason. Edmund, I arrest thee
  On capital treason; and, in thy attaint,
  This gilded serpent. *[Points to Goneril]* For your
    claim, fair sister.
  I bar it in the interest of my wife.   85
  'Tis she is subcontracted to this lord,
  And I, her husband, contradict your banes,
  If you will marry, make your loves to me;
  My lady is bespoke.

Goneril   An interlude!

Albany Thou art armed, Gloucester. Let the trumpet
    sound.   90
  If none appear to prove upon thy person
  Thy heinous, manifest, and many treasons,
  There is my pledge. *[Throws down a glove]* I'll
    make it on thy heart,
  Ere I taste bread, thou art in nothing less
  Than I have here proclaimed thee.

Regan   Sick, O, sick!   95

Goneril *[aside]* If not, I'll ne'er trust medicine.

Edmund There's my exchange. *[Throws down a
    glove]* What in the world he is
  That names me traitor, villain-like he lies.
  Call by the trumpet. He that dares approach,
  On him, on you, who not? I will maintain   100
  My truth and honour firmly.

Albany A herald, ho!

Edmund   A herald, ho, a herald!

Albany Trust to thy single virtue; for thy soldiers,
  All levied in my name, have in my name
  Took their discharge.

Regan   My sickness grows upon me.   105

Albany She is not well. Convey her to my tent.

[Exit REGAN, attended]

83.   *and...attaint:* and accuse with you.

87.   *banes:* notice of intention to marry; read aloud in church for three Sundays preceding the marriage.

89.   *interlude:* a play or dramatic farce.

Goneril fights her sister with poison.

94.   *less:* less guilty.

96.   *medicine:* poison.

97.   *What:* whoever.

103.   *single virtue:* unassisted battle.

[Enter a Herald]
　Come hither, herald. Let the trumpet sound,
　And read out this.

Captain Sound, trumpet! *[A trumpet sounds]*

Herald *[reads]* 'If any man of quality or degree　　110
　within the lists of the army will maintain upon
　Edmund, supposed Earl of Gloucester, that he is a
　manifold traitor, let him appear by the third sound
　of the trumpet. He is bold in his defence.'

Edmund Sound! *[First trumpet]*　　115

Herald Again! *[Second trumpet]*
　Again! *[Third trumpet]*

[Trumpet answers within]

*[Enter EDGAR, armed, at the third sound, a Trumpet
　before him]*

Albany Ask him his purposes, why he appears
　Upon this call o' th' trumpet.

Herald　　　　　　　　　What are you?
　Your name, your quality, and why you answer　　120
　This present summons?

Edgar　　　　　　　Know my name is lost,
　By treason's tooth bare-gnawn and canker-bit;
　Yet am I noble as the adversary
　I come to cope.

Albany　　　　　　　　　Which is that adversary?

Edgar What's he that speaks for Edmund Earl of
　　Gloucester?　　125

Edmund Himself. What say'st thou to him?

Edgar　　　　　　　　　　Draw thy sword.
　That, if my speech offend a noble heart,
　Thy arm may do thee justice. Here is mine.
　Behold it is my privilege,
　The privilege of mine honours,　　130
　My oath, and my profession. I protest—
　Maugre thy strength, place, youth, and eminence,
　Despite thy victor sword and fire-new fortune,
　Thy valour and thy heart—thou art a traitor,

110.　　*degree:* rank.

122.　　*canker-bit:* ruined by maggots.

130.　　*The...honours:* my privilege as a knight.

132.　　*Maugre:* In spite of.

133.　　*fire-new:* newly minted

False to thy gods, thy brother, and thy father,   135
Conspirant 'gainst this high illustrious prince,
And from th' extremest upward of thy head
To the descent and dust below thy foot
A most toad-spotted traitor. Say thou 'no,'
This sword, this arm, and my best spirits are bent   140
To prove upon thy heart, whereto I speak,
Thou liest.

Edmund   In wisdom I should ask thy name,
But since thy outside looks so fair and warlike,
And that thy tongue some say of breeding breathes,
What safe and nicely I might well delay   145
By rule of knighthood I disdain and spurn.
Back do I toss these treasons to thy head,
With the hell-hated lie o'erwhelm thy heart,
Which—for they yet glance by and scarcely bruise—
This sword of mine shall give them instant way   150
Where they shall rest for ever. Trumpets, speak!

[Alarums. Fight. Edmund falls]

Albany Save him, save him.

Goneril   This is practice, Gloucester.
By th' law of war thou wast not bound to answer
An unknown opposite. Thou art not vanquished,
But cozened and beguiled.

Albany   Shut your mouth, dame,   155
Or with this paper shall I stop it.—Hold, sir.—
[To Goneril] Thou worse than any name, read thine
     own evil.
No tearing, lady! I perceive you know it.

Goneril Say if I do—the laws are mine, not thine.
Who can arraign me for't?

Albany   Most monstrous! O,   160
Know'st thou this paper?

Goneril   Ask me not what I know. *[Exit]*

Albany Go after her. She's desperate; govern her.

[Exit an Officer]

Edgar calls Edmund a "most toad-spotted traitor."

142. *wisdom:* prudence

144. *say of breeding:* accent of a gentleman.

150. *instant way:* direct passage to your heart.

152. *practice:* trickery.

155. *cozened:* cheated.

157. *this paper:* Albany has Goneril's love note to Edmund.

162. *govern:* restrain.

Edmund What you have charged me with, that
    have I done,
And more, much more. The time will bring it out.
'Tis past, and so am I.—But what art thou   165
That hast this fortune on me? If thou'rt noble,
I do forgive thee.

Edgar   Let's exchange charity.
I am no less in blood than thou art, Edmund;
If more, the more th' hast wronged me.
My name is Edgar and thy father's son.   170
The gods are just, and of our pleasant vices
Make instruments to plague us.
The dark and vicious place where thee he got
Cost him his eyes.

Edmund   Th' hast spoken right; 'tis true.
The wheel is come full circle; I am here.   175

Albany Methought thy very gait did prophesy
A royal nobleness. I must embrace thee.
Let sorrow split my heart if ever I
Did hate thee, or thy father.

Edgar   Worthy prince, I know't.

Albany Where have you hid yourself?   180
How have you known the miseries of your father?

Edgar By nursing them, my lord. List a brief tale;
And when 'tis told, O that my heart would burst!
The bloody proclamation to escape
That followed me so near (O, our lives' sweetness!   185
That we the pain of death would hourly die
Rather than die at once) taught me to shift
Into a madman's rags, t' assume a semblance
That very dogs disdained; and in this habit
Met I my father with his bleeding rings,   190
Their precious stones new lost; became his guide,
Led him, begged for him, saved him from despair;
Never—O fault!—revealed myself unto him
Until some half hour past, when I was armed,
Not sure, though hoping of this good success,   195
I asked his blessing, and from first to last

166. *fortune on:* victory over.

167. *charity:* forgiveness.

171–172. *The gods...us:* The just gods turn our own evil against us.

173. *got:* begot.

175. *The wheel...here:* I end as I began, as fortune's wheel now grinds me at its lowest point.

176. *prophesy:* indicate.

189. *habit:* dress.

190. *rings:* eye sockets.

Told him our pilgrimage. But his flawed heart—
Alack, too weak the conflict to support—
'Twixt two extremes of passion, joy and grief,
Burst smilingly.

Edmund   This speech of yours hath moved me,   200
And shall perchance do good; but speak you on—
You look as you had something more to say.

Albany If there be more, more woeful, hold it in,
For I am almost ready to dissolve,
Hearing of this.

Edgar   This would have seemed a period   205
To such as love not sorrow; but another,
To amplify too much, would make much more,
And top extremity.
Whilst I was big in clamour, came there in a man,
Who, having seen me in my worst estate,   210
Shunned my abhorred society; but then, finding
Who 'twas that so endured, with his strong arms
Has fastened on my neck, and bellowed out
As he'd burst heaven, threw him on my father,
Told the most piteous tale of Lear and him   215
That ever ear received; which in recounting
His grief grew puissant, and the strings of life
Began to crack. Twice then the trumpets sounded,
And there I left him tranced.

Albany   But who was this?

Edgar Kent, sir, the banished Kent; who in disguise   220
Followed his enemy king and did him service
Improper for a slave.

[Enter a Gentleman with a bloody knife]

Gentleman Help, help! O, help!

Edgar   What kind of help?

Albany   Speak, man.

Edgar What means this bloody knife?

Gentleman   'Tis hot, it smokes.
It came even from the heart of—O, she's dead.   225

204. *dissolve:* cry.

205. *period:* end.

208. *top extremity:* go beyond the limit of endurance.
209. *big in clamour:* loud in grieving.

217. *puissant:* overwhelming.

219. *tranced:* in a faint.

221. *enemy:* hostile.

Albany Who dead? Speak, man.

Gentleman Your lady, sir, your lady; and her sister
By her is poisoned; she confesses it.

Edmund I was contracted to them both. All three
Now marry in an instant.

Edgar   Here comes Kent.   230

[Enter KENT]

Albany Produce the bodies, be they alive or dead.
[Exit Gentleman]
This judgment of the heavens, that makes us tremble,
Touches us not with pity.—O, is this he?
The time will not allow the compliment
Which very manners urges.

Kent   I am come   235
To bid my king and master aye good night.
Is he not here?

Albany   Great thing of us forgot!
Speak, Edmund, where's the King? and where's Cordelia?
[GONERIL'S and REGAN'S bodies brought out]
Seest thou this object, Kent?

Kent Alack, why thus?

Edmund   Yet Edmund was beloved.   240
The one the other poisoned for my sake,
And after slew herself.

Albany Even so. Cover their faces.

Edmund I pant for life. Some good I mean to do,
Despite of mine own nature. Quickly send—   245
Be brief in it—to the castle, for my writ
Is on the life of Lear and on Cordelia
Nay, send in time.

Albany   Run, run, O, run!

Edgar To who, my Lord? Who has the office? Send
Thy token of reprieve.   250

---

230.   *marry:* come together in death.

235.   *very manners:* proper formality.

236.   *aye good night:* good night forever.

239.   *object:* sight.

246.   *writ:* order for execution.

249.   *office:* job of execution.

Edmund Well thought on. Take my sword;
  Give it the captain.

Edgar   Haste thee for thy life.

[Exit Officer]

Edmund He hath commission from thy wife and me
  To hang Cordelia in the prison and
  To lay the blame upon her own despair   255
  That she fordid herself.

Albany The gods defend her! Bear him hence awhile.

[EDMUND is borne off]

*[Enter LEAR, with CORDELIA in his arms, Gentleman,
and others following]*

Lear Howl, howl, howl! O, you are men of stones.
  Had I your tongues and eyes. I'd use them so
  That heaven's vault should crack. She's gone forever.   260
  I know when one is dead, and when one lives.
  She's dead as earth. Lend me a looking glass.
  If that her breath will mist or stain the stone,
  Why then she lives.

Kent   Is this the promised end?

Edgar Or image of that horror?

Albany   Fall and cease.   265

Lear This feather stirs; she lives! If it be so,
  It is a chance which does redeem all sorrows
  That ever I have felt.

Kent   O my good master.

Lear Prithee away.

Edgar   'Tis noble Kent, your friend.

Lear A plague upon you murderers, traitors all;   270
  I might have saved her; now she's gone for ever.
  Cordelia, Cordelia, stay a little. Ha,
  What is't thou say'st? Her voice was ever soft,
  Gentle, and low—an excellent thing in woman.
  I killed the slave that was a-hanging thee.   275

256. *fordid:* destroyed.

263. *stone:* mirror of polished stone.

264. *promised end:* the predicted end of the world.

265. *Fall and cease:* Let the earth come to its end.

Gentleman 'Tis true, my lords, he did.

Lear   Did I not, fellow?
I have seen the day, with my good biting falchion
I would have made them skip. I am old now,
And these same crosses spoil me. Who are you?
Mine eyes are not o' th' best. I'll tell you straight.   280

Kent If fortune brag of two she loved and hated,
One of them we behold.

Lear This is a dull sight. Are you not Kent?

Kent   The same:
Your servant Kent; where is your servant Caius?

Lear He's a good fellow, I can tell you that.   285
He'll strike, and quickly too. He's dead and rotten.

Kent No, my good lord; I am the very man.

Lear I'll see that straight.

Kent That from your first of difference and decay
Have followed your sad steps.

Lear   You are welcome hither.   290

Kent Nor no man else. All's cheerless, dark, and deadly.
Your eldest daughters have fordone themselves,
And desperately are dead.

Lear   Ay, so I think.

Albany He knows not what he says; and vain is it
That we present us to him.

Edgar   Very bootless.   295

[Enter a Messenger]

Messenger Edmund is dead, my lord.

Albany   That's but a trifle here.
Your lords and noble friends, know our intent.
What comfort to this great decay may come
Shall be applied. For us, we will resign,

---

277.   *falchion:* a curved sword.

279.   *crosses:* adversities.

280.   *tell you straight:* recognize you in a moment.

283.   *This...sight:* Lear's sight is unclear.

284.   *Caius:* Kent's name while in disguise.

288.   *see that straight:* understand that in a moment.

289.   *your first...decay:* the beginning of your change for the worse.

295.   *bootless:* useless.

298.   *great decay:* Albany refers here to Lear.

During the life of this old Majesty,   300
To him our absolute power; *[to Edgar and Kent]*
   you to your rights,
With boot and such addition as your honours
Have more than merited. All friends shall taste
The wages of their virtue, and all foes
The cup of their deservings.—O, see, see!   305

Lear And my poor fool is hanged: no, no, no life?
Why should a dog, a horse, a rat, have life,
And thou no breath at all? Thou'lt come no more,
Never, never, never, never, never.
Pray you undo this button. Thank you, sir.   310
Do you see this? Look on her! Look her lips,
Look there, look there—*[He dies]*

Edgar   He faints. My lord, my lord—

Kent Break, heart, I prithee break!

Edgar   Look up, my lord.

Kent Vex not his ghost. O, let him pass! He hates him
That would upon the rack of this tough world   315
Stretch him out longer.

Edgar   He is gone indeed.

Kent The wonder is, he hath endured so long.
He but usurped his life.

Albany Bear them from hence. Our present business
Is general woe. *[to Kent and Edgar]* Friends of my
   soul, you twain   320
Rule in this realm, and the gored state sustain.

Kent I have a journey, sir, shortly to go.
My master calls me; I must not say no.

Edgar The weight of this sad time we must obey,
Speak what we feel, not what we ought to say.   325
The oldest have borne most; we that are young
Shall never see so much, nor live so long.

[Exeunt with a dead march]

306.   *fool:* refers affectionately to Cordelia.

315.   *rack:* instrument of torture.

321.   *gored:* injured.

324.   *obey:* accept.

COMMENTARY

In this final scene of the play, Shakespeare seems to guide us toward a tentative optimism in the midst of deep tragedy. The structure of the scene offers a hint at that optimism. The scene's opening features Lear and Cordelia, two of the characters representing goodness in the play. In the middle of the scene, the focus turns toward evil as Edmund, Goneril, and Regan command the stage one last time. But the scene's ending turns back to the good by bringing Edgar, Albany, Kent, and Lear together. While many critics have emphasized the pessimism inherent in this drama, a scene structure that both begins and ends with the light of the good must offer some hope.

A brief respite

As the scene opens, Lear and Cordelia have been captured by Edmund's troops, and Lear submits to his captivity with joy. The Lear of the opening scenes would never have submitted so peacefully to incarceration; this Lear, however, is a new being. Having suffered immensely, undergoing a purification of sorts, the king is now quite content to envision "setting his rest" upon Cordelia at any cost and in any place, even in a jail. "Setting his rest" upon this dearest, youngest daughter was all that Lear really wanted right from the start, and the poignancy of this brief period of happiness with her stands in sharp relief to the suffering Lear will encounter in the play's final sequences.

Notice how a reunion with his beloved Cordelia has in some measure restored a bit of Lear's old fire. In lines 22–23, Lear proclaims with spirit that "[h]e that parts us shall bring a brand from heaven / And fire us hence like foxes." Caught up in the joy of the moment and in the exhilaration of thinking he is almost in his right mind again, Lear does not see the danger in his present situation. With Edmund's next words, Lear's threat loses its menace.

Having sent Lear and Cordelia off under guard, Edmund initiates the next step in his power play: He orders the Captain to murder the King and his daughter. Edmund reasons that "men / Are as the time is. To be tender-minded / Does not become a sword" (30–32). To convince the Captain to execute this plan, Edmund plays upon his sense of manhood and soldierly swagger. By explaining that he will "thrive by other means" should

the Captain refuse the command, Edmund pricks the Captain's pride (34). Further, by providing the Captain with written authorization, Edmund supplies him with a clear excuse for his actions. When questioned about the deaths of Lear and Cordelia, the Captain can honestly say he was just following orders.

Evil dominates the stage

The entrance of Goneril, Regan, and Albany into this scene creates a sense of overall balance in the play. The play opens with a tableau: trumpets and royalty, ceremony and banishment—and all the major characters either on stage or introduced. This closing scene reminds us of the first. Missing, of course, are the royal trumpets and some of the regalia. But the scene is nonetheless similar in that the major characters all appear, and many are banished—into death.

Edmund's initial role in this tableau is to portray himself as loyal and efficient. Much like in a game of wagering, however, Albany calls Edmund's bluff. Albany is now aware of Edmund's involvement with Goneril; the letter provided by Edgar is Albany's trump card. Both duchesses bare their fangs as they all but come to blows over Edmund; their arguments reveal their spite. When Albany decrees that the marital alliance of Edmund and Regan is solely within his power to decide, Edmund again changes colours, intimating that Albany has no control over the proposed union.

Albany's new strength

Albany here is no longer the "milk-livered" man chided by Goneril. Albany's transformation parallels that of Lear and Gloucester in that Albany learns to recognize the incredible capability for evil that humanity possesses. Fortunately for Albany, the methods by which he learned this lesson were less physically devastating than the trials of Lear and Gloucester. Albany's dry wit and sarcasm here reveal for us a new man—a man who can undermine Edmund's plots with a biting logic. Addressing Regan, Albany says that because Goneril is "subcontracted" to Edmund and Albany forbids that union, then Regan should woo Albany if she wishes to wed (86). This new Albany has discovered—as have Lear and Gloucester before him—that he has been far too inattentive to certain aspects of his life.

Edmund finds himself backed into a corner. Albany has thrown down his own glove, pledging that he himself will fight Edmund if no other champion appears. Though Albany probably finds this a safe challenge to issue—he is aware that another has promised to confront Edmund—Albany is nonetheless set on resolving this strife. Edmund is warned that he must answer alone in this situation, for Edmund's soldiers—"levied" in Albany's name—cannot assist the accused (106).

Trial by combat

As Edgar responds to the trumpet call, the *trial by combat* unfolds. The Herald issues the traditional call for name, lineage, and complaint. Edgar's response carries an ironic truth, for indeed his name is lost; Edgar's rightful title as heir to Gloucester's earldom has been stolen by the bastard Edmund. (This should remind us of the biblical story of Jacob usurping the birthright of Esau.) Although he has no name, Edgar is quick to name Edmund: "False to thy gods, thy brother, and thy father, / Conspirant 'gainst this high illustrious prince" (135–136). Notice again the beast imagery: Edmund is a "toad-spotted traitor" (139).

Surprisingly, Edmund declines to demand the name of his challenger. Many modern critics have questioned why Edmund would fight someone unknown to him. One suggestion is that Edmund, knowing that Albany intends to carry out the challenge himself if necessary, feels he has no choice but to fight the stranger.

Because of the nature of trials by combat, Edmund cannot rely on youth and skill to succeed. A divine judge controls the outcome of this contest, and Edmund knows he is guilty of plotting against Albany. Edmund may possibly feel that he has some hope of success in this battle because the unnamed man could be a charlatan. To win the battle with the stranger would help to vindicate Edmund in the eyes of Albany.

Edgar's vindication

Vindication does occur, but not for Edmund. Defeated by Edgar, Edmund is proven complicit in wrongdoing. Goneril's reaction does not help his case. The conniving Duchess, having seen her hero fall, pronounces the victory unjust because Edmund "wast not bound to answer / An unknown opposite" (153–154). True to her

character, Goneril tries to pull rank on Albany when he reveals the letter proving her alliance with Edmund. Goneril argues that, as a princess of the kingdom, she is above the law: "[T]he laws are mine, not thine. / Who can arraign me for 't?" (159–160). Goneril, much like Regan, Cornwall, and Edmund, does not feel obliged to adhere to moral law; each of these evil characters adheres only to the lower laws of Nature.

Through the trial by combat, Edgar has become the instrument of justice. Respectful of his father and dutiful in every way, Edgar admits that Gloucester's blinding is the result of those "pleasant vices" that the just gods use to "plague us" (171–172). Although he is willing to "exchange charity" with his dying brother, Edgar does not hesitate to unveil Edmund's treachery (167). Edgar could have justifiably challenged Edmund solely to avenge his father, but that would have been selfish. Instead, Edgar also challenges Edmund for his treason against the gods and the rightful princes of the land. Edgar, unlike the evildoers, refuses to subsist on the baser level of Nature and chooses instead a higher order.

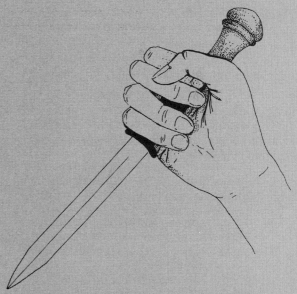

Goneril takes her own life when Edmund loses his.

As Edmund lies dying from a wound Edgar gave him, two other deaths occur offstage: Regan dies from the poison Goneril has given her, and Goneril commits suicide. Edmund expresses, with a sort of amazement, that in death he achieves a love that he never received from the father who laughed about his illegitimacy. For Edmund, being beloved of two women represents a type of victory: "The one the other poisoned for my sake, / And after slew herself" (241–242).

Too late for Cordelia

Seemingly forgotten among the chaos of battle and death, Lear and Cordelia become more than just means to an end for the weakening Edmund. Meaning to do some good "[d]espite of mine own nature," Edmund reveals his death order for the king and his daughter (245). Edmund's last act may be interpreted as a compassionate one. On the other hand, Edmund may be striving to find favour with a superior—in this case, God—with a last-minute good deed.

King Lear Weeping Over the Body of Cordelia, *James Barry, 18th century.*
SuperStock

Tragically, Edmund's attempt at goodwill comes too late. Cordelia has died, hanged by a lowly captain for no crime whatsoever and without the trial that even the reprobate Edmund was afforded. Lear, who tries to catch some breath lingering upon Cordelia's lips, has lost his entire family, as well as his kingdom, title, and sense of self. Even Gloucester is now gone, his heart having "[b]urst smilingly" when Edgar revealed his identity to

his father (200). Only Kent, Edgar, and Albany remain to observe the final moments of the enfeebled king.

Fortune's slight comfort

Even in the midst of so much despair, slight hope remains. Recall that in Act II, Scene 2, while sitting in the stocks at Gloucester's castle, Kent recognized that the wheel of fate turns constantly, promising a better day even when life appears darkest. Edmund, mortally wounded by his own brother, remarks that "[t]he wheel is come full circle" (175). And Edgar, having once told Gloucester that "ripeness is all," now admits that "[t]he weight of this sad time we must obey" (324). The image we should see here is the weighty Wheel of Fortune; its underside seems hard to bear, but at its worst it promises the comfort of continual change.

The Biblical book Ecclesiastes provides a possible key to the fundamental ideology of this play. In Ecclesiastes 1:9, we read that "the thing that hath been, it is that which shall be; and that which is done is that which shall be done, and there is no new thing under the sun." These lines describing the constant turning of life—a cycle that parallels the play's Wheel of Fortune—teach us that both good times and bad will be our lot in life, and whatever suffering or gladness we may experience, someone somewhere has experienced the same thing before.

King Lear also brings to life a specific passage from Ecclesiastes 3:3, which assures us that for everything in life, there is "[a] time to kill, and a time to heal: a time to break down, and a time to build up." The play is rife with killing and death—of persons, titles, and identities. But the play also allows for healing: Lear's mind is at least temporarily healed after his reunion with Cordelia, and the break between Gloucester and Edgar is mended as well. Even though we see a broken kingdom in chaos at the close of the play, we see also a commitment to build up and sustain "the gored state" (321).

The play also teaches lessons about wisdom and foolishness: the foolishness of those who should be wise, and the wisdom of those thought to be fools. Recall the ironic wisdom in the remarks of both the Fool and Poor Tom; remember, too, the foolish acts of the noble and supposedly wise Lear and Gloucester.

Divine justice

To our eyes, Gloucester and Lear suffer excessively for their relatively trivial offenses, and Cordelia's death seems to serve no purpose at all. Yet Shakespeare seems to make a comment in this play about *divine* justice, which differs from other forms of justice. All secrets are finally revealed in *King Lear*, and all things come to judgment. No one is left untouched by the tragedy in this play; all the major characters suffer incredible pain and loss. Though we have a difficult time understanding divine justice in such tragic form, it does have biblical precedents. For example, Exodus 34:7 indicates that the sins of the father are passed to his children, and even to a third generation. In light of this concept, Cordelia's death may make more sense.

Finally, *King Lear* speaks to us repeatedly about fate and chance, destiny and the gods. Is human life like a casino game, completely random, with the house odds stacked against us? What vision of justice do we get, and what picture of loving divinity? *King Lear* reminds us that humanity has free will and choice; as a result, humanity can and does prey upon itself, often blocking the path of virtue and morality so that evil succeeds. But free will can also overcome darkness and restore the light, and we must carry that hope away from the play. If we dwell on the pessimism, we may all end up as mad as Lear.

As noted in the "Introduction to *King Lear*," this final scene of death and crushing sadness prompted a man named Nahum Tate to create a version of this play that has a happy ending. The effects of that change were far-reaching; for more than 150 years, Tate's revision was played before audiences. How fortunate we are that the original ending has been restored to us, despite its vision of woe. So much of Shakespeare's meaning is compromised or lost otherwise. Of Tate's ending, Charles Lamb has written: "A happy ending? As if the living martyrdom that Lear has gone through—the flaying of his feelings alive, did not make a fair dismissal from the stage of life the only decorous thing for him. . . . As if the childish pleasure of getting his gilt robes and sceptre again could tempt him to act over again his misused station—as if at his years, and with his experience, anything was left him but to die." Indeed, after the pure agony of Cordelia's death, Lear has nothing left to do but die.

Notes

King Lear
REVIEW

Use this Review to gauge what you've learned and to build confidence in your understanding of the original text. After you work through the review questions, the problem-solving exercises, and the suggested activities, you're well on your way to understanding and appreciating the works of William Shakespeare.

MULTIPLE CHOICE

1. How does Regan die?

   a. Lear strangles her.

   b. She stabs herself.

   c. Cornwall hangs her.

   d. Goneril poisons her.

2. Who orders the deaths of Cordelia and Lear?

   a. Cornwall

   b. Albany

   c. Edmund

   d. Edgar

3. In this tragedy, what does Gloucester lose?

   a. His earldom

   b. His sight

   c. His life

   d. All of these

4. Flibbertigibbet, Modo, and Obidicut are:

   a. Servants

   b. Demons

   c. Knights

   d. None of these

5. Who kills Oswald?

   a. Edgar

   b. Edmund

   c. Kent

   d. Lear

6. Why does the Duke of Burgundy refuse to marry Cordelia?

   a. He finds her unattractive.

   b. He believes she is unchaste.

   c. He prefers her younger sister.

   d. He won't wed a dowerless princess.

7. Characters who assume disguises in the play are:

   a. Kent and the Fool

   b. Kent and Lear

   c. Kent and Edgar

   d. Edgar and Albany

8. Which characters come to realize that poverty-stricken people need attention?

   a. Lear and Gloucester

   b. Kent and Albany

   c. Cornwall and Goneril

   d. Oswald and Edmund

9. As Poor Tom, Edgar's clothing consists of:

   a. A tattered beggar's suit

   b. A blanket

   c. A rusty suit of armour

   d. A fool's cap and codpiece

10. Who disappears from the play without explanation?

a. Regan

b. King of France

c. Fool

d. Cornwall

11. A coxcomb is a:

a. Rooster

b. Fool's cap

c. Person with little education

d. Cape

12. As he descends into madness, Lear decorates himself with:

a. A crown

b. Lavish garments

c. Flowers

d. Jewels

13. Cornwall insults Lear by:

a. Calling him a fool

b. Slapping him

c. Dismissing his retinue of knights

d. Putting his servant in the stocks

14. Edmund plays on Gloucester's belief in:

a. The power of the stars

b. The power of curses

c. The existence of demons

d. The existence of angels

15. Gloucester receives kind treatment from:

a. One of his tenants

b. Edgar

c. Servants

d. All of the above

TRUE / FALSE

1. T F   Edgar and Edmund have the same mother.

2. T F   Cordelia hopes to inherit Lear's entire kingdom.

3. T F   Kent assumes a disguise so that he can continue to serve Lear.

4. T F   Albany fights Edmund in a trial by combat.

5. T F   Lear and Goneril fight because Lear wants 100 knights to live with him.

6. T F   Gloucester believes that he falls over the cliffs of Dover.

7. T F   Oswald betrays Goneril by telling Regan of her affair with Edmund.

8. T F   Regan invites Lear to come in from the storm.

9. T F   Kent kills Oswald out of loyalty to Lear.

10. T F   The French troops defeat the British and capture Albany.

11. T F   Lear assures Gloucester that he will not die for adultery.

12. T F   Edgar delays revealing his identity to the blinded Gloucester because he is still angry with his father.

13. T F   Lear had hoped to spend his old age in Cordelia's care.

14. T F   The Fool offers some of the play's wisest remarks.

15. T F   Lear is the first character in literature to use the love test.

SHORT ANSWER

1. What does Edmund mean by saying he was "contracted to them both"?

2. Why is Kent banished?

3. Who is Caius?

4. During what ceremony does Edmund die?

5. What is the literary term for a monologue in which the speaking character reveals his true thoughts and nature?

6. Regan reveals that Lear bears what relationship to Edgar?

7. Why does Edgar assume two different identities when guiding Gloucester toward and away from the "cliffs"?

8. Why would Early Modern audiences have been particularly concerned about Lear's plans to divide his kingdom and renounce his position as king?

9. In what way are Kent and Oswald similar? What differentiates them despite this similarity?

10. What prompts Albany to finally take a stand against Goneril?

IDENTIFY THE QUOTATION

Answer the following questions as you identify the quotations listed below:

* Who is speaking? Who (if anyone) is listening?

* What does the quotation reveal about the speaker's character?

* What does the quotation tell you about other characters within the play?

* Where does the quotation occur within the play?

* What does the quotation show you about the play's themes?

* What significant imagery do you see in the quotation, and how do images in this passage relate to images in the rest of the play?

1. O reason not the need! Our basest beggars
   Are in the poorest thing superfluous.
   Allow not more than nature needs,
   Man's life's as cheap as beast's.

2. The weight of this sad time we must obey,
   Speak what we feel, not what we ought to say.
   The oldest hath borne most; we that are young
   Shall never see so much, nor live so long.

3. Haply, when I shall wed,
   That lord whose hand must take my plight shall carry
   Half my love with him, half my care and duty.
   Sure I shall never marry like my sisters,
   To love my father all.

4. As flies to wanton boys are we to th' gods;
   They kill us for their sport.

5. They'll have me whipped for speaking true; thou'lt have me whipped for lying; and sometimes I am whipped for holding my peace. I had rather be any kind o' thing than a fool, and yet I would not be thee, nuncle: thou hast pared thy wit o' both sides and left nothing i' th' middle. Here comes one o' the parings.

6. He'll shape his old course in a country new.

7. Thou, Nature, art my goddess; to thy law
   My services are bound. Wherefore should I
   Stand in the plague of custom, and permit

The curiosity of nations to deprive me,
For that I am some twelve or fourteen moon-
shines
Lag of a brother?

8. This milky gentleness and course of yours,
Though I condemn not, yet under pardon,
You are much more atasked for want of
wisdom
Than praised for harmful mildness.

9. A knave, a rascal, an eater of broken meats;
a base, proud, shallow, beggarly, three-suited,
hundred-pound, filthy worsted-stocking knave;
a lily-livered, action-taking, whoreson,
glass-gazing, super-serviceable, finical rogue.

10. O, sir, you are old;
Nature in you stands on the very verge
Of his confine. You should be ruled, and led
By some discretion that discerns your state
Better than you yourself.

11. O strange and fast'ned villain!
Would he deny his letter, said he? [I never got
him.]

12. Is man no more than this? Consider him well.
Thou ow'st the worm no silk, the beast no
hide, the sheep no wool, the cat no perfume.
Ha! here's three on's are sophisticated. Thou art
the thing itself; unaccommodated man is no
more but such a poor, bare, forked animal as
thou art. Off, off, you lendings!

13. We two alone will sing like bird i' th' cage.
When thou dost ask me blessing, I'll kneel
down
And ask of thee forgiveness. So we'll live,

And pray, and sing, and tell old tales, and laugh
At gilded butterflies, and hear poor rogues
Talk of court news.

14. I cannot think my sister in the least
Would fail her obligation. If, sir, perchance
She have restrained the riots of your followers,
'Tis on such ground, and to such wholesome
end,
As clears her from all blame.

15. You are not worth the dust which the rude
wind
Blows in your face. I fear your disposition:
That nature which contemns its origin
Cannot be bordered certain in itself.
She that will sliver and disbranch
From her material sap, perforce must wither
And come to deadly use.

IDENTIFYING PLAY ELEMENTS

Find examples of the following in the text of
King Lear:

* **Iambic pentameter:** Lines of the play that have
(about) 10 syllables with five clearly stressed syllables are written as iambic pentameter.

* **Rhyming couplet:** Shakespeare sometimes
rhymes two consecutive iambic pentameter lines
to create a *rhyming couplet.*

* **Wordplay:** This device often takes the form of
puns—instances when a word can have more than
one meaning. Wordplay is often used for comic
effect but can also draw attention to the flexibility of language (and the difficulty of pinning
down specific meaning).

* **Verbal irony:** An instance in which what a character says has a vastly different literal meaning
than what the character actually means.

* **Dramatic irony:** This is what occurs when the audience knows more than the characters on stage do. Because the audience is in a privileged position, it can anticipate what may happen to a character even though the character himself is caught by surprise.

* **Soliloquy:** Shakespeare often uses this device in his tragedies. Soliloquies are monologues that occur when a character is alone. These speeches tell the audience a great deal about the character's inner thoughts, feelings, and intentions. They are also very useful for creating dramatic irony, because they let the audience in on secrets that other characters in the play know nothing about.

* **Foreshadowing:** This device allows the playwright to drop hints about what's to come in the play. Sometimes characters' words offer these hints, and sometimes the action indicates that the audience can anticipate certain events later.

* **Apostrophe:** This device occurs when a character speaks either to someone who not within hearing distance or to an object or animal—something that cannot understand his words. An apostrophe allows the speaker to think aloud.

* **Symbol:** A symbol is a person, place, or thing in a literary work that figuratively represents something else. Symbols are often physical entities that represent abstract ideas.

* **Oxymoron:** This figure of speech combines two apparently contradictory words (such as "wise fool").

DISCUSSION QUESTIONS

The major themes and concepts of this play respond well to extended, detailed discussion. A good way to start discussion is by rephrasing the questions below to create thesis statements. Then use supporting evidence from the play to develop those statements and create solid arguments.

1. Contrast the differing concepts of Nature expressed in the play. Pay particular attention to the views of Nature expressed by Edgar, Edmund, Gloucester, and Lear. Look also for instances in the play where characters use the word "unnatural" to describe another character or a situation. What would various characters consider to be unnatural?

2. Discuss the theme of age and the older generation, specifically addressing the issue of how children treat their parents. Why do Regan and Goneril treat their father so poorly? What qualities do Cordelia and Edgar demonstrate in their treatment of Lear of Gloucester that the other sisters and Edmund don't have? What does being "old" mean in this play? Is Lear old at the beginning, or does he become old as the play progresses?

3. One of the themes in this play is "reason in madness, madness in reason." Discuss what this phrase means, taking care to account for the different types of madness on display in this play. Consider the madness portrayed in various characters, such as Lear, Edgar, the Fool, Regan, Goneril, and Edmund.

4. Recount Lear's descent into madness, offering specific examples to define each stage of that process. Where do you find the first evidence that his sanity is deteriorating? What are the sources of his madness? What events seem to propel him toward madness? Are there any indications that he could recover?

5. Draw parallels between the Lear plot and the Gloucester subplot, emphasizing specific similarities. Which characters resemble each other in the plot and subplot? Which actions resemble each other? Consider Shakespeare's motivation for using this type of construction to

emphasize the themes of the play. If a play were staged eliminating the Gloucester subplot, what impact would that have on the audience?

6. Consider Lear's use of a love test to determine which daughters receive the largest portion of his kingdom. What motivates Lear to use this type of device? What does Shakespeare seem to say about the type of love Lear seeks? Does Lear seem to learn his lesson after the disastrous results of the love test in Act I, Scene 1? Has love been redefined for him by the end of the play?

7. We do not see the character of the King of France after the first scene. What do we learn about his character from his brief appearance? How does he differ from the more prominent characters in the play? How, specifically, does he contrast with Lear?

8. Lear seems to make an important discovery in the company of Poor Tom on the heath. He calls Tom "the thing itself," and the stage directions tell us that he "begins to disrobe" immediately after this revelation. Discuss what seems to be happening in Lear's mind at this moment in the play. What does he learn that he never knew before? Why does that knowledge lead him to remove his clothing?

9. Of all the cruel punishments Cornwall and the evil sisters could have chosen for Gloucester, consider why they settle on removing his eyes. Why does Shakespeare script this horrible act, and why does he choose to portray it onstage instead of allowing the violence to occur outside of our view?

10. Why do you think that Shakespeare has Cordelia and Lear die at the play's end? What is the impact of those deaths? Would the play's messages change if they were still living when the curtain closes?

ACTIVITIES

This section provides teachers with suggestions for classroom activities that can serve as springboards for further discussion. Tailor the activities to meet the needs of your specific classroom.

1. Have a small group of students perform the closing scene from Shakespeare's *Lear* and the closing scene from Nahum Tate's 1681 revised version of *Lear* (the one with a happy ending). Note what effects the different endings have on the audience. Discuss how the themes of the play may be altered by this revision. Also consider why Tate's version was preferred over Shakespeare's for so many years. Poll the audience to determine which ending each student would choose if he or she were directing a production of this play.

2. Have students research the history of the *trial by combat* and the details of the ceremony involved in its enactment. Ask them to create a collage that shows the types of weapons and armor most often used in that type of combat and the coats-of-arms most likely seen in the conflicts.

3. Ask students to work in small groups to design a Web site for *King Lear*. The site can include character descriptions and plot summaries for each scene, but it should also provide access to more analytical information. Ask students to create links to other sites that offer criticism of the play, information about its production history, and contemporary films that are based on the play.

4. Have students develop a *Lear* teaching kit: a kit that each of them could use to teach the play or to demonstrate its main themes and elements. Students should collect modern-day items that symbolize age discrimination, disrespect for parents, belief in the supernatural, and

other major play themes. They can package the items in a sturdy container and include an itemized, descriptive pamphlet of what is in the kit and the purpose each item serves when teaching the play.

5. Ask students to write a short book that tells and illustrates the *King Lear* story on an elementary school level. Share the stories with other students in your class to generate discussion about what elements of the play stayed when it was stripped down to this length. Ask students to describe the difficulties they may have experienced when trying to tell the story in its simplest form.

6. Show a recent film based on the story of *King Lear* to your students. Some suggestions include *A Thousand Acres, The Dresser,* and the Kurosawa film (in Japanese with subtitles) *Ran.* After watching the film, discuss with your students the ways in which the film version directly parallels Shakespeare's play and ways in which it diverges from the original. Discuss reasons why a modern writer and film director would choose to revisit the story of Lear and update its themes for today's audiences.

7. As your students read the play, ask them to keep a reading journal that tracks the action and themes as well as their responses and questions. To do this effectively, students should have a notebook devoted to the play in which they divide each page into two columns. In one column, they should write brief summaries of the play's plot, including new information they learn about characters and any themes that are being explored in the course of that action. In the other column, they should note their individual responses to what they are reading, including questions they have. Students should mark act and scene numbers on each journal page so they can quickly identify which pages to turn to during class discussion.

8. Stage a debate between students representing various characters in the play. For example, ask one student to take on the role of King Lear and another student to take on the role of Goneril. Have other class members generate debate questions that address the issues these two characters seem to disagree about in the play. In this instance, the debate may centre on the amount of respect that is due to our parents and to the elderly. Ask class members listening to the debate to judge which character makes the most effective arguments. Debates could be staged between any number of pairings: Lear and Cordelia, Edgar and Edmund, Gloucester and Edmund, the Fool and Lear, Cordelia and Goneril, and so on. After each debate, discuss how the arguments made by each character impacts students' views of the issues that Shakespeare presents.

ANSWERS

Multiple Choice

1. d 2. c 3. d 4. b 5. a 6. d 7. c 8. a 9. b 10. c 11. b 12. c 13. d 14. a 15. d.

True / False

1. False 2. False 3. True 4. False 5. True 6. True 7. False 8. False 9. False 10. False 11. True 12. False 13. True 14. True 15. False

Short Answer

1. He was promised to both Goneril and Regan as a lover and potential husband.

2. Kent is banished because he defied Lear's authority by questioning his treatment of Cordelia in the first scene.

3. Caius is the name that Kent takes to disguise his identity so that he can continue to serve Lear.

4. He dies during a *trial by combat* in which Edgar proves his virtue.

5. A soliloquy.

6. Edgar is Lear's godson.

7. He wants his father to believe that he was led to the cliff by a "fiend." He must assume a second identity after the fall to convince Gloucester of the fiend's existence.

8. Early Modern belief held that kingship was held by divine right; a king was chosen by God. Any attempt to renounce that position could only spell trouble for the king and the entire country.

9. Kent and Oswald both display fierce loyalty— Kent to Lear and Oswald to Goneril. But Kent despises Oswald because his loyalty is to an evil master.

10. Albany becomes disgusted when he learns how Goneril and Regan have treated their father. He cannot tolerate his wife's villainous behaviour any further.

Identify the Quotation

1. In Act II, Scene 4, Lines 261–264, Lear says these words to Goneril and Regan. Lear argues that even poor people have more than they need. He offers this argument in defense against his daughters' insistence that he cut his retinue of knights down from 100 to 50, 25, or even zero.

2. Edgar speaks these lines in the final moments of the play, in Act V, Scene 3, Lines 324–327. He speaks to the small assembly of those who remain living at the end of the play. The speech closes the play and emphasizes the sadness of the situation and the role of fate in all our lives.

3. In Act I, Scene 1, Lines 101–103, Cordelia says these words to Lear. She argues that unlike her sisters, she will not claim to love only her father after she has married.

4. These lines are spoken by Gloucester to Edgar and an Old Man in Act IV, Scene 1, Lines 36–37. Gloucester feels that the gods are being wicked and cruel, playing with humanity for the fun of it.

5. The Fool says these words to Lear in Act I, Scene 4, Lines 187–191. The Fool emphasizes that everything he does seems to be in error and that Lear is in gross error as well for giving up his authority to his wicked daughters.

6. Kent says this in Line 188 of Act I, Scene 1. Speaking to Lear's court after being banished for defending Cordelia, Kent says that he plans to find a new home but continue to practice his accustomed loyalty.

7. Edmund speaks these lines as a soliloquy in Act I, Scene 2, Lines 1–6. In this revealing passage, Edmund pledges himself to be a follower of an animalistic level of Nature. He denies the value of the laws of Nature that Lear and other characters follow.

8. In Act I, Scene 4, Lines 344–347, Goneril chides her husband Albany for his weak personality. She reveals that the traditional roles of a strong man and a more dependent woman have been reversed in their relationship, and she lacks respect for him because of it.

9. Kent uses these and other words in Act II, Scene 2, Lines 15–19 to insult Oswald. Despite Oswald's confusion, Kent berates him and draws him into a swordfight. The incident lands Kent in the stocks.

10. In Act II, Scene 4, Lines 143–147, Regan says these words to Lear. Showing her full disrespect for the older generation, she urges Lear to allow himself to be controlled.

11. Gloucester uses these words in Act II, Scene 1, Lines 77–78 to display his anger at his supposedly traitorous son Edgar. He says the lines to Edmund, adding to the irony of the situation. Gloucester, like Lear, is quick to judge and therefore easily duped by his illegitimate son.

12. In Act III, Scene 4, Lines 102–107, Lear describes a revelation he experiences after seeing in Poor Tom the bare essence of man. He removes his clothing in response to this revelation, presumably to strip himself of all pretenses and arrive at the essential man.

13. In Act V, Scene 3, Lines 9–14, Lear speaks kindly to Cordelia. Having been captured by Edmund, Lear realizes that he does not mind imprisonment as long as Cordelia is with him. This is one of Lear's few moments of comfort in the play, and it proves to be short-lived.

14. In Act II, Scene 4, Lines 138–142, Regan proves her loyalty to Goneril and disloyalty to Lear by insisting that her sister cannot have meant ill toward her father. With these words, Regan indicates that Lear will not find sympathy, or a home, with this daughter either.

15. In Act IV, Scene 2, Albany finally stands up to Goneril and proves himself to be a strong man as indicated by lines 30–36. His transformation occurs after learning of his wife's treatment of Lear.

RESOURCE CENTRE

The learning doesn't need to stop here. This Resource Centre shows you the best of the best: great links to information in print and on film.

EDITIONS

Different editions of Shakespeare's plays incorporate not only various versions of the dramas but also insightful and interesting background information and critical comments. Each of the editions listed below will provide unique perspectives while covering the basics.

Evans, G. Blakemore, ed. *The Riverside Shakespeare*. Boston: Houghton, 1974.

Gollancz, Israel, ed. *The Larger Temple Shakespeare*. London: J. M. Dent, 1899.

Greenblatt, Stephen, ed. *The Norton Shakespeare*. New York: W. W. Norton, 1997.

BOOKS / CHAPTERS

This title is one of many great books about *King Lear* and William Shakespeare available. To read more about the play or the playwright, look for the following:

Bate, Jonathan, and Russell Jackson, eds. *Shakespeare: An Illustrated Stage History*. Oxford: Oxford UP, 1996.

A dazzling display of illustrations enhances the study of Shakespearean plays, actors, and stagecraft in this easy-to-use, well-written reference text.

Bradley, A.C. *Shakespearean Tragedy*. London: Macmillan, 1904.

Bradley's text includes a lengthy discussion of tragedy. The volume is also the most important example of psychological criticism of Shakespeare's plays as records of real people.

Coleridge, S.T. *Shakespearean Criticism*. Boston: Harvard UP, 1811–1834.

In two volumes, Coleridge offers some of the most important commentary of Shakespeare's work from among the Romantic writers. This work prompted excessive admiration of Shakespeare in the Victorian period and remains a frequently quoted reference today.

Crowl, Samuel. "Free Style: Adrian Noble's *King Lear* and *As You Like It*." *Shakespeare Observed: Studies in Performance on Stage and Screen*. Athens: Ohio UP, 1992. 122–141.

This chapter from a thoughtful and well-organized text offers insight into directorial and production decisions that must be made when staging both Shakespeare's *King Lear* and *As You Like It*. The book's first chapter on "The Art of Observation" also provides interesting background information on Shakespearean performance criticism.

Doyle, John and Ray Lischner. *Shakespeare For Dummies*. Foster City: IDG Books Worldwide, Inc., 1999.

This guide to Shakespeare's plays and poetry provides summaries and scorecards for keeping track of who's who in a given play, as well as painless introductions to language, imagery, and other often intimidating subjects.

Foreman, Walter C., Jr. *The Music of the Close: The Final Scenes of Shakespeare's Tragedies*. Lexington: UP of Kentucky, 1978.

Foreman's book looks at the ending of *King Lear* along with those of several other Shakespearean tragedies. His discussion of the differences and similarities among the structures of the dramas' final scenes sheds light on both Shakespeare's craft and purpose.

Frost, William. "Shakespeare's Rituals and the Opening of *King Lear*." *Shakespeare: The Tragedies*. Ed. Clifford Leech. Chicago: U of Chicago P, 1965. 190–201.

This fine essay examines Shakespeare's knowledge and uses of ritual, looking specifically at the opening tableau of *King Lear*.

Frye, Northrop. *Northrop Frye on Shakespeare*. Ed. Robert Sandler. New Haven: Yale UP, 1986.

Frye's text offers a good discussion of the differing levels of Nature in *King Lear*, as well as the consideration of myth and history in the play.

Granville-Barker, Harley. *Prefaces to Shakespeare*. London: Sedgwick and Jackson, 1927.

Long called the most important and stimulating of all modern criticism, this work includes descriptions from Granville-Barker's own dramatic productions.

Hazlitt, William. *Hazlitt's Characters of Shakespeare's Plays*. Ed. Ernest Rhys. London: J. M. Dent, 1910.

Hazlitt's commentary on Shakespeare's characters provides important insights on character development and function in the plays.

Hazlitt, W. C., ed. *Shakespeare's Library*. London: Reeves and Turner, 1875.

Presented in six volumes, this work discusses the source books used by Shakespeare as background and story foundations for his plays.

Jorgens, Jack. *Shakespeare on Film*. Bloomington: Indiana UP, 1977.

Jorgens's book provides well-written and informative essays on a number of Shakespeare's plays as filmed. The text offers a solid basis for comparing and contrasting different versions.

Knight, G. Wilson. Wheel of Fire. Oxford: Oxford UP, 1930.

Knight supplies an imaginative interpretation of Shakespeare's poetic imagery in *King Lear*, including an interesting argument concerning the grotesque comedic effects in the play.

Kott, Jan. *Shakespeare, Our Contemporary*. Trans. Boleslaw Taborski. Garden City: Doubleday, 1964.

Kott compares classical theatrical tragedy to the theatre of the grotesque, with comments about modern theatre. This is a scholarly and insightful text.

Lusardi, James P., and June Schlueter. *Reading Shakespeare in Performance: King Lear*. London: Associated University Presses, 1991.

A fine resource, *Reading Shakespeare* divides *King Lear* into six primary segments and offers critical commentary, explanations, and photographs of *Lear* in production.

Ralli, Augustus. *A History of Shakespearian Criticism.* Oxford: Oxford UP, 1932.

Ralli's two-volume set looks back at the entire history of Shakespeare criticism in an elaborate and fairly objective set of summaries. The work covers commentary up until 1925.

Spurgeon, Caroline F.E. *Shakespeare's Imagery and What It Tells Us.* Boston: Beacon, 1961.

Spurgeon offers an elaborate and detailed study of Shakespeare's imagery. She also makes some effort to examine Shakespeare's personality and thought as displayed through the characters and themes of the plays he wrote.

Stoll, Elmer E. *Art and Artifice in Shakespeare.* Cambridge: Cambridge UP, 1933.

Stoll considers the aesthetic effect of the play as the primary concern of the dramatist. He argues against criticism that looks at Shakespeare's plays as social documents.

Styan, J.L. *Shakespeare's Stagecraft.* Cambridge: Cambridge UP, 1971.

Styan's book offers interesting and detailed discussions of technique in staging Shakespeare's plays, including specific commentary on *King Lear* productions.

FILMS AND OTHER RECORDINGS

All of Shakespeare's plays were meant to be performed, and *King Lear* has been interpreted in a wide variety of ways on stage and film. The films and other recordings listed below can lend new insight into the play and increase your appreciation for the Bard's works.

Shakespeare's Soliloquies and Scenes for Actors, by Edwards, Hilton, and Michael Machienour. Spoken Arts. June 1986.

This audiocassette collection of recordings of soliloquies from *King Lear* and *Julius Caesar* is an excellent drama coaching and student memorization tool.

The Dresser. Dir. Peter Yates. 1983. 118 min.

This film, starring Albert Finney and Tom Courtenay, takes a backstage look at a touring stage company in war-torn England. As the company struggles to put *Lear* on stage in the midst of wartime chaos, the actor portraying Lear begins to resemble the king himself and struggles with his own seeming descent into madness.

Ran (Chaos). Film. Dir. Akiro Kurosawa. 1985. 135 min.

This Japanese version of *King Lear* features astounding photography. (Filmed in Japanese with English subtitles.)

King Lear. Dir. Peter Brook. Orson Welles as Lear. 1953. B/W. 75 min.

This version eliminates the Gloucester subplot and expands the character of Poor Tom.

King Lear. Dir. Grigor Kozintsev. Yuri Yarvet as Lear. 1970. B/W. 140 min.

This film contains panoramic outdoor scenes. (Subtitles.)

King Lear. Dir. Peter Brook. Paul Scofield as Lear. 1971. B/W. 137 min.

The text of the play is severely cut and rearranged in this film version, which is an existential production that partners well with Jan Kott's "King Lear or Endgame," a chapter in *Shakespeare, Our Contemporary.*

King Lear. Dir. Jonathan Miller. Michael Hordern as Lear. 1982. 180 min.

Tame and with little realism, this BBC version closely follows the play text.

King Lear. Dir. Michael Eliot. Laurence Olivier as Lear. 1984. 158 min.

This was Laurence Olivier's last Shakespearean role. The film features a Stonehenge set and also stars Diana Rigg (from the original *Avengers*) and John Hurt.

King Lear. Dir. Alan Cooke. Mike Kellan as Lear. 1984. 182 min.

Poorly acted with American actors, this film is fairly close to the play text in length.

King Lear. Dir. Richard Eyre. Ian Holm as Lear. 1998. 150 min.

Holm gives a superb performance in this film, which displays unspeakable wickedness in the Regan/Goneril duo.

ARTICLES

Armstrong, William. "Shakespeare and the Acting of Edward Alleyn." *Shakespeare Survey.* 9 (1954): 82–92.

This article offers a fine discussion of the dramatic abilities of Edward Alleyn and his experiences as a Shakespearean actor.

Carroll, William C. "'The Base Shall Top th' Legitimate': the Bedlam Beggar and the Role of Edgar in *King Lear.*" *Shakespeare Quarterly.* 38 (1987): 96–118.

Shakespeare Quarterly is the standard in the field of Shakespeare criticism, and this article offers a detailed and scholarly discussion of Bedlam beggars in history and in *King Lear.*

Lynch, Stephen J. "Sin, Suffering, and Redemption in Leir and Lear." *Shakespeare Studies.* 18 (1986): 161–74.

Lynch's interpretation compares the folk legend with Shakespeare's Lear and includes reference to religious themes in each play.

Shaw, John. "*King Lear:* The Final Lines." *Essays in Criticism.* 16 (1966): 263–264.

The Folio and Quarto versions of *King Lear* assign the play's closing lines to different characters. Shaw's essay discusses how the close of *Lear* is affected by the assignment of those final lines.

KING LEAR

READING GROUP DISCUSSION GUIDE

Use the following questions and topics to enhance your reading group discussions. The discussions can help get you thinking—and hopefully talking—about Shakespeare in a whole new way!

DISCUSSION QUESTIONS

1. Throughout *King Lear*, you can interpret many of the characters' actions as based on choice *(free will)*, based on fate *(destiny)*, or influenced by some supernatural force. Which of Lear's actions seem to be driven by his own free will? Which seem to be driven by destiny? What actions seem to be influenced by a higher force? What about the actions of Edgar? Edmund? Goneril? Regan? Cordelia? What relationship between free will, destiny, and supernatural forces does Shakespeare suggest?

2. Directors of stage and film productions of *King Lear* often have a difficult time casting the role of Lear. The character in the play is an old man, but the play's long speeches, emotions, and strenuous physical activity require a strong, nimble (and often younger) actor. If you were directing a new production of *King Lear*, what casting choices would you make? What are the pros and cons of casting an actor in his 50s in the role of Lear? Of casting an older actor?

3. The role of the Fool puzzles many actors, directors, and readers. In fact, some directors have been so puzzled by the character that they've cut him entirely from the play. If you were directing the play, would you cut the Fool or keep him in? How would you cast the role of the Fool? Is he old and weary like Lear? Young and spry? How well does he sing and dance? How sane is he? How would you costume him? How do you explain the Fool's disappearance halfway through the play?

4. *King Lear* features a large cast of supporting characters. Why did Shakespeare include the characters of Kent? Oswald? Burgandy? Cornwall? Albany? What do these characters add to the play? How would the play be different if you took away each of these characters?

5. Take another look at the first scene of the play. Directors of *King Lear* usually stage this scene in two distinct ways: as a formal public appearance with much pomp and ritual, or as an intimate family conversation behind closed doors. What are the pros and cons of staging the scene as a public event? Of staging the scene as a private family meeting? Does the scene work better one way or the other? Which way would you stage it?

6. In many ways, *King Lear* is unique among Shakespeare's plays because the female characters make many major decisions and frequently take action on their own. Find examples of the three women making decisions and taking control of the action of the play. What are the consequences of these actions? Is Shakespeare making any specific statements about the role of women in society? About the role of women in family relationships?

7. In 1681, Nahum Tate introduced a rewritten version of *King Lear* that became more popular and was performed more frequently than Shakespeare's original work until 1823. In Tate's version, Lear and Cordelia survive. Lear is restored to the throne, and Cordelia marries Edgar. Is it necessary for both Lear and Cordelia to die at the end of the play for the story to be truly tragic? How does having one or both of them alive at the end of the play change the play's meaning and effectiveness?

8. The roles of Lear's daughters are among the most popular for Shakespearean actresses. Directors have cast the roles in a variety of ways throughout the ages. How old should Goneril be? Regan? Cordelia? How physically attractive should each of these women be? How would you costume each female character?

9. Throughout the nineteenth and twentieth centuries, stage directors have desperately tried to create realistic storms for Lear to rage against in Act III. Real wind and rain, as well as extensive thunder and lightning special effects, have been used with mixed success. More recent productions have tried to make the storm more symbolic and stylized, relying less on special effects and more on the actors to create the impression of a great storm. How important is a realistic storm? What are the benefits of having the actors pretend to be out in the wind, rain, and lightning? What is the downside of using minimal special effects? How much of the storm is in Lear's mind?

10. Film and stage productions of *King Lear* have been set in hundreds of different locations and historical time periods. Select a location or historical time period (medieval Europe, Victorian England, a modern corporate boardroom, a futuristic space colony, and so on) and suggest how you would stage the following:

Lear dividing up his kingdom

Goneril and Regan plotting to overtake their father

Lear raging against the storm

The blinding of Gloucester

Lear carrying in the dead body of Cordelia

Notes

Notes

Notes